Enhance your parenting style by recognizing and developing your children's motivational gifts. Don and Katie Fortune guide you and your child in learning whether he is a perceiver, teacher, administrator, compassion person, giver, server, or exhorter. (Or a combination of these!) The Fortunes alert you to the talents, tendencies, special interests, strengths and weaknesses, and personality traits of each gift and present effective means of discipline related to each of the gifts.

This interesting, practical book is one no Christian parent — or grandparent or youth worker — should be without. Whether your children are infants, toddlers, grade-schoolers, high schoolers, or newlyweds, the teaching in this book relates to them. Through charts, diagrams, and self-examination questions, children from pre-school age to adulthood can discover the gifts with which they have been blessed. Take the time today to *Discover Your Children's Gifts*.

Don't miss the Fortunes' first book, a fascinating guide to realizing and practicing your own motivational gifts!

"This book will enable every believer to discover his gifts so that he can better serve God among the body of believers. I wholeheartedly and enthusiastically endorse this book."

The Rev. Paul Yonggi Cho, Pastor
Yoido Full Gospel Church
Seoul, Korea

"I found it fascinating! Invaluable! A long-overdue idea presented with skill, charm, and common sense. Every Christian should own a copy, certainly every Christian leader."

Marjorie Holmes
author of *Two from Galilee*
and many other books
McMurray, Pa.

"It is such an attractive and well-organized publication!"

Jane Hansen, International President
Women's Aglow Fellowship
Edmonds, Wash.

(continued on back)

"The most comprehensive work on the topic I have ever seen...a tremendous help both to me and my wife, Sandy. A superb work....We'll continue to reap benefits for years to come."

The Rev. David Noel, Pastor
Morning Star Church
Anderson, Ind.

"It's been a terrific inspirational instrument to me and the clergy I am working with."

Agnes Jenkins, Assimilation Coordinator
Church of the Good Samaritan
Paoli, Pa.

"This book helps laypersons discover their areas of ministry in the local church and opens up new understanding of the complementary relationship of pastor and people."

The Rev. Vince Hart, Pastor
United Methodist Church
Goldendale, Wash.

"Three groups have gone through the book already. We have many testimonies of the release that has come from the 'discovery' individuals have made about God's gifting in their lives."

Gary Geesey, Associate Pastor
El Centro First Assembly of God
El Centro, Calif.

"The book answers marvelously and biblically so many questions asked today, not only about ourselves, but of the relationships we have with others. It frees us to relate wholeheartedly!"

Jim and Adele Noetzelman, missionaries
Nuremberg, West Germany

"While working on my Master of Ministry thesis at Northwest Baptist Theological Seminary I have been studying gift identification programs and was quite impressed with your material."

The Rev. Kenton Anderson, Pastor
Prince Rupert Fellowship Baptist Church
B.C., Canada

DISCOVER
YOUR CHILDREN'S
GIFTS

DISCOVER YOUR CHILDREN'S GIFTS

Don & Katie Fortune

Chosen Books

A Division of Baker Book House Co
Grand Rapids, Michigan 49516

Library of Congress Cataloging-in-Publication Data

Fortune, Don.
    Discover your children's gifts / Don and Katie Fortune.
      p.   cm.
    Bibliography: p.
    ISBN 0-8007-9151-7
    1. Child rearing—United States.   2. Gifts, Scriptural.
    I. Fortune, Katie.   II. Title.
    HQ769.F67   1989
    234'.13—dc20   89-32990
                                                  CIP

Published by Chosen Books
a division of Baker Book House Company
P.O. Box 6287, Grand Rapids, MI 49516-6287

Fourteenth printing, November 2002

Printed in the United States of America

For current information about all releases from
Baker Book House, visit our web site:
http://www.bakerbooks.com

To our three wonderful children who are such a delight to us, through whom we have learned so much about the motivational gifts . . .

Linda Fortune
David Fortune
Dan Fortune
And to our delightful grandson, Jon!

CONTENTS

CONTENTS

INTRODUCTION

I got an early morning phone call from our editor at Chosen Books, Jane Campbell.

"This is Jane. I have just one thing to say to you: We want another book!"

"What?" I replied.

"Your book is doing so well we'd like to publish another of the same general nature and quality."

"Oh!" I declared. "Another book? Yes. I'd like to do that. In fact, we have one in mind."

"Great!"

"Jane, remember when our first manuscript was too long, and I decided to condense what we'd researched about children and their motivational gifts into one chapter? I told you we had enough on this subject for a whole book."

"That would be good. A natural sequel." Jane seemed pleased.

Shortly after the call Don returned home from early morning prayer meeting.

"Chosen wants a second book," I announced.

"On children and their motivational gifts, of course," Don replied quickly. "Now we can make use of all that research we did. Wonderful! I'm excited!"

I chuckled at Don's "I'm excited." He'd become so well-known for those words, our friends gave him a turquoise T-shirt with "I'm excited!" emblazoned across the front in large white Roman bold letters at our twenty-fifth wedding anniver-

9

sary celebration. I received a matching colored shirt imprinted with "I'm motivated." We wore them proudly.

Now it was time to write again. How grateful I was for a computer! We even bought a compatible lap computer so we could begin the book while ministering in Europe for the next two-and-a-quarter months. But when we got our detailed schedule of speaking engagements from Sweden and Germany we realized there would be no time for writing. The computer stayed home and we took off to share about the motivational gifts.

Our first book, *Discover Your God-Given Gifts*, had been translated into Swedish, and we led three consecutive weekend retreats in the south, north, and central parts of Sweden. We did a quick course in Denmark, and then moved on to six weeks of intensive teaching throughout Germany.

Everywhere we went people asked, "I've discovered my children's gifts, but how do I train them up in those gifts?" "How do I discipline my stubborn perceiver and my gentle compassion child and appear fair to them?" "Should my server go to college?"

During our nine weeks of ministry in Japan last spring many parents asked us, "How do I help my children develop in their motivational gifts in a conformity-oriented culture?" Others wanted to know what to do if the child was already grown; was it too late to benefit from the teaching?

As guests for five live one-hour programs on the nationally broadcast *It's a New Day*, produced in Winnipeg, we received calls from parents who were eager to learn about the gifts of their children. When we mentioned we were going to write a book especially about training up children in their gifts, the response was overwhelmingly enthusiastic.

So, here we are. Our book is targeted to you—the parent. What a responsibility you have! We know. We've been there. It seems almost audacious of God to entrust us with children. But what a blessing, even through the challenges!

We are grateful we learned about the motivational gifts when our boys were just seven and nine, so we could encourage and develop their giftedness. It helped us to understand them and to delight in the development of their exceedingly different personalities. Dave, an administrator/teacher combination, was a striking contrast to Dan, a perceiver/compassion combination.

Our daughter, Linda, was already grown, but knowing about her gentle gift of compassion has helped us to build a beautifully close relationship to her as an adult.

Those of you who are grandparents will undoubtedly discover, as we have, the joy of knowing your grandchildren's gifts. Our grandson, Jon, is a remarkable server/administrator child. It's fun to watch his joy in serving mingled with his leadership abilities.

We hope you who have special responsibilities with children—as teachers, counselors, social workers, youth leaders, and Sunday school teachers—will find insights and information useful for working with children and youth of all ages.

May we all work together to help young people blossom into all God has designed them to be! They are the leaders of tomorrow. We long for them to use their God-given gifts in society's service, and to have internal joy, the natural by-product of operating in their gifts.

We hope you will enjoy the book. For a complete presentation of the motivational gifts we refer you to our first book, *Discover Your God-Given Gifts*, published in the fall of 1987 by Chosen Books, a division of the Fleming H. Revell Company. It is available at most Christian bookstores, or you may write to us and order an autographed copy.

Parenting is an adventure! We trust the Lord will guide you as you train up your children in their God-given gifts.

With love in Jesus,

Don & Katie Fortune
Edmonds, Washington, 1989

DISCOVER
YOUR CHILDREN'S
GIFTS

PART I

DISCOVER YOUR CHILDREN'S GIFTS

EVERY CHILD IS GIFTED BY GOD

1

During our seminar on motivational gifts we ask the audience to quote Proverbs 22:6 from memory. They quote it faithfully in one accord from the King James Version of the Bible as follows: "Train up a child in the way he should go: and when he is old, he will not depart from it."

"You've left part of it out!" we exclaim. Astonished looks appear on many faces as they repeat it to themselves, trying to figure out what they've omitted.

Then we go on to explain. In translating from the original Hebrew language, which is more precise than our English, the Amplified Bible reads:

> Train up a child in the way he should go [and in keeping with his individual gift or bent], and when he is old, he will not depart from it.
>
> Proverbs 22:6, TAB

Other versions seem to imply that if parents discipline and train their children properly they will mature into well-behaved adults. While this is generally true, all children should not be disciplined and trained in the same way. Each child is uniquely gifted by God and that will help determine the most effective type of training.

From the original Hebrew we see each child has a *gift*—a motivational gift—or a *bent*—a direction in life to be fulfilled by using his motivational gift(s). As parents we have a responsibility to discover our children's gifts and to encourage their development, so that when they come of age they will use their gifts to the glory of God. Proper usage of God's gifts yields true fulfillment.

This book should help you discover your children's gifts. It also offers practical information to help you to do the best possible job of training up your children according to their individual gifts. We don't pretend to have all the answers, but we've learned a lot in fifteen years of researching, teaching, and applying this subject.

WE'VE HAD OUR SHARE OF EXPERIENCE!

We've raised three children ourselves. Before we were married Don was a widower with a daughter who was eleven going on fifteen. How I wish I had known about the motivational gifts then. It would have made stepping into instant motherhood so much easier.

My primary gift is administration, with a secondary gift of teaching, and a third, perception. All three work together to make me a highly analytical and logical person.

Linda's gift of compassion caused her to function in the *feeling* mode—constantly. Our methods of operation were worlds apart.

I'd sit down with Linda and explain a dozen reasons why her father and I did not want her to go to a particular unsupervised party. I was sure she'd understand how logical our point of view was.

"But I feel like going," she'd reply. "All my friends will be there and I want to go!"

I'd call Don for help and we'd explain all the reasons again.

"Please let me go," she'd plead. "Everything will be okay."

I could not understand why she could not understand! My logic was getting us nowhere. But I was the one who did not understand our differing motivational gifts and the contrasting modes in which we functioned.

When David was born our neighbor gave us a lovely rocking chair. I had visions of cuddling our newborn and rocking him for hours. He was only six days old when I tried it. He screamed. I tried an hour later. More complaints. After several days I concluded it was a losing battle. David did not want to be rocked, and would allow only a certain amount of cuddling. We saw an independent streak in him from the beginning.

When Dan came along two-and-a-half years later, I tried out the rocking chair gingerly. Bingo! He loved it. The more I cuddled him the better; rocking always settled him down.

A psychology professor who championed a behavioristic perspective once said to my college class: "A child is a clean slate yet to be written upon." Obviously this man never had children!

While it's true parents and environment have an impact on a child's life, it's also true each child comes into this world with gifts giving him a distinct personality even in infancy.

THE BASIS FOR OUR TEACHING

The basis for our teaching on motivational gifts is found in the New Testament:

> Having gifts (faculties, talents, qualities) that differ according to the grace given us, let us use them: [He whose gift is] prophecy, [let him prophesy] according to the proportion of his faith; [He whose gift is] practical service, let him give himself to serving; he who teaches, to his teaching; (He who exhorts, encourages), to his exhortation; he who contributes, let him do it in simplicity and liberality; he who gives aid and superintends, with zeal and singleness of mind; he who does acts of mercy, with genuine cheerfulness and joyful eagerness.
>
> Romans 12:6–8, TAB

We believe Peter referred to this category of gifts in 1 Peter 4:10, suggesting we should *employ them* to benefit one another, just as Paul says here we are to *use them*.

We *possess* these gifts! God built them into us to be used for His glory and for the benefit of others. They provide the basis for and help to shape our personalities and motivate our lives.

These are *grace* gifts. We do not deserve them. Because God has created us with free will we can choose to use them appropriately, neglect them, or even abuse them.

In order to cooperate with God's will for our lives and to help our children do the same, it is important to have some understanding of what the gifts are and how they function. Here are the seven key words we have chosen to identify the gifts, and a brief definition of each.

1. *Perceiver*, one who clearly perceives the will of God. We have purposely chosen this word over *prophet* to avoid negative connotations and possible confusion, since the same root word is used in the other two categories of gifts, found in 1 Corinthians 12:10 and in Ephesians 4:11.

2. *Server*, one who loves to serve others. Another appropriate word is *doer*.

3. *Teacher*, one who loves to research and communicate truth. We almost selected the word *researcher* since that interest is so strong.

4. *Exhorter*, one who loves to encourage others to live a victorious life. These extremely positive people are often called *encouragers*.

5. *Giver*, one who loves to give of his time, talents, energy, means, and money to benefit others or advance the Gospel. This person could also be called a *contributor*.

6. *Administrator*, one who loves to organize, lead, or direct. Other identifying words could be *facilitator* or *leader*.

7. *Compassion person*, one who shows mercy, love, and care, especially to those who have great needs. We've chosen *compassion* over *mercy* since it is more comprehensive in today's usage.

The apostle Peter points out the universality of the motivational gifts:

> As each one has received a special gift, employ
> it in serving one another, as good stewards of the
> manifold grace of God.
>
> 1 Peter 4:10, NAS

Everyone has a motivational gift! No one has been left out. We have tested tens of thousands of people and each has discovered his specific giftedness in one of the seven categories, or sometimes more than one. This is true of our children as well.

OUR GIFTS WERE BUILT INTO US WHEN GOD FORMED US

Our gifts were not afterthoughts, but part of God's plan to equip us to accomplish His purposes for our lives.

One of the most beautiful Old Testament passages about our creation is found in the Psalms:

> For You did form my inward parts, You did knit me together in my mother's womb.
>
> I will confess and praise You, for You are fearfully wonderful, and for the awful wonder of my birth! Wonderful are Your works, and that my inner self knows right well.
>
> My frame was not hidden from You, when I was being formed in secret and intricately and curiously wrought (as if embroidered with various colors) in the depths of the earth [a region of darkness and mystery].
>
> Your eyes saw my unformed substance, and in Your book all the days of my life were written, before ever they took shape, when as yet there was none of them.
>
> Psalm 139:13–16, TAB

What a magnificent expression of the design and development of the child in the womb!

God uses what scientists now call DNA (deoxyribonucleic acid) in the genetic process. When a child is conceived, half of his DNA inheritance comes from the father and half from the mother. And in that microscopic fertilized egg the joined DNA forms a helix-shaped genetic ladder more than six feet long. How incredible!

Every detail of our physical being is programmed by DNA. Its intricacies outweigh the most sophisticated computer system on the market today. All our physical characteristics—our hair color, our nose shape, our height, our body frame, our complexion type—were determined by DNA at the moment of conception.

If God planned so precisely for the development of our physical bodies—which are eventually subject to degeneration and death—how much more would He plan for our giftedness! We believe we receive our motivational gifts at conception and, just as DNA produces our physical characteristics, so our motivational gifts produce interests, abilities, enthusiasms, and actions to make us effective members of the Body of Christ.

OUR GIFTS COLOR ALL WE SEE AND DO

If we go outside on a sunny day and put on sunglasses, all we see will be colored accordingly.

It's the same with a person's motivational gift. A perceiver looks at life through a perceiver's eyes. Everything looks good or bad, right or wrong, in God's will or out of God's will. The perceiver cannot see life any other way.

A server, on the other hand, approaches life thinking, "What can I do to help in this situation?" He constantly sees opportunities to do things for others.

A teacher searches for truth in everything he encounters. Like the persistent Diogenes of Greek literature, searching with a lantern for an honest man, the teacher persistently seeks, investigates, analyzes, and researches.

An exhorter sees opportunities to encourage people, to build them up. Exhorters always approach life positively.

The giver looks for ways to invest his time, talent, energy, money, and resources to provide for the needs of others and/or to advance the Gospel.

The administrator's broad vision grasps the overall perspective of a situation. Administrators naturally want to organize or lead.

The person of compassion recognizes hurts and wounds needing healing, and sees endless opportunities to express love.

Yet each one may think, "Why don't others see things the way I see them? It's so clear to me!"

The family setting always holds potential for great conflict and hurt when there is misunderstanding. Those outside the family usually cannot hurt us as deeply. Many conflicts within the family arise because its members fail to discern each other's gifts. Conflicts between family members disappear quickly as each discovers his own gifts and begins to make room for the gifts of others.

EACH GIFT IS OF EQUAL VALUE

We use this diagram when teaching about motivational gifts.

Notice that *all* gifts are *equal*, both in the sight of God and in their contributions to the collective functioning of the family and of the Body of Christ. No gift is higher than or better than another gift. If one gift is not in operation there is a lack, a void.

Each child receives God's best gift(s) for the working out of His plans and purposes in that child's life, and for the benefit of other lives he will touch. It is a parent's privilege and responsibility to help each child develop in his giftedness!

This can be summed up in the oft-quoted slogan:

What you are is God's gift to you;
What you make of your life is your gift to God.

People often ask us if the parents' giftedness determines their offspring's motivational gifts. Our answer is no. Two parents with the gift of compassion are just as likely to produce a server or an exhorter as a child with the gift of compassion. In a large family almost every gift may be represented.

God seems to bestow some gifts more frequently than others. That's because more people are needed in certain functions. We have compiled data showing the percentages of people who have each gift:[1]

Perceiver	12%	Giver	6%
Server	17%	Administrator	13%
Teacher	6%	Compassion person	30%
Exhorter	16%		

The most prevalent gift is compassion, perhaps because we desperately need love and compassion in the world.

Servers and exhorters almost tie for second place. Servers get the work done and exhorters offer encouragement to keep us all going.

Administrators and perceivers nearly tie for third place. Givers and teachers tie for fourth.

But the prevalence of a certain gift does not invest it with more importance. Neither does its rarity make it more special. All the gifts are equally important, and should be so treated within the family circle. All the gifts are necessary. All the gifts, when used properly, are blessings.

EACH GIFT MEETS SPECIFIC HUMAN NEEDS

Even in young children the various gifts begin to focus on meeting specific human needs. As children mature, so does the capability of their gifts, becoming more precise in meeting needs. All children, however, will naturally meet all of these needs to some degree.

The following chart offers a brief overview of the motivational gifts, the needs they meet, and what the gifts do in general:

[1] This information is based on detailed response sheets from approximately 1,000 people over 10 years and from more than 100 groups in a variety of states, provinces, and countries.

GIFT	DEFINITION	NEEDS MET	WHAT IT DOES
PERCEIVER	Declares the will of God	Spiritual	Keeps us centered on spiritual principles
SERVER	Renders practical service	Practical	Keeps the work of ministry moving
TEACHER	Researches and teaches the Bible	Mental	Keeps us studying and learning
EXHORTER	Encourages personal progress	Psychological	Keeps us applying spiritual truths
GIVER	Shares material assistance	Material	Keeps specific needs provided for
ADMINISTRATOR	Gives leadership & direction	Functional	Keeps us organized and increases our vision
COMPASSION PERSON	Provides personal & emotional support	Emotional	Keeps us in right attitudes & relationships

This is only a bird's-eye view of how the motivational gifts function. Some overlapping or interaction may occur, and secondary gifts color or modify the operation of a primary gift. The seven major needs are not met exclusively by the gift specified, but that gift will meet that need on a more consistent basis.

GOD'S PURPOSES CAN BE FULFILLED

The fact that you are reading this book indicates that you are interested in your children, and you want to experience the greatest joy of Christian parenthood: seeing God's purposes fulfilled in their lives.

Remember: Each child has been gifted by God. Discover those gifts and train him up to use them for the glory of God and to fulfill God's purposes for his life!

We hope the following chapters will help you in both the discovery and training processes.

MOTIVATIONAL GIFTS: A PORTRAIT

2

From one thousand responses to our motivational gifts questionnaire we've assembled a composite portrait of the qualities associated with each of the seven gifts. The portrait should serve as a tool, enabling parents not only to discover their children's gifts, but also to know better how to train them up in their giftedness (Proverbs 22:6).

The feedback questionnaires were collected from a broad cross-section of people from both the United States and Canada, representing all walks of life, ages, and most denominations. Allowing for the variables that impact people's lives, we've found normative characteristics that show up consistently even in the lives of young children, depending on their motivational gifts.

Each of the 21 categories for the seven gifts received a wide range of response, but eighty to ninety percent usually fell into clearly defined, indicative areas. We eliminated the minor areas of response for each category and developed 147 (7 x 21) definitive characteristics. Based upon this research we developed testing material for various age groups.

THE SURVEY

Here is the actual survey questionnaire from which we have tallied more than a thousand responses:

Please answer all the following questions about your childhood experiences and feelings as descriptively as possible:

1. *Emotions:*   Describe your emotional makeup as a child.
2. *Expression:*   How easy was it for you to communicate verbally?
3. *Self-Image:*   How do you feel about yourself as a person?
4. *Approach to Life:*   Describe your general approach to life (i.e., realistic, idealistic, systematic).
5. *Imagination/Reality:*   To what degree were you imaginative or realistic?
6. *Behavior:*   Describe your usual behavior patterns.
7. *Personal Habits:*   What were your good and bad habits?
8. *Friends:*   How many friends did you usually have? How did you feel about it?
9. *Relationships:*   How did you relate to peers, older children, parents, and teachers?
10. *Intellect:*   Describe your mental capacity as a child.
11. *Leadership:*   To what degree were you a leader or follower?
12. *School:*   How well did you do in school?
13. *Best Subjects:*   What were your best subjects in school?
14. *Reading:*   What did you like to read for enjoyment?
15. *Sports:*   In what sports did you participate regularly?
16. *Games/Toys:*   What were your favorite games and toys?
17. *Pets:*   Did you have pets? How did you feel about them?
18. *Qualities:*   List three positive qualities evident in you as a child.
19. *Interests:*   What were your general interests?
20. *Joy:*   What brought you the most joy as a child?
21. *Other comments on your childhood:*

We have summarized the various responses from our survey in the chart at the end of chapter 3 based on gifts evident in the adults who filled out the questionnaire. The age span covers earliest memories to high school age. While the data is typical for each gift, please remember: A child's secondary gift, the variables in life, and the freedom from polluting factors can all affect the degree to which he may match this data.

The category column lists the 21 subjects covered in our questionnaire survey, using only the key words for reference. (Some categories, like those referring to school age activities, will not be relevant to preschoolers.)

PARENTING STYLES AND CHILDREN'S GIFTS

Children's differing motivational gifts require different types of care, discipline, and training in the family setting. Our perceiver son required about four times the amount of discipline as did our administrator son or our compassion daughter. Compassion children are most easily wounded and most often in need of protection. They also must learn how to express negative feelings appropriately, in order to avoid deep emotional damage.

Teachers exasperate us with their questions and challenges while exhorters talk our ears off. Servers delight us with their helpfulness but get hurt if we don't show appreciation. Givers amaze us with their frugality, yet often prove to be stingy. And administrators may try to take over the organization of family activities, yet thrill us with their accomplishments.

TWO TYPES OF CHILDREN: SPEAKERS AND SERVERS

In respect to the motivational gifts there are two basic types of children: speakers and servers. This is identified in the verse following immediately after 1 Peter 4:10, a verse referring to the motivational gifts with a command to use them.

> As each one has received a special gift, employ it in serving one another, as good stewards of the manifold grace of God. Whoever *speaks*, let him speak, as it were, the utterances of God; whoever *serves*, let him do so as by the strength which God supplies; so that in all things God may be glorified through Jesus Christ, to whom belongs the glory and dominion forever and ever. Amen.
> 1 Peter 4:10–11, NAS

The first category of children consists of those whose motivational gifts enable them to be effective speakers: perceivers, teachers, exhorters, and administrators. These children fit our Western modes of education: They are naturally competitive, quick learners, articulate, and comfortable when speaking in front of the class.

The second category includes those whose motivational gifts enable them to be naturally helpful, cooperative, and supportive of others: servers, givers, and compassion children. They are *not* competitive. Meaningful relationships and working together for the benefit of all are more important to them. Less likely to excel in our educational systems, they are overwhelmed by the children with speaking gifts who thrive on competition.

CHILDREN'S LEARNING STYLES

Just as children's different learning styles have been recognized in secular educational circles, so the study of the motivational gifts in action shows that these gifts cause children to learn more effectively in various ways.

Children with serving gifts (serving, giving, and compassion) are generally more reserved and perform better when grouped together and separated from the more aggressive "speaking gift" children (perceivers, teachers, exhorters, and administrators).

Teachers who have developed subgroups for children with serving gifts for some learning sessions or activities have found that servers do much better academically and socially in the subgroups. When they are not overshadowed by their speaker counterparts, they overcome their shyness and speak up more readily. They thrive on more cooperative frameworks for learning. Personalities begin to blossom. Confidence builds.

How we wish all teachers would recognize these differences and provide more compatible learning opportunities for children with serving-type gifts! We go into this in more detail in chapter 26, "Insights for Those Who Teach and Work with Children."

Parents also benefit from this knowledge. Within most families the children have a variety of gifts. By knowing and understanding their children's giftedness parents can help them gain the most from school, providing the help and encouragement each child needs. It's good to be aware of these differences in the earliest years of a child's education.

Additional individual testing sets are available for each age group: preschool, primary (ages 6–8), junior (ages 9–12), youth (ages 13–21), and adult. We have also designed testing materials for situations where testing must be totally objective, for secular testing, for ministry discovery, and for occupational success determination. These are listed under "Additional Material Available" on page 293 in the back of the book.

With these thoughts in mind it's time to use the testing materials in the following chapters to discover your children's motivational gifts.

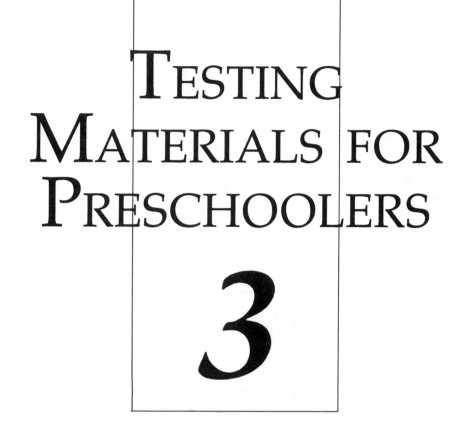

TESTING MATERIALS FOR PRESCHOOLERS

3

In this section we present testing materials parents of preschoolers can use to discover a general idea of their children's gifts. Gifts in preschool children are sometimes not as well-defined or easily discernible as with older children.

Recognizing children's motivational gifts makes us aware of the need to treat each child differently. There is no such thing as a model child. Rather, there are seven!

You will be using the composite portrait of the seven gifts beginning on page 27. Select a different colored pencil for each child. Then read the description across from each of the 21 categories, and circle the descriptions that match one child. The heading with the most circles should represent his primary gift. The one that has the next highest number of circles may be his secondary gift. Do the same for each child.

Record the information on the Early Childhood Scoring Records Chart on page 26. Note that there is provision for you to reevaluate each child at a later time. We suggest you do so every year since preschool children continue to develop so significantly. The older the child, the more likely you will be able to determine his giftedness clearly.

When a child enters first grade, or is five or six years old, we recommend you use the Primary Children's Questionnaire found in chapter 4 to test him. When he enters the fourth grade, or is eight or nine years old, give him the Junior Children's Questionnaire in chapter 5. When he enters seventh grade, or is eleven or twelve years old, he's ready for the Youth Questionnaire in chapter 6.

EARLY CHILDHOOD SCORING RECORDS CHART

Name of child	Color code	Age	Date	Primary gift	Secondary gift
		Age	Date	Primary gift	Secondary gift
		Age	Date	Primary gift	Secondary gift
Name of child	Color code	Age	Date	Primary gift	Secondary gift
		Age	Date	Primary gift	Secondary gift
		Age	Date	Primary gift	Secondary gift
Name of child	Color code	Age	Date	Primary gift	Secondary gift
		Age	Date	Primary gift	Secondary gift
		Age	Date	Primary gift	Secondary gift
Name of child	Color code	Age	Date	Primary gift	Secondary gift
		Age	Date	Primary gift	Secondary gift
		Age	Date	Primary gift	Secondary gift
Name of child	Color code	Age	Date	Primary gift	Secondary gift
		Age	Date	Primary gift	Secondary gift
		Age	Date	Primary gift	Secondary gift
Name of child	Color code	Age	Date	Primary gift	Secondary gift
		Age	Date	Primary gift	Secondary gift
		Age	Date	Primary gift	Secondary gift

Testing Materials for Preschoolers

CATEGORY	PERCEIVER	SERVER	TEACHER	EXHORTER	GIVER	ADMINISTRATOR	COMPASSION
1. Emotions	Sensitive Intense Extremes of secure & insecure	Shy Sensitive Emotional Easily embarrassed	Stable disposition Unemotional Reserved	Happy Sensitive Balanced	Happy Expressive of feelings Sometimes shy	Stable Confident Sensitive Happy Enthusiastic	Sensitive Shy Hard to express negative feelings
2. Expression	Verbalizes easily	Verbalizes with difficulty Quiet Shy in class	Verbalizes easily Articulate Dislikes small talk	Very verbal! Likes public speaking	Some verbalize easily Some verbalize with difficulty	Very verbal Expresses self easily	Verbalization hard to easy depending on feelings Softspoken
3. Self-image	Self-image problems Negative Introspective	Low self-image Needs to be appreciated Security in doing	Good self-image Objective	Most have good self-image Positive personality	Average self-image	Average to very good self-image Basically secure	Poor to good self-image Insecure Takes guilt for conflict
4. Approach to life	Idealistic Practical Creative Can get depressed	Practical Idealistic & realistic Oriented toward doing	Realistic Idealistic Practical Searcher for truth	Idealistic Creative Realistic Practical Adaptable	Balanced between realistic & idealistic Wholehearted	Practical Systematic Creative Wide areas of interest	Idealistic Creative Subjective Loving Peacemaker
5. Reality/ imagination	Can be both but mostly imaginative	Excellent imagination Good at pretending Realistic	Very realistic Poor imagination	Imaginative and also practical	Very imaginative	Both realistic & imaginative	Very imaginative Daydreamer

CATEGORY	PERCEIVER	SERVER	TEACHER	EXHORTER	GIVER	ADMINISTRATOR	COMPASSION
6. Behavior	Obedient Extremes of good/bad Very strong-willed	Obedient Quiet Likes to do things on own terms	Obedient Independent Entertains self easily	Obedient Outgoing Adaptable	Obedient Industrious	Obedient Gregarious Competitive Pleasing	Obedient Loving Indecisive Crusader for good causes
7. Personal habits	Dependable Wants to be right! Tattletale	Neat, tidy Helpful Completes projects	Neat Good study habits Punctual Intolerant	Neat, clean Helpful Accepting Not saver Interrupts	Neat Helpful Friendly Makes money Saves money	Studious Plans ahead Saves things Procrastinates	Neat, clean Helpful Disorganized Not punctual "Now" people
8. Friends	Few or no friends Loner	Only a few friends	Just a few friends Often a loner	Many friends Gregarious Joiner Well-liked	Just a few friends Supportive	Average to many friends Likes large groups Joiner	A few close friends Drawn to friendless
9. Relationships	Relates best to adults & teachers Relates poorly to peers	Relates best to parents Good to teachers Shy toward peers	Relates best to parents & teachers Some difficulty with peers	Relates well to everyone	Relates well to everyone	Relates very well to all Tends toward broad relationships	Relates best to adults & teachers Average to peers
10. Intellect	Above average	Average to good Good at details	Very intelligent Highest IQs Investigative	Above average to excellent	Average to good	Good to excellent Investigative	Average to above average Concern for feelings

CATEGORY	PERCEIVER	SERVER	TEACHER	EXHORTER	GIVER	ADMINISTRATOR	COMPASSION
11. Leadership	Can be either leader or follower	Follower Prefers smaller groups	Some are leaders	Mostly leaders	Primarily follower Sometimes will lead	Excellent leader Organizer Delegates	Follower Occasionally will lead
12. School	Above average Focuses on facts and truths	Average to good Meticulous	Excellent student! Self-motivated Overprepares	Above average	Average to good	Excellent student Excels Enjoys a challenge	Average to above average
13. Best subjects	1. English 2. Math 3. History 4. Art 5. Drama	1. Math 2. English 3. History 4. Science 5. Home ec/shop	1. History 2. English 3. Good in all subjects	1. English 2. Math 3. History 4. Likes most subjects	1. English 2. Math 3. Business 4. History/geography	1. English 2. Math 3. History 4. Good in all subjects	1. English 2. Math 3. Art/music 4. History
14. Reading	1. Biography 2. Romance 3. Adventure 4. Mystery	1. Adventure 2. Mystery 3. Romance 4. Historical novel	1. Prolific reader 2. Historical novel 3. Mystery	1. Biography 2. Fiction 3. Nonfiction	1. Loves to read 2. Fiction 3. Adventure 4. Animal	1. Wide range of interests 2. Mystery 3. Biography	1. Romance 2. Mystery 3. Fairy tale & fantasy 4. Animal
15. Sports	Prefers individual sports—swim, ski, bicycle	Group sports Noncompetitive sports—swim, skate Some: none	Not much interest Prefers watching or books	Loves active sports Group sports Swimming	Most like group sports Some don't like any sports	Group sports Competitive sports	No sports or noncompetitive sports

CATEGORY	PERCEIVER	SERVER	TEACHER	EXHORTER	GIVER	ADMINISTRATOR	COMPASSION
16. Games & toys	Makes up own games, Plays alone, Toys—real things	Card games, Table games, Manual skill & crafts, Puzzles	Table games, Active games, Prefers books	Active games, Group games, Toys with a purpose—ball, skates	Outdoor games, Construction toys, Creative play	Table games, Group games, Creative play	Table games, Card games, Quiet imaginative play
17. Pets	Loves pets	Loves pets, Feels they are special friends	Indifferent about pets, Would rather read a book	Likes them but prefers people	Enjoys pets but people even more	Loves pets but not the routine care	Adores pets, They are their friends, Brings home strays
18. Qualities	1. Sensitive 2. Honest 3. Loyal 4. Responsible	1. Helpful 2. Reliable 3. Sensitive 4. Obedient	1. Intelligent 2. Honest 3. Diligent 4. Dependable	1. Friendly 2. Loving 3. Obedient 4. Happy	1. Industrious 2. Generous 3. Honest 4. Thrifty	1. Capable 2. Responsible 3. Honest 4. Gregarious	1. Loving 2. Caring 3. Helpful 4. Obedient
19. Interests	1. Reading 2. Sports 3. Music	1. Handwork 2. Animals 3. Homemaking skills/build/fix	1. Reading 2. Studying 3. The arts	1. People 2. Outdoor activities 3. Reading	1. Reading 2. Friends 3. Making & giving money	1. Wide areas of interest 2. Doing things with others 3. Reading	1. Music/art 2. Reading 3. People
20. Joy	1. Family activities 2. Nature 3. Feeling approved	1. Family activities 2. Appreciation 3. Serving	1. Family activities 2. Learning 3. Being accepted	1. Family activities 2. Making others happy 3. People	1. Family activities 2. Helping others 3. Travel	1. Family activities 2. Accomplishments 3. People	1. Family activities 2. Friendships 3. Being appreciated
21. Other	Strong conscience, Opinionated, Blunt	Good dexterity, Not college-oriented	Bookworm, Teacher's pet	Encourager, Gives lots of advice	All-around personality, Gives generously	Makes lists, Writes notes, Plans	Easily hurt, Easily moved to tears

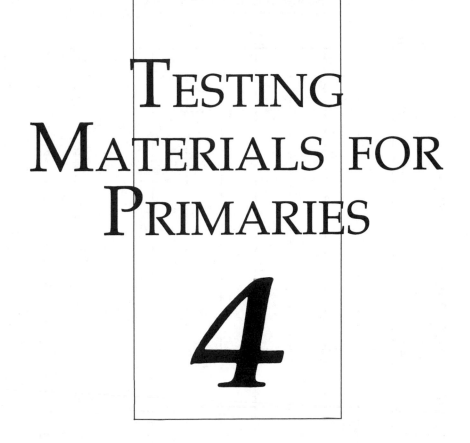

TESTING MATERIALS FOR PRIMARIES

4

The following Primary Children's Questionnaire is designed for children ages six through eight, or who are in grades one through three. The testing should be done by the parent or teacher.

THE SCORING PROCEDURE

Only five options are given: never (0), seldom (1), sometimes (2), usually (3), and always (4). Score the child according to how true the statement is about him by placing an "X" in the appropriate box. Then record the numerical scores in the point column. When all 25 characteristics of a gift have been completed, total the scores. Then shade in the total from left to right on the profile sheet bar graph matching the gift. Complete all the gifts. Comparison of the seven scores will reveal the child's strongest gifts.

Fill out the information at the bottom of the profile sheet. Teachers should keep a photocopy of each student's completed profile sheet for future use or reference. Parents, remember: You may want to retest your children every year or so since gifts can be identified more precisely as children get older.

A separate questionnaire should be used for each child. Additional copies of the Primary Children's Questionnaire are available through the ordering information at the end of the book.

In chapters 8 through 14 of Part II, "Train Up Your Children in Their Gifts," we will go into extensive detail about the characteristics.

David - 7.5 - 1st grade - Feb 2005 #1
#2
#3

Primary Children's Questionnaire

Discover Your Children's Gifts

PRIMARY CHILDREN'S MOTIVATIONAL GIFT PROFILE SHEET

Gift	0	10	20	30	40	50	60	70	80	90	100
Perceiver											
Server											
Teacher											
Exhorter											
Giver											
Administrator											
Compassion Person											

#1 GIFT Perception 71

#2 GIFT Giving 70

#3 GIFT Exhortation 65

NAME Alex

AGE 6 GRADE K DATE Feb 2005

PARENT/TEACHER _____

Primary Children's Questionnaire

GIFT OF PERCEPTION

1. Is very sensitive to God's will, with a desire to please Him.
2. Emotions vacillate from one extreme to the other.
3. Sees everything as black or white, good or evil, right or wrong.
4. Finds it easy to talk because of strong opinions.
5. Is frank and outspoken.
6. Prone to have self-image problems.
7. Tends to be negative.
8. Is often too idealistic.
9. Has a strong conscience.
10. Tends to feel he is always right.
11. Can get depressed easily.
12. Tends to be strong-willed and stubborn.
13. Longs to be obedient and feels guilty when disobedient.
14. Often a tattletale.
15. Has few or no friends.
16. Enjoys playing alone.
17. Easily senses the character of other children.
18. Prefers to be around adults more than others his own age.
19. Does above average in school.
20. Shows early signs of leadership ability, but bossy.
21. Prefers active individual sports best.
22. Prefers realistic games and toys to fantasy types.
23. Loves pets but can get along fine without them.
24. Is very dependable, but almost legalistic about his promises.
25. Has a strong belief in the power of prayer; prays easily.

#	Never 0	Seldom 1	Sometimes 2	Usually 3	Always 4	POINTS
1.		X		1		
2.			1		1	
3.		X		X		
4.	X			1		
5.	X			1		
6.			X			
7.		1	X			
8.		X	X			
9.			X		1	
10.			X	1		
11.				X	1	
12.				X		
13.			X	1		
14.		X			1	
15.			1		1	
16.		1				
17.				X		
18.					X	
19.			1	X		
20.				X		
21.				X		
22.				1		
23.		X	X			
24.		X			1	
25.		X			1	
						TOTAL

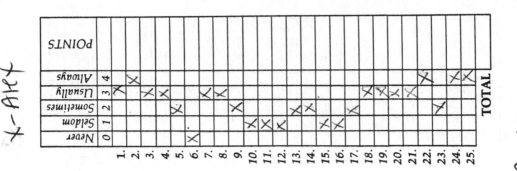

	Never	Seldom	Sometimes	Usually	Always	POINTS
	0	1	2	3	4	
1.				X		
2.					X	
3.				X		
4.				X		
5.			X			
6.	X					
7.				X		
8.				X		
9.			X			
10.		X				
11.		X				
12.		X				
13.			X			
14.			X			
15.		X				
16.		X				
17.			X			
18.				X		
19.				X		
20.				X		
21.				X		
22.					X	
23.			X			
24.					X	
25.					X	
					TOTAL	

Primary Children's Questionnaire

THE GIFT OF SERVING

1. Finds the greatest joy is in helping others.
2. Loves to work with his hands and is exceptionally good at it.
3. Is shy and easily embarrassed.
4. Tends to be very quiet in school or other group situations.
5. Doesn't like to speak in front of the class.
6. Is prone to have a low self-image.
7. Needs lots of verbal appreciation.
8. Is very realistic and practical.
9. Has excellent imagination.
10. Is very independent about the way he likes to do things.
11. Keeps his room tidy and neat.
12. Always wants to finish what he starts.
13. Seems to be content with just a few close friends.
14. Relates better to adults than to peers.
15. Is an average student but especially good at details.
16. Is definitely a follower, not a leader.
17. Prefers noncompetitive sports.
18. Loves to work on things like crafts, collections, and puzzles.
19. Feels a pet is like a special friend.
20. Always agrees to help when asked.
21. Proves to be consistently reliable.
22. Likes to build, create, or fix things.
23. Tends to be a perfectionist.
24. Shows love for others by what he does for them.
25. Seems to have endless energy.

Primary Children's Questionnaire

THE GIFT OF TEACHING

1. Finds the greatest joy in learning.
2. Has the ability to be exceptionally objective.
3. Has very stable emotions.
4. Not only speaks easily and well but is exceptionally articulate.
5. Has a good self-image and self-confidence.
6. Has strong convictions and opinions.
7. Loves to search for truth.
8. Has a poor imagination; not good at pretending.
9. Is exceptionally independent.
10. Is self-disciplined.
11. Consistently punctual.
12. Has a few friends but also enjoys being alone.
13. Relates better to parents, adults, and teachers than to peers.
14. Has exceptionally high I.Q.
15. Is a top-of-the-class student.
16. Develops and uses a large vocabulary.
17. Motivated to study without being told.
18. Very good at leadership.
19. Tends to excel in every subject.
20. Loves to read books on almost any subject; a "bookworm."
21. Is not much interested in sports.
22. Especially enjoys word games and table games.
23. Is indifferent about pets; prefers books.
24. Likes things like operas, art, music and ballet.
25. Often considered a teacher's pet.

	Never 0	Seldom 1	Sometimes 2	Usually 3	Always 4	POINTS
1.				✓		
2.			✓			
3.			✓			
4.				✓		
5.				✓		
6.				✓		
7.				✓		
8.		✓				
9.			✓			
10.			✓			
11.			✓			
12.		✓				
13.			✓			
14.				✓		
15.				✓		
16.					✓	
17.				✓		
18.				✓		
19.				✓		
20.			✓			
21.			✓			
22.			✓			
23.				✓	✓	
24.			✓			
25.				✓		
					TOTAL	

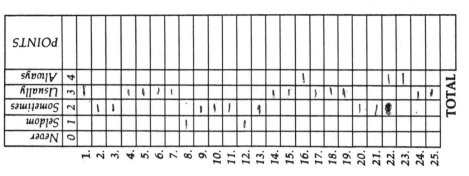

35

Primary Children's Questionnaire

THE GIFT OF EXHORTATION

	Never	Seldom	Sometimes	Usually	Always	POINTS
	0	1	2	3	4	
1. Greatest joy is encouraging others.				/		
2. Is a happy child with a balanced personality.				/		
3. Is talking constantly.					/	
4. Loves opportunity to talk in front of a class or group.				/ /		
5. Has a very positive personality.			/			
6. Is sensible and practical about everything.					/	
7. Would rather be with people than anything else.				/ /		
8. Accepts himself and others unreservedly.				/		
9. Is amazingly adaptable.						
10. Throws away anything that is not useful.			/			
11. Tends to interrupt in his eagerness to express himself.				/	/	
12. Has lots of friends.				/ /		
13. Is well-liked by peers.				/		
14. Gets along well with parents, teachers, and friends.					/	
15. Is a very good student.				/ /		
16. Enjoys being a leader, but can also be a good follower.				/ /		
17. Likes active and group sports.			/			
18. Prefers toys with a purpose.			/			
19. Enjoys pets but would rather be with friends.			/			
20. Is exceptionally friendly to everyone.				/		
21. Loves to make others happy.				/		
22. Learns his best lessons from experience.			/			
23. Loves to give advice.				/		
24. Is not very skilled with his hands.			/			
25. Enjoys looking for ways to make tasks easier.			/			
					TOTAL	

Primary Children's Questionnaire

THE GIFT OF GIVING

	Never 0	Seldom 1	Sometimes 2	Usually 3	Always 4	POINTS
1. Greatest joy is in giving to others.				/		
2. Is typically a happy child.				/		
3. Expresses his feelings well, but is sometimes shy.					/	
4. Has an average self-image.			/			
5. Is wholehearted in whatever he does.				/		
6. Has a positive personality.				/		
7. Is very imaginative.			.			
8. Is amazingly industrious.			/			
9. Is exceptionally good at making money.			/			
10. Is thrifty and tends to save money rather than spend it.			/			
11. Has just a few friends but is very loyal to them.			.	/		
12. Relates to adults and peers equally well.			/			
13. Is an average to good student.		/	/			
14. Prefers to be a follower, but occasionally will lead.			/			
15. Has about an average interest in sports.		/	/			
16. Likes toys and games that build or create.			/			
17. Enjoys creative play.		/				
18. Is quick to help whenever he sees a need for help.					/	
19. Loves to help entertain visitors in his home.					/	
20. Is consistently honest.					/	
21. Is eager to tithe and give even more of his money.					/	
22. Wants his gifts to be the best he can make or buy.				/		
23. Often gives away what he has to others.					/	
24. Likes to pray often for missionaries and unsaved people.					/	
25. Loves to tell others about Jesus.					/	
TOTAL						

A-70

Primary Children's Questionnaire

THE GIFT OF ADMINISTRATION

	Never 0	Seldom 1	Sometimes 2	Usually 3	Always 4	POINTS
1.					ı	
2.				ı		
3.				ı		
4.				ı		
5.				ı		
6.		ı				
7.					ı	
8.				ı		
9.			ı			
10.			ı			
11.			ı			
12.			ı			
13.				ı		
14.					ı	
15.					ı	
16.					ı	
17.			ı			
18.					ı	
19.			ı			
20.			ı			
21.		ı				
22.				ı		
23.		ı				
24.		ı				
25.		ı				
TOTAL						

1. Greatest joy is in accomplishing something.
2. Confident and enthusiastic about whatever he does.
3. Is very good at self-expression and loves to speak in class.
4. Self-accepting, with a good self-image.
5. Definitely has a wide area of interests.
6. Can be either realistic or imaginative, depending on the situation.
7. Thrives on competition; always wants to be first or best.
8. Always planning ahead.
9. Tends to save everything thinking he'll have a use for it later.
10. Usually has a messy room, meaning to put things away "later."
11. Has many friends and enjoys large groups.
12. Is a joiner who may also create a group for others to join.
13. Gets along well with parents, teachers, and peers.
14. Respects and obeys authority.
15. Is an excellent student who enjoys a challenge.
16. Tends to excel in school in all subjects.
17. Loves to be a leader and to organize.
18. Enjoys being in charge and telling others what to do.
19. Loves to plan and to create projects.
20. Enjoys reading in a wide range of subjects.
21. Loves competitive sports.
22. Likes group games and challenging table games.
23. Is an exceptionally capable child.
24. Does not enjoy doing routine tasks.
25. Constantly makes lists of things to do and writes notes to himself.

Primary Children's Questionnaire

THE GIFT OF COMPASSION

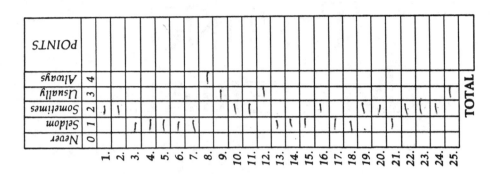

	Never	Seldom	Sometimes	Usually	Always	POINTS
	0	1	2	3	4	
1.			✓			
2.			✓			
3.		✓				
4.		✓				
5.		✓				
6.		✓				
7.		✓				
8.					✓	
9.			✓			
10.			✓			
11.				✓		
12.				✓		
13.		✓				
14.		✓				
15.			✓			
16.		✓				
17.		✓				
18.		✓				
19.			✓			
20.			✓			
21.		✓				
22.			✓			
23.			✓			
24.			✓			
25.				✓		
						TOTAL

1. Greatest joy is showing love to someone who is hurting.
2. Finds it very difficult to admit and express negative feelings.
3. Shy about speaking up in class or in groups.
4. Tends to have a poor self-image when he doesn't feel loved.
5. Tends to feel insecure.
6. Finds it hard to stand up for his own rights.
7. Becomes so idealistic that he's often unrealistic.
8. Is an incredibly loving and cuddly child; a constant hugger.
9. Tries to be a peacemaker whenever that role is needed.
10. Is often a daydreamer.
11. Is extremely imaginative and creative.
12. Eager to please and be obedient.
13. Tends to be indecisive.
14. Tends to be unorganized and does not plan ahead.
15. Seems unaware of the importance of time and is usually not punctual.
16. Is drawn to be a friend to those who have no friends.
17. Is an average student who focuses more on relationships than studies.
18. Would rather be a follower than a leader.
19. Loves animal, fantasy, and/or mystery stories.
20. Prefers noncompetitive sports or none at all.
21. Enjoys quiet, imaginative play and noncompetitive games.
22. Adores pets and feels they are his special friends.
23. Always looks for the good in people and ignores the bad.
24. Is thin-skinned and easily hurt.
25. Often prays for those who have needs or who hurt.

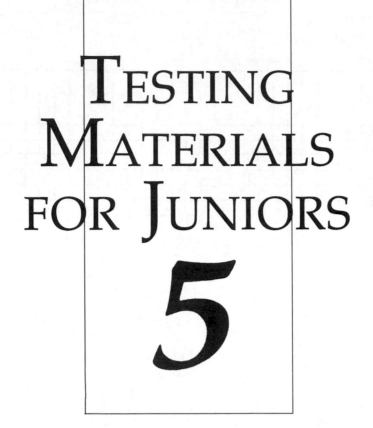

TESTING MATERIALS FOR JUNIORS

5

The following children's questionnaire is designed for young people nine to twelve years old, or in grades four through six. A parent, teacher, or leader should help with the testing. We recommend you have a copy of the *Junior Children's Questionnaire Scoring Set*, available by mail, for each junior being tested. See the ordering information at the end of the book.

HERE'S HOW TO SCORE

The parent or teacher should read the following instructions and then assist the student(s) in scoring this test. The characteristics of the seven motivational gifts have been written at the upper grade school level. Some concepts, however, will require your explanation.

There are 25 characteristics for each gift. As the student considers each characteristic have him ask himself, "How true is this of me?" His first response will probably be most accurate. Tell him not to answer the way he'd *like* to be or the way he thinks he *ought* to be, but to score the way he *is*. Have him be honest! There are no right or wrong answers; this is simply a self-discovery process. Parents may want to assist a child with some of the scoring choices, but be sure to give him the opportunity to try first. If he has not been realistic or has misunderstood the characteristic, talk it over with him and have him adjust his score accordingly.

EXPLAIN THE SCORING PROCESS

If the characteristic is never true of him, have him put an "X" in the box under *never*, and place a "0" in the points column.

If the characteristic is true of him only on rare occasions, have him score under *seldom*, and place a "1" in the points column.

If the characteristic is sometimes true of him, perhaps up to 49% of the time, have him score under *sometimes*, and place a "2" in the points column.

If the characteristic is usually true of him, more than 50% of the time, have him score under *usually*, and place a "3" in the points column.

If the characteristic is true of him all of the time, have him score under *always*, and place a "4" in the points column.

After finishing all 25 characteristics of a gift he can total those scores at the bottom of the scoring sheet. When he has completed all seven gifts, have him transfer the scores to the profile sheet on the next page by shading in the horizontal columns from left to right up to the number of points he scored for each gift.

Now the student will have a composite profile of himself. The score standing farthest out to the right, like a nose on a person's facial profile, is his primary motivational gift. He will also be able to see which is his secondary gift, third, and so forth.

Knowing his giftedness will enable a child to use and develop it, and to understand, value, and appreciate himself more. The self-discovery process will improve his interpersonal relationships and enlighten future career choices.

The profile also helps a child identify areas where he is *least* gifted so he will not feel he must excel in everything.

Have your child fill out the information at the bottom of the profile sheet. Teachers should keep a photocopy of each student's profile sheet for future use or reference. Parents may want to retest a child every year or so. The older the child, the more well-defined the test scores usually are.

Junior Children's Questionnaire

JUNIOR CHILDREN'S MOTIVATIONAL GIFT PROFILE SHEET

Gift	0	10	20	30	40	50	60	70	80	90	100
Perceiver											
Server											
Teacher											
Exhorter											
Giver											
Administrator											
Compassion Person											

NAME _____ #1 GIFT _____

AGE _____ GRADE _____ DATE _____ #2 GIFT _____

PARENT/TEACHER _____ #3 GIFT _____

Junior Children's Questionnaire

GIFT OF PERCEPTION

	Never	Seldom	Sometimes	Usually	Always	POINTS
	0	1	2	3	4	
1.						
2.						
3.						
4.						
5.						
6.						
7.						
8.						
9.						
10.						
11.						
12.						
13.						
14.						
15.						
16.						
17.						
18.						
19.						
20.						
21.						
22.						
23.						
24.						
25.						
					TOTAL	

1. My greatest joy is seeing God's will being done.
2. I want to help people do what is right.
3. I'm so idealistic that I can get depressed easily.
4. I'm always trying to analyze myself.
5. My emotions seem to go from one extreme to the other.
6. It's easy for me to talk because what I say is the truth.
7. I am strong-willed.
8. I always know what God wants me to do.
9. I am basically a loner with few or no friends.
10. I'd rather be around adults than others my own age.
11. I would usually rather be a leader than a follower.
12. I do above-average work in school.
13. I prefer to read biographies.
14. I am very dependable.
15. I like active individual sports best.
16. I prefer real things to toys.
17. I have a strong conscience.
18. I see things as black or white, good or evil, right or wrong.
19. I can easily sense the character of others.
20. I see problems as opportunities for growth.
21. I am frank and outspoken.
22. I view the Bible as the basis for truth.
23. My opinions are strong and right.
24. I get very sad over the sins of others.
25. I feel God wants me to spend much time praying for others.

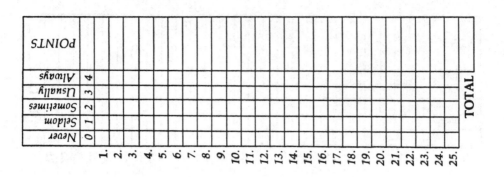

POINTS	Always	Usually	Sometimes	Seldom	Never
	4	3	2	1	0
1.					
2.					
3.					
4.					
5.					
6.					
7.					
8.					
9.					
10.					
11.					
12.					
13.					
14.					
15.					
16.					
17.					
18.					
19.					
20.					
21.					
22.					
23.					
24.					
25.					
TOTAL					

Junior Children's Questionnaire

THE GIFT OF SERVING

1. My greatest joy is doing things for others.
2. I like to do things with my hands.
3. I am very realistic and practical.
4. I need appreciation in order to feel good about myself.
5. I am shy and easily embarrassed.
6. I don't like to speak in front of a class.
7. I like to do things the way I like to do them.
8. I'm good at imitating and pretending.
9. I have just a few close friends.
10. I feel more comfortable around my parents than around other kids.
11. I would rather be a follower than a leader.
12. I am an average student and good at details.
13. I prefer to read adventure stories.
14. I am very helpful.
15. I prefer noncompetitive sports.
16. I love to work on things like crafts, collections, and puzzles.
17. I am especially good with my hands.
18. I am very neat.
19. I always want to finish what I start.
20. I have a hard time saying no when asked to help.
21. I usually do more than I'm asked to do.
22. I'd rather work on a short project than a long one.
23. I want everything I do to be perfect.
24. I show love for others by what I do for them.
25. I always have lots of energy.

Junior Children's Questionnaire

THE GIFT OF TEACHING

	Never	Seldom	Sometimes	Usually	Always	POINTS
	0	1	2	3	4	
1.						
2.						
3.						
4.						
5.						
6.						
7.						
8.						
9.						
10.						
11.						
12.						
13.						
14.						
15.						
16.						
17.						
18.						
19.						
20.						
21.						
22.						
23.						
24.						
25.						
						TOTAL

1. My greatest joy is learning.
2. I'd rather read a book than anything else.
3. I love to search for truth.
4. I am very objective about myself.
5. My emotions are very stable.
6. I can speak easily and well.
7. I am very independent.
8. It's hard for me to pretend or to use my imagination.
9. I have a few friends but also enjoy being alone.
10. I'd rather be with my parents or teacher than with other kids.
11. I enjoy being a leader.
12. I am an excellent student.
13. I love to read books on almost any subject.
14. I am always on time.
15. I'm really not interested in sports.
16. I prefer word games.
17. I am a bookworm.
18. I like things like operas, art, music, and ballet.
19. I love to study and do research.
20. I like things to be logical, systematic, and organized.
21. I like to develop and use a large vocabulary.
22. I believe Scriptures should always be used in the right context.
23. I believe truth has the power to change people.
24. I have strong convictions and opinions.
25. I am self-disciplined.

45

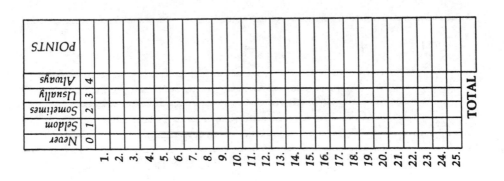

	Never	Seldom	Sometimes	Usually	Always	POINTS
	0	1	2	3	4	
1.						
2.						
3.						
4.						
5.						
6.						
7.						
8.						
9.						
10.						
11.						
12.						
13.						
14.						
15.						
16.						
17.						
18.						
19.						
20.						
21.						
22.						
23.						
24.						
25.						
TOTAL						

Junior Children's Questionnaire

THE GIFT OF EXHORTATION

1. My greatest joy is encouraging others.
2. I'd rather be with people than anything else.
3. I am very adaptable.
4. I have a positive personality.
5. I am a happy person.
6. I absolutely love to talk.
7. I always look for ways to make tasks easier.
8. I am very practical about everything.
9. I have lots of friends.
10. I get along well with my parents, teachers, and all my friends.
11. I enjoy being either a leader or a follower.
12. I am an above-average student.
13. I prefer to read biographies.
14. I'm very accepting of others.
15. I like active and group sports.
16. I like toys with a purpose.
17. I am not good with my hands.
18. I love to show others how to be happy.
19. I prefer to learn about things I can apply in my daily life.
20. I believe that truth is best learned in everyday experience.
21. I love to help others solve their problems.
22. I think problems help me grow and develop character.
23. I clear up problems with others as quickly as possible.
24. I find that others like me because I'm so positive.
25. I prefer to share the Lord by how I live rather than by what I say.

Junior Children's Questionnaire

THE GIFT OF GIVING

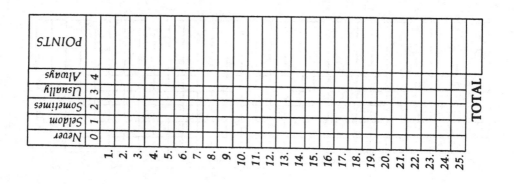

	Never	Seldom	Sometimes	Usually	Always	POINTS
	0	1	2	3	4	
1.						
2.						
3.						
4.						
5.						
6.						
7.						
8.						
9.						
10.						
11.						
12.						
13.						
14.						
15.						
16.						
17.						
18.						
19.						
20.						
21.						
22.						
23.						
24.						
25.						
TOTAL						

1. My greatest joy is giving to help others.
2. I do everything I can to witness to others.
3. I try to live my life wholeheartedly.
4. I think I am about average in how I feel about myself.
5. I am a happy person.
6. I am about average in my ability to express myself.
7. I am industrious.
8. I have a good imagination.
9. I have a few friends and I'm very supportive of them.
10. I enjoy everyone.
11. I usually prefer to be a follower rather than a leader.
12. I am usually a good student.
13. I love to read, especially fictional stories.
14. I am good at making and saving money.
15. I have about an average interest in sports.
16. I like toys and games that are constructive.
17. I believe in giving a tithe and even more if possible.
18. I like to give quietly, without others knowing about it.
19. I am delighted when my gift is an answer to prayer.
20. I want my gifts to be the best I can make or buy.
21. I pray often for those who are sharing the Gospel a lot.
22. I love to help entertain visitors in our home.
23. I am quick to help whenever I see a need for help.
24. I'm not gullible.
25. I think I have a well-rounded personality.

	Never	Seldom	Sometimes	Usually	Always	POINTS
	0	1	2	3	4	
1.						
2.						
3.						
4.						
5.						
6.						
7.						
8.						
9.						
10.						
11.						
12.						
13.						
14.						
15.						
16.						
17.						
18.						
19.						
20.						
21.						
22.						
23.						
24.						
25.						
						TOTAL

Junior Children's Questionnaire

THE GIFT OF ADMINISTRATION

1. My greatest joy comes in accomplishing something.
2. I have a wide span of interests.
3. I love to plan and to work on projects.
4. I am basically self-accepting.
5. I am confident and enthusiastic about whatever I do.
6. It's easy for me to express myself.
7. I always want to be first or best.
8. I can be either realistic or imaginative, depending on the situation.
9. I have many friends and enjoy large groups.
10. I feel I get along well with parents, teachers, and friends.
11. I love to be a leader and to organize.
12. I am an excellent student who enjoys a challenge.
13. I love to read on a wide range of subjects.
14. I have to admit that my room is usually untidy.
15. I love competitive sports.
16. I like group games.
17. I'm always making lists and writing notes to myself.
18. I've always felt it's important to obey authority.
19. I'm quick to take a leadership role if no one else will.
20. It's easy to see the overall picture and set long-range goals.
21. I do not enjoy doing routine tasks.
22. I like to be in charge and tell others what to do.
23. I'm willing to take criticism in order to get something done.
24. I'll work hard to get something done even if another gets the credit.
25. I really enjoy working with people.

	Never	Seldom	Sometimes	Usually	Always	POINTS
	0	1	2	3	4	
1.						
2.						
3.						
4.						
5.						
6.						
7.						
8.						
9.						
10.						
11.						
12.						
13.						
14.						
15.						
16.						
17.						
18.						
19.						
20.						
21.						
22.						
23.						
24.						
25.						
						TOTAL

Junior Children's Questionnaire

THE GIFT OF COMPASSION

1. My greatest joy is showing love to those who are hurting.
2. I want to make sure everyone feels good.
3. I'm so idealistic that I'm sometimes unrealistic.
4. I don't always feel good about myself.
5. I am shy and quiet.
6. I am very softspoken.
7. It's hard for me to stand up for my own rights.
8. I am a daydreamer.
9. I try to be a friend to those who have no friends.
10. I am eager to please everyone.
11. I would rather be a follower than a leader.
12. I am an average student.
13. I love to read romance, fantasy, or mystery stories.
14. I am very loving.
15. I prefer noncompetitive sports or none at all.
16. I enjoy quiet, imaginative play and games.
17. I realize that I am easily hurt.
18. I am eager to help people who are hurting on the inside.
19. I always look for the good in people and ignore the bad.
20. I want everyone to get along with everyone else.
21. It's easy for me to tell when someone is insincere.
22. I am very trusting of others.
23. I feel happy when others are happy and sad when others are sad.
24. I often pray for those who have needs or who hurt.
25. I don't like to be rushed in what I do.

TIE BREAKERS FOR JUNIOR CHILDREN

If you find that your first two scores are tied or very close, use the tie-breakers below. Look for the choice that fits you.

Answer every question, even if you feel, "I really like to do both." *Make a choice, even if the margin of choice is very small.*

If your answer is (a), your main gift is the first of the two gifts named. If your answer is (b), your gift is the second one named.

You can also use these tie-breakers to distinguish between other gifts ranking close together on your profile sheet.

PERCEIVER/SERVER
Would you rather
____ a. win an argument (or)
____ b. work with your hands?

PERCEIVER/TEACHER
Do you prefer to
____ a. tell others what to do (or)
____ b. read a book?

PERCEIVER/EXHORTER
Would you rather tell others
____ a. what their problems are (or)
____ b. how to solve their problems?

PERCEIVER/GIVER
Would you rather
____ a. give advice (or)
____ b. do something for someone?

PERCEIVER/ADMINISTRATOR
Would you rather
____ a. tell others where they're right or wrong (or)
____ b. organize a project?

PERCEIVER/COMPASSION
Do you most often help others with
____ a. their spiritual needs (or)
____ b. their emotional needs?

SERVER/TEACHER
Would you enjoy
____ a. serving on a committee (or)
____ b. giving a report in front of the class?

SERVER/EXHORTER
Would you rather
_____ a. work with your hands (or)
_____ b. speak with your mouth?

SERVER/GIVER
Would you rather help someone in need by
_____ a. doing something for him (or)
_____ b. giving him money without his knowing who gave it?

SERVER/ADMINISTRATOR
If a room needed to be cleaned, would you
_____ a. get a broom and sweep it (or)
_____ b. figure out who could do the job best?

SERVER/COMPASSION
Do you care more about
_____ a. helping people (or)
_____ b. how people feel?

TEACHER/EXHORTER
Would you prefer to
_____ a. read a good book (or)
_____ b. be with people?

TEACHER/GIVER
Would you rather
_____ a. study (or)
_____ b. save money?

TEACHER/ADMINISTRATOR
Do you find you more often
_____ a. read a good book (or)
_____ b. make lists of things to do?

TEACHER/COMPASSION
Do you
_____ a. keep your emotions in control (or)
_____ b. feel deeply and cry easily?

EXHORTER/GIVER
Would you prefer to
_____ a. speak in front of a group (or)
_____ b. serve quietly in the background?

EXHORTER/ADMINISTRATOR
Do you like to
_____ a. encourage others (or)
_____ b. be a leader?

EXHORTER/COMPASSION
Are decisions
_____ a. easy for you to make (or)
_____ b. hard for you to make?

GIVER/ADMINISTRATOR
Would you rather
_____ a. support others (or)
_____ b. be a leader?

GIVER/COMPASSION
Are you more interested in
_____ a. people's needs (or)
_____ b. people's feelings?

ADMINISTRATOR/COMPASSION
Would you rather work with
_____ a. a group (or)
_____ b. one person at a time?

If you are still unsure which gift is your strongest one, talk about it with your parents. They know you well, and can help you decide.

Testing Materials for Teenagers

6

Teenagers are eager to know about themselves, and we have enjoyed working with them individually, and in school, church, and retreat settings. Since they are getting ready to make lifelong career decisions, discovering their motivational gifts helps point them in fruitful and satisfying directions.

Awareness of their motivational gifts also helps teens build acceptable self-images and understand some of the problems and stresses they are experiencing. Stronger interpersonal relationships with peers and parents, and more responsible decisions about life partners can also result. Adults often say to us, "How I wish I had known about my motivational gifts when I was a teenager!"

If you're a parent, we suggest you allow your teenager to read this chapter for himself and to follow the testing procedure.

If you are teaching a group of young people, prepare them for the test by presenting some background information about the motivational gifts. This is available in our first book, *Discover Your God-Given Gifts*, and also on cassette tapes listed under "Additional Material Available" at the back of the book.

Older teens enjoy getting involved in the teaching process. Try assigning each of the seven specific gift chapters in Part II of this book, *Discover Your Children's Gifts*, to different students or teams, to study and present to the rest of the group. Each student or team could lead the others step by step through the scoring of the gift he studied, giving examples or illustrations that he has gleaned. Or, you could do this yourself.

College students can use this youth test or, if married, the adult one. Each student should have his own Youth Questionnaire. Additional copies are available at a nominal cost; see the ordering information at the end of the book.

FOR TEENAGERS ONLY

Dear student,

You are about to embark on an exciting personal adventure—discovering *your* God-given gifts. Every human being is endowed at creation with one or more of the seven gifts described in Romans 12:6–8. No one has been left out, for God has a plan for each life and has equipped each person accordingly.

> For I know the thoughts and plans that I have for you, says the Lord, thoughts and plans for welfare and peace, and not for evil, to give you hope in your final outcome.
> Jeremiah 29:11, TAB

> As each of you has received a gift (a particular spiritual talent, a gracious divine endowment), employ it for one another. . . .
> 1 Peter 4:10, TAB

You may already have some awareness of your giftedness. This test may merely serve as confirmation. Or, you may discover gifts that you have never before identified. Since these gifts were built into you by God at the moment of your creation, they do not change, although your *awareness* of them—or the way in which you use them—may change.

We hope knowledge of your giftedness will help you to cooperate fully with God's plan for *your* life and to experience increasing amounts of joy.

Learning about these seven gifts enables people to understand and appreciate themselves more, to get along better with others, to be better students, to set and accomplish realistic goals, to enter fields of study and work successfully, and to contribute significantly to society.

The following testing material is the result of more than fifteen years of research and teaching about these motivational gifts to thousands of people in the United States and in twenty countries of the world. The tests have proven to be highly indicative, and we trust they will be for you!

Yours in Christ,
Don & Katie Fortune

P.S. If you're interested in discovering the jobs or careers in which you'd be most successful, take a look at chapter 22, "Off to College, or Where?"

HOW TO SCORE YOURSELF

As you consider each characteristic in the following pages, ask yourself, "How true is this of me?" Your first response will probably be most accurate. Don't answer the way you'd *like* to be or the way you think you *ought* to be. Be honest! Remember, *there are no right or wrong answers!* This is a self-discovery process. You alone know yourself well enough to be able to score properly.

If the characteristic is never true of you, put an "X" in the box under *never*. Place a "0" in the points column.

If the characteristic is true of you only on rare occasions, score under *seldom*. Place a "1" in the points column.

If the characteristic is sometimes true of you, up to 49% of the time, score under *sometimes*. Place a "2" in the points column.

If the characteristic is usually true of you, 50% to 75% of the time, score under *usually*. Place a "3" in the points column.

If the characteristic is true of you most of the time, score under *mostly*. Place a "4" in the points column.

If the characteristic is true of you all of the time, score under *always*. Place a "5" in the points column.

After you have scored yourself on all twenty characteristics, tally your score. It does not matter whether you tend to score high, low, in the middle, or in extremes. Remember, this is a subjective test. It is the *comparison* of your seven scores that will help you to determine your motivational gifts.

Now take a look at the profile sheet on page 57, which provides space for scores of 0 to 100 for each of the seven gifts. Transfer your score for each gift to the profile sheet, shading in the appropriate horizontal column from left (0) to right, stopping where your score is in relation to the scale at the top of the chart.

After you have transferred all seven scores you will have a composite profile of yourself. The score standing farthest out to the right, much like a nose on a person's facial profile, is your primary motivational gift. You will also be able to see which is your secondary gift, and so forth.

It is also important to identify areas where you are *least* gifted, so you can:

1) recognize *your* areas of incapability;

2) rejoice in those persons who *are* gifted in those areas;

3) avoid trying to be what you are *not* and wasting time doing what you are *not* gifted to do; and

4) say, "No, thank you," with *confidence* when asked to do things outside the sphere of your giftedness. On the other hand, knowing your giftedness will release you to accept gift-appropriate responsibilities, in which you will enjoy maximum success and bless others as well.

Note: Do *not* add the five negative characteristics to your score or to the profile sheet. Score these separately and view them as areas in which you can change and grow prayerfully.

Each of the seven motivational gifts has its own set of problems and challenges. One student said to us, "It's a relief to know my problems are typical for my gift.

I thought I was the only one in the world wrestling with these things. Now I have hope and direction."

Without problems there would be no opportunity for spiritual growth!

As you take an honest look at your problem areas:

1) You will be relieved you are not alone.

2) Your identification of the problems will assist you in discovering specific solutions.

3) You will know how to pray for God's help and grace in overcoming the problems.

Score the same as for the twenty positive characteristics, but do *not* transfer your scores to the profile sheet. Use the negative scores to gauge your maturity level. Your primary and secondary gifts will probably have higher negative scores, but as you grow spiritually those scores will decrease. Here's the scale:

    0 to 5 points = mature
    6 to 10 points = growing in grace
    11 to 15 points = average
    16 to 20 points = immature
    21 to 25 points = needs help!

Youth Questionnaire

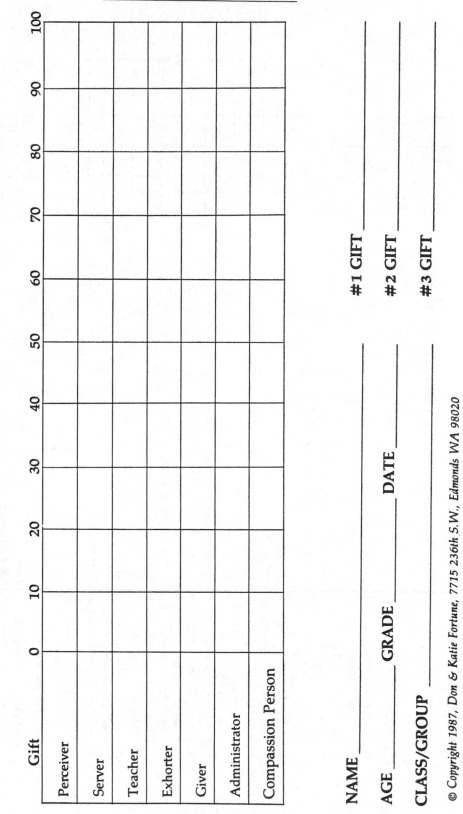

YOUTH MOTIVATIONAL GIFT PROFILE SHEET

Gift	0	10	20	30	40	50	60	70	80	90	100
Perceiver											
Server											
Teacher											
Exhorter											
Giver											
Administrator											
Compassion Person											

NAME _____

AGE _____ GRADE _____ DATE _____

CLASS/GROUP _____

#1 GIFT _____

#2 GIFT _____

#3 GIFT _____

THE GIFT OF PERCEPTION

	Never 0	Seldom 1	Sometimes 2	Usually 3	Mostly 4	Always 5	POINTS
1.							
2.							
3.							
4.							
5.							
6.							
7.							
8.							
9.							
10.							
11.							
12.							
13.							
14.							
15.							
16.							
17.							
18.							
19.							
20.							
							TOTAL

Characteristics:

1. Quickly sees what is good or evil and hates evil.
2. Sees everything as either right or wrong.
3. Can easily tell the character of others.
4. Encourages others to be sorry for doing wrong.
5. Believes problems and difficulties can produce spiritual growth.
6. Has only a few or no close friendships.
7. Views the Bible as the basis for truth, belief, and action.
8. Boldly lives by spiritual principles.
9. Is frank, outspoken, and doesn't have much tact.
10. Is very convincing with words.
11. Feels bad when others sin.
12. Is eager to see his own blind spots and help others see theirs, too.
13. Desires above all else to see God's will done in everything.
14. Loves to encourage the spiritual growth of others.
15. Prays a lot for others and for God's will to be done.
16. Likes to dramatize what he "sees."
17. Looks inside self a lot.
18. Has strong opinions and beliefs.
19. Has strict personal standards.
20. Feels strong desire to be obedient to God.

1.		
2.		
3.		
4.		
5.		
		TOTAL

Typical problem areas:

1. Tends to be judgmental and blunt.
2. Forgets to praise others for accomplishments.
3. Pushy in trying to get others to grow spiritually.
4. Doesn't like opinions and views that differ from his own.
5. Struggles with self-image problems.

POINTS	Never 0	Seldom 1	Sometimes 2	Usually 3	Mostly 4	Always 5	
1.							
2.							
3.							
4.							
5.							
6.							
7.							
8.							
9.							
10.							
11.							
12.							
13.							
14.							
15.							
16.							
17.							
18.							
19.							
20.							
TOTAL							

1.			
2.			
3.			
4.			
5.			
TOTAL			

THE GIFT OF SERVING

Characteristics:

1. Is quick to meet the needs of others.
2. Especially enjoys working with hands.
3. Keeps everything neat and in order.
4. Remembers details easily.
5. Enjoys having people at his house.
6. Wants to complete what is started.
7. Has a hard time saying no to requests for help.
8. Is more interested in meeting the needs of others than own needs.
9. Enjoys working on projects that can be finished in a short time.
10. Shows love for others in deeds and actions more than words.
11. Needs to feel appreciated.
12. Tends to do more than asked to do.
13. Finds highest joy in doing something that is helpful to someone.
14. Does not want to lead others.
15. Has a high energy level.
16. Cannot stand to be around clutter.
17. Wants everything to be perfect.
18. Thinks serving is the most important thing in life.
19. Would rather do a job than ask someone else to do it.
20. Likes to help others who are in leadership get the job done.

Typical problem areas:

1. Upset with others who do not offer to help out with needs.
2. May forget to help family by being too busy helping others.
3. May become pushy in eagerness to help.
4. Hard to accept being served by others.
5. Easily hurt when not appreciated.

THE GIFT OF TEACHING

	Never	Seldom	Sometimes	Usually	Mostly	Always	POINTS
	0	1	2	3	4	5	
1.							
2.							
3.							
4.							
5.							
6.							
7.							
8.							
9.							
10.							
11.							
12.							
13.							
14.							
15.							
16.							
17.							
18.							
19.							
20.							
							TOTAL

Characteristics:

1. Likes to present truth in a logical way.
2. Always likes to check out the facts.
3. Enjoys studying.
4. Enjoys learning the meaning of words.
5. Likes to use biblical illustrations to make a point.
6. Does not like Scripture to be used out of context.
7. Wants truth to be established in every situation.
8. Able to analyze without personal feelings getting in the way.
9. Easily develops and uses a large vocabulary.
10. Believes facts are more important than feelings.
11. Always wants to be sure that what is learned is true.
12. Prefers helping believers grow as opposed to witnessing.
13. Feels this gift is the best one for a strong Christian life.
14. Solves problems by using principles found in the Bible.
15. An excellent student.
16. Self-disciplined.
17. Emotionally self-controlled.
18. Has only a few close friends.
19. Has strong beliefs and opinions.
20. Believes truth has the power to produce change in people.

1.		
2.		
3.		
4.		
5.		
		TOTAL

Typical problem areas:

1. Tends to forget to apply truth in practical ways.
2. Slow to accept viewpoints of others.
3. Tends to feel smarter than most others the same age.
4. Tends to be a "know-it-all."
5. Easily sidetracked by new interests.

Youth Questionnaire

THE GIFT OF EXHORTATION

Characteristics:

1. Loves to encourage others to live fully and happily.
2. Watches for the response of others when speaking.
3. Would rather apply truth than research it.
4. Prefers learning things that can be used in practical ways.
5. Loves to tell others what to do in order to grow.
6. Loves to work with people.
7. Encourages others to develop in their ability to help others.
8. Finds truth most often in experience.
9. Loves to help others with their problems.
10. Will stop helping others with their problems if they don't change.
11. Prefers teaching that can be applied to life.
12. Believes trials and problems can help people grow.
13. Accepts people as they are.
14. Is positive about everything.
15. Prefers to witness through the way he lives his life rather than talking about it.
16. Makes decisions easily.
17. Completes what is started.
18. Wants to clear up problems with others quickly.
19. Expects a lot of self and others.
20. Needs a close friend to share ideas and thoughts with.

Typical problem areas:

1. Tends to interrupt others in eagerness to give opinions.
2. Will use Scriptures out of context in order to make a point.
3. May tend to give the same advice again and again.
4. Speaks out boldly on opinions and ideas.
5. Can be too self-confident.

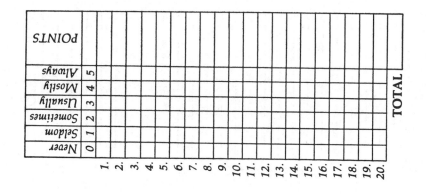

	Never	Seldom	Sometimes	Usually	Mostly	Always	POINTS
	0	1	2	3	4	5	
1.							
2.							
3.							
4.							
5.							
6.							
7.							
8.							
9.							
10.							
11.							
12.							
13.							
14.							
15.							
16.							
17.							
18.							
19.							
20.							
							TOTAL

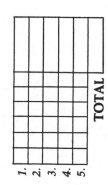

1.			
2.			
3.			
4.			
5.			
			TOTAL

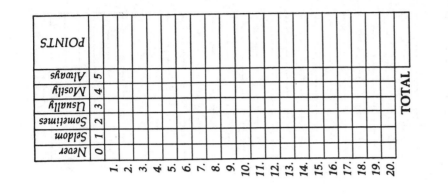

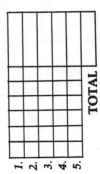

	Never	Seldom	Sometimes	Usually	Mostly	Always	POINTS
	0	1	2	3	4	5	
1.							
2.							
3.							
4.							
5.							
6.							
7.							
8.							
9.							
10.							
11.							
12.							
13.							
14.							
15.							
16.							
17.							
18.							
19.							
20.							
							TOTAL

1.	
2.	
3.	
4.	
5.	
	TOTAL

Youth Questionnaire

THE GIFT OF GIVING

Characteristics:

1. Gives freely of money, things, time, and love.
2. Loves to give quietly, without others' knowing about it.
3. Wants to feel a part of the ministry he gives to.
4. Prays a lot for the salvation of others.
5. Delighted when his gift is an answer to someone's prayer.
6. Wants gifts to be the best he can give.
7. Gives only by the leading of the Holy Spirit.
8. Gives to support and bless others or to help a ministry.
9. Sees having people in his home as an opportunity to give.
10. Has ability to handle money wisely and well.
11. Quick to help where a need is seen.
12. Prays about the amount to give.
13. Believes in tithing and in giving more besides.
14. Loves to share the Gospel more than anything else.
15. Believes God will take care of all his needs.
16. Works hard to earn money so more can be given away.
17. Good at making money.
18. Careful not to waste money on self.
19. Not easily fooled.
20. Has both natural and God-given wisdom.

Typical problem areas:

1. May try to control how money given is used.
2. Pushy in trying to get others to give.
3. May upset others who do not understand how and why he gives.
4. May spoil someone by giving too much.
5. May become stingy.

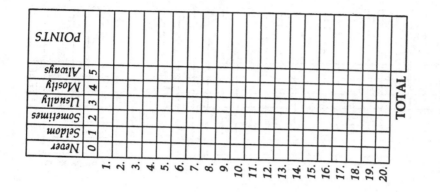

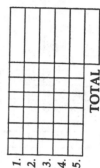

	Never	Seldom	Sometimes	Usually	Mostly	Always	POINTS
	0	1	2	3	4	5	
1.							
2.							
3.							
4.							
5.							
6.							
7.							
8.							
9.							
10.							
11.							
12.							
13.							
14.							
15.							
16.							
17.							
18.							
19.							
20.							
						TOTAL	

1.	
2.	
3.	
4.	
5.	
	TOTAL

THE GIFT OF ADMINISTRATION

Characteristics:

1. Loves to organize anything.
2. Can explain ideas and organization to others clearly.
3. Is glad to be under authority in order to have authority.
4. Will not try to take leadership unless given by those in authority.
5. Will take leadership when needed if there is no leadership.
6. Enjoys working on long-range goals and projects.
7. Can easily see the broad picture of what needs to be done.
8. Knows how to pick the right people to get a job done.
9. Enjoys getting others to do things and to grow in responsibility.
10. Doesn't mind criticism as long as things get done.
11. Has great interest and enthusiasm for whatever he does.
12. Finds greatest fulfillment and joy in working toward a goal.
13. Is willing to let others get the credit in order to get a job done.
14. Prefers to move on to something new once a goal is completed.
15. Constantly writes notes to self.
16. Is a natural and good leader.
17. Knows when to change ways of doing things and when not to.
18. Enjoys working with and being around people.
19. Wants to see things completed as quickly as possible.
20. Does not enjoy doing the same things over and over.

Typical problem areas:

1. Becomes upset when others do not work together well toward a goal.
2. Can hold in hurts due to being a target for criticism.
3. Can sometimes "use" people to accomplish own goals.
4. Can tend to drive self and neglect personal needs.
5. Can neglect home chores due to intense interest in activities.

THE GIFT OF COMPASSION

	Never 0	Seldom 1	Sometimes 2	Usually 3	Mostly 4	Always 5	POINTS
1.							
2.							
3.							
4.							
5.							
6.							
7.							
8.							
9.							
10.							
11.							
12.							
13.							
14.							
15.							
16.							
17.							
18.							
19.							
20.							
						TOTAL	

Characteristics:

1. Great ability to show love.
2. Always looks for the good in people.
3. Senses the spiritual and emotional condition of others.
4. Attracted to people who are hurting or in distress.
5. Takes action to remove hurts and relieve distress in others.
6. More concerned for mental and emotional hurts than physical hurts.
7. Helps others have right relationships.
8. Loves to give others the better place or opportunity.
9. Careful with words and actions to avoid hurting others.
10. Can easily tell when others are insincere or have wrong motives.
11. Drawn to others with the gift of compassion.
12. Loves to do thoughtful things for others.
13. Trusting and trustworthy.
14. Avoids conflicts with others.
15. Doesn't like to be rushed in a job or activity.
16. Usually cheerful and joyful.
17. Ruled by heart rather than head.
18. Rejoices to see others blessed and grieves to see others hurt.
19. A crusader for good causes.
20. Prays a lot for the hurts and problems of others.

1.					
2.					
3.					
4.					
5.					
TOTAL					

Typical problem areas:

1. Has a hard time making decisions.
2. Can easily take up another person's offense.
3. Feelings are easily hurt.
4. Concern for the suffering of others can produce depression.
5. Can be taken advantage of by others.

TIE-BREAKERS FOR TEENAGERS

If you find your first two scores are tied or very close, use the tie-breakers below. Answer every question even if you want to say, "I really like to do both." *Make a choice*, even if the margin of choice is very small.

If your answer is (a), your main gift is the first of the two gifts named. If your answer is (b), your gift is the second one named. You can also use these tie-breakers to distinguish between other closely scored gifts.

PERCEIVER/SERVER
1. Would you rather
_____ a.   win an argument (or)
_____ b.   work with your hands?
2. Would you rather help a person get rid of
_____ a.   sin in his life (or)
_____ b.   clutter in his house?

PERCEIVER/TEACHER
1. Do you prefer to
_____ a.   tell someone what to do (or)
_____ b.   read a book?
2. Do you form opinions based on
_____ a.   your current beliefs (or)
_____ b.   careful research?

PERCEIVER/EXHORTER
1. Would you rather tell someone
_____ a.   what his problem is (or)
_____ b.   how to solve his problem?
2. In giving advice do you
_____ a.   quote Scripture as a basis for action (or)
_____ b.   give practical steps of action to follow?

PERCEIVER/GIVER
1. To help someone would you prefer to
_____ a.   pray for him (or)
_____ b.   do something for him?
2. Would you rather
_____ a.   help someone get his life in order (or)
_____ b.   provide for him?

PERCEIVER/ADMINISTRATOR
1. In giving advice to someone would you
_____ a.   tell him where he's right or wrong (or)
_____ b.   first try to gain perspective about his problems?

2. Would you rather spend time
_____ a. getting a group to do things right (or)
_____ b. organizing an important project?

PERCEIVER/COMPASSION

1. In helping someone do you tend to meet
_____ a. his spiritual needs first (or)
_____ b. his emotional needs first?
2. When someone is hurting do you
_____ a. show him how to overcome the hurt (or)
_____ b. identify with the hurt, staying with him until it's gone?

SERVER/TEACHER

1. If someone needs something would you rather
_____ a. provide it for him (or)
_____ b. show him how to provide for himself?
2. Would you rather
_____ a. serve on a committee (or)
_____ b. give a report in front of the class?

SERVER/EXHORTER

1. Would you rather
_____ a. work with your hands (or)
_____ b. speak with your mouth?
2. If a person didn't follow your instructions properly would you
_____ a. go ahead and do it yourself (or)
_____ b. explain more thoroughly so he could do it?

SERVER/GIVER

1. Would you rather
_____ a. help others in practical ways (or)
_____ b. share your personal testimony?
2. Would you rather help someone in need by
_____ a. doing something for him (or)
_____ b. anonymously giving money?—

SERVER/ADMINISTRATOR

1. If a room needed to be cleaned, would you
_____ a. get a broom and sweep it (or)
_____ b. figure out who could do the job best?
2. Do you
_____ a. take things as they come (or)
_____ b. plan ahead?

SERVER/COMPASSION
1. Do you care more about
___ a. the help people need (or)
___ b. how people feel?
2. Would you rather
___ a. help with a church work party (or)
___ b. visit shut-ins or nursing home patients?

TEACHER/EXHORTER
1. Would you prefer to
___ a. read a good book (or)
___ b. be with people?
2. Do you like
___ a. a few select friends with similar interests (or)
___ b. lots of friends, the more the better?

TEACHER/GIVER
1. Would you rather
___ a. study (or)
___ b. save money?
2. Would you prefer to
___ a. read a good book (or)
___ b. witness to a friend?

TEACHER/ADMINISTRATOR
1. Do you find you more often
___ a. read a good book (or)
___ b. make lists of things to do?
2. Would you rather
___ a. do thorough research on a subject (or)
___ b. organize and lead a group project?

TEACHER/COMPASSION
1. Is your decision making
___ a. based on research (or)
___ b. difficult for you?
2. Do you
___ a. keep your emotions in control (or)
___ b. feel deeply and cry easily?

EXHORTER/GIVER
1. Do you encourage someone
___ a. by sharing your own experiences (or)
___ b. by giving him practical help and support?

2. Would you prefer to
_____ a. lead or speak in front of a group (or)
_____ b. serve quietly in the background?

EXHORTER/ADMINISTRATOR
1. Do you like to
_____ a. encourage others (or)
_____ b. lead others?
2. When working on a project do you
_____ a. stay with it until it is finished (or)
_____ b. try to delegate as much as you can to others?

EXHORTER/COMPASSION
1. Are you
_____ a. able to see a problem as a challenge (or)
_____ b. sometimes overwhelmed by a problem?
2. Are decisions
_____ a. easy for you (or)
_____ b. hard to make?

GIVER/ADMINISTRATOR
1. Would you rather
_____ a. assist with a project (or)
_____ b. organize a project?
2. Would you rather be
_____ a. a support person (or)
_____ b. a leader?

GIVER/COMPASSION
1. Is your prime interest in
_____ a. a person's needs (or)
_____ b. a person's feelings?
2. If you're working on a project and someone expresses a need,
_____ a. would you finish the project and then meet the need (or)
_____ b. would you meet the need and then finish the project?

ADMINISTRATOR/COMPASSION
1. When you look at things do you focus on
_____ a. the long-range view (or)
_____ b. what's happening now?
2. Would you rather
_____ a. lead a group (or)
_____ b. work with one person at a time?

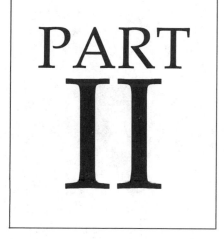

PART
II

TRAIN UP YOUR
CHILDREN IN
THEIR GIFTS

EVERY CHILD HAS A GIFT

7

Every child is a gift from God. He belongs to God. Yet God entrusts us to raise him even though we are not parenting experts. What a privilege! What a responsibility!

Our discoveries about the motivational gifts have been a constant source of help in raising our children. Now that you have used the testing materials in Part I to help your children discover their gifts, we want to share some practical advice in training up children according to their motivational gifts. We base the following material on our many years of experience teaching this subject all around the United States and in many nations of the world, our continued research, our own parenting experience, and one thousand responses from a cross-section of the population to our three-page feedback questionnaire mentioned in chapter 2.

HERE'S THE PLAN

As we consider each of the seven motivational gifts we will discuss twenty specific areas of strength and need, and offer appropriate parenting ideas. The twenty areas coincide with the order of information on the feedback questionnaire as follows:

1. Emotions.
2. Expression: Communication Skills.

   3. Self-Image.
   4. Approach to Life.
   5. Imagination/Reality.
   6. Behavior (and Effective Discipline).
   7. Personal Habits and Irritants.
   8. Friendships: One or Many?
   9. Relationships to Peers and Others.
  10. Intellectual Endowments.
  11. Leaders or Followers?
  12. Scholastic Achievements.
  13. School Subject Interests.
  14. Reading Interests.
  15. Sports.
  16. Games and Toys.
  17. Pets.
  18. Outstanding Qualities and Traits.
  19. General Interests.
  20. Special Joys.

Each chapter will deal with what we call the *classical* gift, the motivational gift as it is typically expressed through a person who does not have a close secondary gift. More than two-thirds of those we have tested, however, do have strong secondary gifts, and some have a third dominant gift as well. A few people have two motivational gifts of equal strength in their lives.

Understanding the characteristics and needs of children in relation to the seven gifts will enable you to see how a child with a combination gift or strong secondary gifts can be trained and encouraged in his giftedness. You'll see that extreme traits are modified and mellowed. Similar traits become more pronounced. Positive traits are enhanced and negative traits create even greater challenges for the task of parenting.

If your child has more than one strong gift, we suggest you read the two chapters relating to his gift simultaneously: Read item one about the first gift's emotions and then read item one in the other chapter. Ponder how they interact in your child. Ask the Lord how you can effectively train your child in this area of his life. Then proceed the same way with item two in each chapter, and so on.

In chapter 15, "How to Cope with Combination Gifts," we discuss some of the typical problems and challenges encountered in children with gift combinations, and include helpful comparison graphs.

Train Up Your Perceiver

Alex's top

8

The perceiver is, perhaps, the most challenging child to raise. But we know from experience that the investment in training the perceiver in God's ways can produce unimaginable blessings and joys. We absolutely delight in our son Dan, a now-adult perceiver, and his beautiful server wife, Ileana.

1. The Perceiver's Emotions.

Perceivers are frequently insecure, with intense emotions swinging from one extreme to the other. This roller-coaster disposition is hard to live with. One minute the perceiver child is tender; the next minute his yet-to-be-tamed temper is exploding. One day he is upbeat, on top of the world; the next finds him moody—under an invisible cloud of gloom.

Much of his moodiness stems from unresloved. hidden anger. Teach him to identify the anger, talk about it, and then forgive. He may be mad at God—for doing, or not doing something. Assure him God is in control: He knows what He's doing. Have him forgive God and ask God to forgive him for being angry. Have him say the words out loud. If another person is involved, have him try to resolve the conflict fact to face. If he can't, at least have him release all judgments and criticisms of the person.

Perceivers are keenly sensitive to right and wrong, and desire to be right—all the time. When a perceiver realizes he's done wrong, or not lived up to his own standards, he feels angry at himself. He's his own worst enemy. Depression often follows.

Parents need to realize the perceiver's internal struggle and draw him out, encouraging him to talk about it. Perceiver Pat wrote on her questionnaire, "I had a lot of negative feelings growing up, but I didn't express much of what I felt because of my parents' reactions. They were so quick to tell me what I felt was wrong. But it was real to me, and I desperately needed to talk about those feelings and work them through so the pain would go."

Perceivers often believe their parents don't understand them. This, coupled with their lack of self-understanding, creates inner turmoil. Defuse this problem by being open and available. Put the welcome mat out for communication. Your perceiver often can't or doesn't know how.

The peaks and valleys plotted on a chart describing this child's emotional ups and downs can be modified until they look more like rolling hills with occasional plains. You can accomplish such behavioral conditioning by affirming his positive attitudes and actions, and by defusing the negative with quality listening time. Remember: His feelings are not necessarily right or wrong, they just are.

In the 1940s a popular tune exhorted, "Accentuate the positive, eliminate the negative, latch on to the affirmative, and don't mess with Mr. In-Between." We think it must have been written by the exhausted parent of a perceiver child!

2. Expression: The Perceiver's Communication Skills.

Verbal communication is not usually a problem for perceiver children. They are good at expressing their thoughts openly, which is fine when they are in positive modes. In negative modes they dump a lot of garbage on others, lacking a sense of responsibility for what pours out of their mouths. Tact, social graces, and concern for others are not natural perceiver qualities.

Bluntness may get them into trouble, causing them to lose friends with cutting remarks, or preventing the development of friendships. Boys, especially, can trigger fights with rude and undiplomatic declarations. We often refer to perceivers' foot-in-mouth disease.

Work privately with your perceiver on taking responsibility for what he says and how he says it. Instill the sowing and reaping principle. He must learn obedience and responsibility for words and behavior that hurt others. If he does not learn obedience from you he will struggle with wholehearted obedience to God.

Offer suggestions from your own experiences in learning to get along with people. It may help to tell him you'll stop him anytime you hear him misusing his mouth so he can begin to catch himself. Discuss what is wrong right then. This takes extra effort but it is good training.

Perceivers are opinionated. Sometimes they are right, sometimes they aren't. Margaret, from Colorado, admitted, "My worst habit was expressing my opinion without praying first. If I'd ask the Lord about something first, I'd find out His opinion. If not, I'd usually come on as a know-it-all without any basis for it."

Mike, a classic perceiver, wrote about his childhood years: "How often I said, 'Lord, why did I open my mouth and say that?' I embarrassed myself so many times. I repeatedly asked the Lord to help me to be more careful with what came out of my mouth. I knew He wanted me to speak the truth—but with wisdom and love, and in His timing, not mine!"

Teach your perceiver to pray first and opinionate second, so he'll have something worthwhile to say.

3. The Perceiver's Self-Image.

Perceivers' introspective natures, coupled with their strong, almost perfectionistic desire to be right, cause recurring, occasionally ongoing self-image problems. They are inclined to be negative about themselves, feeling they fail to live up to their own expectations.

Cheryl, from Canada, said, "As a child I was always looking inward and checking things out. I wanted to see how my attitudes and feelings related to what I knew of God's Word. If they seemed to be in harmony I felt good about myself. But whenever they were contrary I felt bad—actually mad at myself."

Only about twenty percent of the perceivers we surveyed said they had good self-images during childhood. Eighty percent made comments like: "I thought I was a horrible person"; "I hated myself"; "I felt like an outsider"; "I had a terrible inferiority complex"; "I blamed myself a lot"; "I was self-conscious and felt so imperfect"; "I felt others were better than me"; "I felt lousy about myself"; "I longed for the approval of my parents."

Your child may not be as bad as he thinks he is, but his feelings are real, dictating sorrow, a sense of failure, and a suspicion of hopelessness. "For as he thinks within himself, so he is" (Proverbs 23:7, NAS).

It's important for parents to help a perceiver build a good self-image. He must be trained in positive ways of thinking about himself. The preschool perceiver needs repeated affirmation of his intrinsic value and your unconditional love for him. Give him lots of hugs. The perceiver often must be *convinced* that verbal affirmation is true.

Assure him of God's love. When he's in a negative mode he may believe his behavior has caused the withdrawal of God's love. He may feel God is angry with him, projecting onto God what he feels toward himself.

You can help your older preschool or primary perceiver by teaching him about his motivational gifts. Many adult perceivers have told us they wish they'd known about the motivational gifts when they were children. Some have confessed self-hatred because they assumed they were constant failures. They suffered from both real and false guilt.

Knowing that his introspection and high self-expectations are God-given will bring the perceiver a measure of relief and self-acceptance. Explaining that these tendencies, properly channeled, will help him to become a godly person should result in spurring him on to spiritual growth.

Perceivers tend to be super-serious. Teach them to laugh at themselves, to see blunders as stepping-stones, and imperfections as reminders of their need for God's grace and help.

4. The Perceiver's Approach to Life.

Idealism is the strongest influence in the perceiver's approach to life. Some perceivers' realism balances their idealism.

Suki Laney, a friend who grew up in Japan, told us, "I was always the idealist, but a realist as well. I never expected anything that was not within reach or possibly attainable."

But not all perceivers are that well-balanced. Many desperately want a perfect world and a perfect family situation and when life does not measure up they are upset, disillusioned, angry.

Help your child to see life as it is, with idealism as a goal. We live in a fallen world, filled with sin, sickness, death, imperfect people, and imperfect parents. The perceiver must learn to do his best in given circumstances and aim for the ideal as best he can.

Perceivers must also conquer a tendency to fall into depression when things don't go well. Karen told us, "As a child I had a strong sense of fairness and demanded *justice* (as I saw it) in those around me—not just for myself, but for everyone. When justice did not prevail I got angry, which often led to depression. Now I realize I was mad because I was not getting 'my way.' "

Most perceivers handle life's traumatic experiences with an amazing ability to snap back. One perceiver tells how a bad home situation resulted in her doing many things that were not wise. "By the time I was fifteen I had learned to roll with the punches and not let anything keep me down too long. I adopted the attitude, 'I'll chalk that one up to experience and not do it again.' "

Perceivers are able to face and deal with blind spots, both their own and others', too. Many of us are unable to separate the sin and the sinner, disliking a person because we dislike his sin. Perceivers can love the person and yet hate and deal with the sin.

Kay shared her childhood abhorrence of cheating. "If I suspected there might be even a little blind spot about it in my life," she said, "I immediately asked the Lord to show me and help me to change. But I also saw other students who had blind spots, who thought if they could get away with cheating it was somehow okay. I encouraged them to see it for what it was and to be willing to get a lower grade rather than to cheat. They didn't always listen, but some did, and I rejoiced at that."

Encourage your child to seek out and deal with his blind spots. Warn him to be careful about trying to help others with theirs, doing so only if they are open—and realizing that even then it can backfire, causing him to be rejected.

Stubbornness is typical of the perceiver child, seen even in the high chair as he repeatedly spits out his spinach. He doesn't want to eat what he doesn't want to eat. He doesn't want to do what he doesn't want to do. This child leaves the proverbial black heel marks all over the floor.

One reason for his stubbornness is his innate belief he is always right, even when he isn't. When taught the clear difference between right and wrong, he will want to do what is right. Be patient with his argumentativeness; you have to convince him. Repeat your explanations, if necessary, until he understands. An early start on this process will make it easier to help him transform his stubbornness into a positive defense of truth and a championing of righteousness.

Teaching your child to choose forgiveness as a lifestyle is essential if he is going to live a happy and victorious life. Otherwise, his own idealism and stubbornness will make him miserably judgmental.

5. Imagination, Reality, and the Perceiver.

Perceiver children are normally imaginative, but you can help them to nurture and encourage their creativity.

Preschool perceivers enjoy quiet, imaginative play. Older children find creative outlets at school. Some, like our friend Vicky, get carried away with it. "I loved making up stories, sometimes to the point where they were so real to me I wasn't sure if they were based on reality or not," she said.

Don't let imagination take over when it shouldn't. Debbie said of her strong imagination, "When I didn't want to face reality—a problem, a difficulty, something unpleasant—I'd turn loose my imagination. . . . I'd create my own 'world,' but that wouldn't solve my problem."

As a child I attended a special art school on Saturday mornings sponsored by the Seattle Music & Art Foundation. There were no lessons. It was the director's theory that given the media in which to work, children would become creative. We could ask for whatever we wanted—paper, paint, crayons, pastels, clay, collage materials—and create whatever we wanted. The director offered no evaluations, constructive criticisms, or suggestions unless we requested them. Imaginations cut loose. Creativity flourished. Many students went on to become professional artists.

Give your child the tools he needs to bring out his creativity—love, caring, interest, time, hugs, and even paper and paint if that is his bent—and see him blossom.

6. The Perceiver's Behavior (and Effective Discipline).

The perceiver's emotional extremes cause vacillation between obedience and disobedience. The less the parental discipline the more the disobedience. Conversely, consistent discipline produces obedience, and eventually, a mature, responsible, joy-filled adult.

An attractive couple in their mid-thirties brought their nine-year-old daughter, Jennifer, to me for counseling.

"She has an anger problem," the mother explained. "She can't seem to control her temper. She won't obey us; sometimes she screams and bites and throws fits. We can't do anything with her."

A few indicative questions told me they had a perceiver on their hands. "How do you discipline her?" I asked.

"We tell her not to do something, but she won't listen to us. Sending her to her room doesn't help either."

"Do you ever spank her?" I queried.

"Well, no. We've never thought that was right."

Here was a classic case of an undisciplined perceiver child. But the parents were the problem, not the child.

I took the parents aside and explained the biblical teaching on disciplining with a rod.[1] Representing authority, the rod is far more effective than spanking with anything else, including the hand.

To alleviate potential fears I reminded them that children's bottoms come nicely padded; the rod applied with firmness, but never to wound, effectively encourages obedience to parental authority.

A parent should never spank in anger, I explained, but with a calm recognition of spanking as part of the training process. The child should be told clearly why she is being disciplined. Afterward, she should be physically loved (rocked, held on the lap, hugged—whatever is appropriate for her age) and verbally affirmed that she is loved.

"Never let your daughter get away with any kind of sassing, disrespectful language, hitting, disobedience, or other inappropriate behavior again," I told them. "Be consistent. Don't repeat a command; you will train her only to obey after the second or third command. Getting the rod immediately will take some extra effort on your part in the beginning, but once she realizes you mean business she will obey without challenging you."

I assured them Jennifer would feel more secure and loved, and would obey readily if they tried the biblical pattern for discipline.

Then we returned to the girl. I sat down directly in front of her and looked her in the eye.

"Jennifer," I said firmly, "your parents have not been disciplining according to God's Word. But I've explained to them how to do so." Then I told her most of what I'd told them.

"You must learn to be obedient! Because your parents love you they are going to spank you whenever you misbehave. It will be up to *you* how often that happens. You can choose to start obeying them. Things are going to be different at home from now on. Do you understand?"

"Yes," she replied, a mixture of shock and astonished relief on her face.

Four days later I received a call from Jennifer's father.

"I've never believed in miracles before," he began, "but I do now! I want to thank you for helping us. Jennifer has made a complete turnabout. She's become a model child. And we only had to spank her twice. We can hardly believe it!"

I could. I was glad these parents had found out the truth before it was too late.

---

[1] The rod should be a dowel stick about 7/8" in diameter and 18" long. Lumber stores carry them, or an old broomstick will supply two of them nicely. Be sure to sand the ends to avoid any sharp edges. We kept one at each end of the house, always within easy reach. Once consistency of discipline restores parental authority, even a few steps in the direction of the rod will usually produce immediate obedience.

Perceivers are typical strong-willed children, pressing against parental authority as hard as they can. If parents give in, perceivers take over, becoming tyrants. Without discipline the teen years are filled with even more rebellion, and the adult years are polluted with disrespect for all authority and rebellion against God.

7. The Perceiver's Personal Habits and Irritants.

Each type of gift carries positive and negative habits or traits. One of the perceiver's positive traits is dependability. He will nearly always do what he says he will do. And unless he's terribly polluted he will always tell the truth, even if it is self-incriminating.

Tattletaling is one of the perceiver's negative habits, especially in relation to his siblings. He loves to tell his parents what a brother or sister is doing wrong, almost as if he feels responsible for facilitating their correction or punishment. This, of course, does not make him very popular.

Parents must try consistently to modify this tendency. Don't eliminate it altogether; his disclosures may prevent dangerous or life-threatening situations. One perceiver reported quickly that his younger sister was eating red berries from a neighbor's bush, thus preventing a possible case of poisoning.

Discuss what is appropriate to tell and what is not. Set the ground rules for what you will accept as helpful. "The baby is playing with a sharp object!" is information the parent needs. A brother's refusal to let the perceiver have a turn on the swing is not. His sister being lured off by a stranger is critically important news. A sibling pinching him is not.

Another negative habit is judgmentalism. He's quick to size up others—or situations—and decide who's right and who's wrong. "I alone am right and everyone else is wrong" can develop into a sort of "super-spirituality." The perceiver needs to be subject to a higher authority, and at this time in his life that's you. Nip his superiority complex in the bud. No one but God is *always* right. Teach him the difference between awareness that someone is wrong, or in sin, and judgmentalism. God alone is the judge; the judging we do boomerangs right back onto us, and we will be judged accordingly (Matthew 7:1–5).

Teach your perceiver to pray for those he perceives are wrong. (See Matthew 7:1–2.) A very wise perceiver parent from Canada told us she had taken the problem list from the adult scoring sheets and made it a prayer list. It helped her so much she had her three teenage children do the same from the youth scoring sheets. It worked wonders.

8. The Perceiver's Friendships.

A perceiver may go through childhood with one or two good friends, or none at all. He may worry about this—wondering why he doesn't want to reach out to more youngsters his own age. Or, he may feel comfortable in his aloneness.

But *parents* are often overly concerned, feeling their perceiver should be friend-lier, more involved with other children.

We faced this with our younger son, Dan, before we understood his gift. During his primary years Dan seemed to prefer playing alone after school, or with his older brother, Dave.

"Why don't you invite the boy down the street to come over, Dan?" we would ask.

"I don't want to."

"Why not?"

"He's dishonest. I've seen him steal things from other kids at school."

"Then why not ask the boy who lives on 76th to come?"

"Not him! He's got a temper. I can't stand him!"

"How about Johnny, then?"

"No way! He lies. I don't like to be around him!"

And so it would go. Dan couldn't seem to find a friend who lived up to his standards.

One time we forced the issue and insisted Dan invite over the boy from down the street. After he left we noticed that some of Dan's foreign car models, gifts from our European trip, were missing. And about two dozen quarters had disappeared from his coin bank. Our hearts sank. Dan had been right: The boy was a thief.

We went to the boy's house to confront the issue, but his parents refused to consider the possibility that their son had stolen anything. A week later the boy showed up at school with one of the cars, claiming his parents had bought it for him—yet the cars were not available in this country.

We could see that Dan had a type of discernment we did not have. We took the pressure off, letting him play alone if that's what he preferred. When we learned about the motivational gifts some time later, we recognized Dan as a perceiver, with a tendency to be a loner or have highly selective friendships. Dave, on the other hand, was an administrator, naturally drawn to a wide range of broad friendships.

Interestingly, soon after we enrolled our boys in a Christian school, Dan made several close friends who shared his standards. Our perceiver son found this a more congenial atmosphere in which to develop friendships without compro-mising standards.

Just as the Levites were set apart from the rest of the twelve tribes of Israel to minister to the Lord in the Temple, so, we believe, perceivers have been called apart to spend much time in prayer, to bring God's Word to the Body of Christ, and to uphold God's highest standards. They will not have the luxury of broad friendships for several reasons:

a) Time for friendships is limited by their call to a ministry of prayer.

b) Broad friendships require a degree of concession and/or tolerance for people with different standards and beliefs. Perceivers must not compromise.

c) God's gifting draws the perceivers to enjoy aloneness so they can enjoy being "alone with Him."

Don't pressure a perceiver about friendships: Let him find his own. But do encourage relationships that promise to be beneficial.

9. The Perceiver's Relationships to Peers and Others.

Our survey showed perceiver children relating better to adults than to peers. We've already pointed out some of their relational problems—their loner tendencies, tattletaling, and judgmentalism. But while they may never be popular, perceivers can be respected by other kids.

Encourage your perceiver's inclination to be honest, loyal, and responsible. These qualities appeal to peers as well as to teachers and other adults.

More mature perceivers sometimes find especially fulfilling relationships with older children. This may contribute to increasing social skills with their peers as well.

Perceivers focus so much on justice, integrity, and righteousness that they appear older. They take life very seriously. Perceivers take stands that amaze their parents, often calling them to greater accountability.

One parent related a typical example of how her perceiver teenager keeps her honest: "One day I was talking on the phone to a friend who wanted to borrow our utility trailer. Feeling inwardly irritated because this particular person borrowed things frequently and did not always return them in good shape, I made up an excuse. 'Sorry, the trailer's being used right now,' I said.

" 'Mom!' my daughter said in a shocked tone of voice after I hung up. 'The trailer's just sitting there! It's *not* being used. We're supposed to give to those who ask of us and not turn away from those who would borrow from us!'

"She was right," the mother continued. "She had quoted a principle from Matthew 5:42. Feeling amply reproved by a daughter I had grown to respect for her principled life, I called my friend back and told her the trailer was available after all."

Encourage a perceiver who shows interest in special relationships with adults or teachers. He will frequently benefit, especially in improved social skills.

10. The Perceiver's Intellectual Endowments.

Perceivers are usually intelligent, above-average students with B to B+ grades. Most parents do not have to push their perceivers to study because their desire to do so comes quite naturally.

Perceivers take pride in learning and accomplishment. Given an assignment, a perceiver wants to do it well, to feel proud of what he's done, to feel he's done his best, even if the grade is not an A.

If the perceiver is in one of his negative moods, however, or is currently experiencing a measure of depression, his academic achievement can suffer. His attitude may degenerate into, "Who cares?"

You can help him to deal with his feelings, to express what's really bothering him. Keep probing to get to the bottom of the matter. Don't let him wallow in anger, self-pity, or real or imagined injustice. Teach him to forgive those who have hurt him. It's the only way to get free of depression.

Argumentativeness seems to come with the gift. Remember, the perceiver thinks he's always right. And when he is not right, he will continue to feel he is until someone can convince him otherwise. In the early school years he may be awed by his teachers' authority. In his teen years he begins to realize teachers are not infallible, and may feel free to confront them on specific issues he feels are not quite right. He is not argumentative just because he enjoys an argument, but because he wants to promote another viewpoint.

Actually, many teachers enjoy a child who will challenge them, seeing it as evidence that he is questioning and learning in the process. But if argumentativeness becomes a behavioral or attitudinal problem and the teacher disciplines him or calls you in on it, you'll need to discuss seriously with him his student role in showing respect for authority. Explain that it's okay to have a difference of opinion, but that the teacher's final judgment on the matter is to be respected and obeyed.

Perceivers are always searching for truth, and consequently are good candidates for college and even graduate school. If it's at all possible they should be encouraged to go on in higher education. If they are called to Christian service (and many of them are) they should consider a Bible school, Christian college, or seminary.

Suitable occupations for perceivers include: air traffic controller, airplane pilot, ambassador, criminologist, evangelist, guidance counselor, inspector, judge, lawyer, life insurance agent, market researcher/analyst, military officer, minister, missionary, paramedic, philosopher, reporter, scientist, systems analyst, drama teacher, science teacher, or theologian. These are the jobs in which they would most likely be successful. Depending on secondary gifts and other factors, there are many other options. For a complete look at the occupational success probabilities see the test charts in chapter 22, beginning on page 249.

11. The Perceiver: Leader or Follower?

Perceivers generally are more prone to be leaders than followers, though they can be either or both, depending on the circumstances. They often lead because of their strong convictions or because they want to further a cause.

Some perceivers lead by example, *showing* others the way to live, the way to do things, the proper attitudes to have. They believe they should walk their talk.

Confident perceivers will not waver in their leadership or compromise their value systems. They may demand extremely high standards and lose followers along the way. But they will carry on.

If your perceiver is more comfortable being a leader of those younger than himself—neighborhood or school kids—let him get experience and build confidence. Later he'll probably lead his peers in some way.

Darlene recalled that she was often a spontaneous leader. "I seemed to have a burden for helping other kids to improve their minds. I organized everyone for nature walks, leading the way and pointing out sights they should observe."

Kay, another perceiver, said, "I wanted to be a leader, but others didn't necessarily follow. My bossiness got in the way."

You can affirm your child's leadership efforts and see him develop greater confidence. Bring inappropriate behavior, especially bossiness, to his attention, and show him why it's not good leadership procedure. Suggest alternatives.

Many young perceivers fail to identify their potential leadership abilities because they are thwarted or intimidated at home, rather than encouraged. A poor self-image does not lay a good foundation for confident leadership. Perceivers make good followers, providing the leadership is acceptable to them. They are supportive of *good* leadership, and resistive to *bad*. Joe told us, "I wouldn't follow someone unless he had the same values I had."

12. The Perceiver's Scholastic Achievements.

Secure perceivers will be excellent students. Many report getting mostly A's and B's and being high achievers, working for good grades—not to please their parents or teachers but because they want to do their best. Our son Dan says that even though he was not as smart as some other top students, he determined in his heart to work hard for good grades. "I'd be disappointed in myself," he explained, "if I didn't try wholeheartedly to do my very best."

Encourage your perceiver to work hard and do his best.

Insecure perceivers—who have been hurt a lot, squelched, or raised in negative atmospheres—are likely to be underachievers. Grades will average out closer to Cs, with occasional Ds or even Fs. Unresolved inner conflicts and simmering anger can produce contemptuous, "I-don't-care" attitudes toward school and authority. These perceivers may become behavioral problems.

You can help your underachieving perceiver talk and pray about his problems and feelings. Take him to a Christian counselor if necessary. If you, your spouse, or a sibling are part of the problem you'll need objective counseling for the whole family.

Perceivers are also natural achievers in sports and music. Give yours the opportunity to get training in one or both of these areas, if possible.

Programs like Scouts, Awana, Pioneer Girls, and Boys' Brigade provide achievement groups in which perceivers can blossom. Perceivers seem to like working within defined rules to earn badges and awards. This challenges them to achieve for their own satisfaction of accomplishment.

13. The Perceiver's School Subject Interests.

Responding to our survey, perceivers reported they enjoyed the following subjects: 1) English; 2) math; 3) history; 4) art; 5) drama.

English and math require students to learn and define rules. Perceivers are secure and work well with easily discernible rules and defined boundaries.

History and art nearly tied for next place. Many perceivers also indicated an interest in foreign languages.

Perceiver respondents were the only ones who mentioned drama. Perceivers are characteristically dramatic, even melodramatic, when they feel strongly about something. Their intense feelings make them more expressive than most.

Joy, a young wife, was in many plays throughout grade school and junior high, and starred in her senior class play. When I asked her why she enjoyed drama so much she replied, "I'm good at getting into the mind of the character. It's fun to pretend. It's challenging, exhilarating, and I feel a sense of accomplishment. It's a good outlet for someone who is intense, and it's fun to have the audience captivated. I'm a ham at heart!

"My friend Jennifer, also a perceiver, has been acting all her life. Now she's involved in drama at Biola. Her goal in life is to establish a drama team to go on the mission field or to local churches to communicate the Gospel and other truths about the Christian life."

Give your perceiver every possible opportunity for creative expression, especially through church, school, and community dramatic productions.

14. The Perceiver's Reading Interests.

Our survey showed the four most popular types of books for perceivers to be: 1) biography; 2) romance; 3) adventure; 4) mystery. Perceivers' interest in people explains their interest in biographies. The other three preferences reflect their interest in drama and their intense personalities. They not only like to be where the action is, they like to read about it, too.

Develop your child's reading abilities by providing him with books from these categories. Girls love romances and both boys and girls respond to adventures, biographies, and mysteries. Perceivers want every story to have a moral and a happy ending.

Consider biographies about people like Helen Keller or Joni Eareckson, who have overcome difficult circumstances or handicaps. True stories of outstanding Christians like David Livingstone, Hudson Taylor, and Dwight L. Moody have great appeal. For older girls try romances like *Christy* and *Julie* by Catherine Marshall. England's prolific Barbara Cartland has written hundreds of romances about heroines who are virgins and heroes of admirable character. Mark Twain's adventure classics about Tom Sawyer and Huckleberry Finn along with Robert Louis Stevenson's *Treasure Island* will delight older perceivers. Mystery series about the Bobbsey Twins and Nancy Drew were popular on our survey. We recommend the Tyler Twins mystery and adventure series by Hilda Stahl for seven- to ten-year-olds, and the Adventure Series by Lee Roddy for nine- to thirteen-year-olds.

Start your children off early with books. Even preschoolers love them. It's best to buy for that age group since books are so easily damaged or lost. Once your perceiver is in school, take him to your local library and guide his selection in areas you know he'll respond to well. Books make good gifts for special occasions throughout the growing-up years.

References from which you can select books to fit your child's interests are available at your library. Ask for *Honey for a Child's Heart* or *How to Grow a Young Reader*. Or, ask your child's teacher for recommendations.

15. The Perceiver and Sports.

Most perceivers who answered our questionnaire preferred individual sports like swimming, skiing, bicycling, and hiking. Yet about forty percent liked active competitive sports as well or even better, indicating a preference for baseball, with basketball and volleyball coming in second and third. Their interest in individual sports shows how the loner tendency affects their activities; their desire to compete results from wanting to win and to be part of the best group.

Sports activities will help your perceiver. Starting him in community or school sports by fourth or fifth grade will dissipate some of his intense energy and improve his self-image.

Whether he will do better in group or individual sports will be obvious from his early interests. Observe him on the playground and in neighborhood activities. If he expresses a preference for an individual sport like skiing or swimming, try to make lessons available, either through group sessions offered at ski schools or public swimming pools, or through private contacts.

One fourth grader who especially enjoyed swimming lessons joined the swim team at our community pool and faithfully got up every morning at five o'clock in order to swim laps at six. We wondered how he could endure such a schedule. But he was a loner perceiver who enjoyed a challenge. He did well in competitions all the way through high school; it was his one claim to fame.

Other individual sports mentioned by perceivers in our survey were: roller skating, ice skating, horseback riding, tumbling, and track. Other dual or group sports included tennis, soccer, football, badminton, tetherball, and kickball.

16. Games and Toys for Perceivers.

Perceivers' independence and creativity cause them to enjoy making up their own games. If they allow other kids to play they'll insist all play by the newly created rules, assuming the judge position if there's a difference of opinion.

Perceivers also like to play alone, sometimes for hours on end. One rather poetic perceiver wrote:

In the fall I'd rake up the leaves and jump in them.

In the winter I'd build snowmen and snowwomen and igloos.

In the spring I'd hunt for pussy willows in the woods.

In the summer I could hardly wait to move to our summer cabin where I'd walk for miles on the isolated beach, swim, beach-comb, row the boat, and build sand castles by the hour.

Other perceiver favorites are hiking, jogging, running, tree climbing, hop-scotch, jump rope, and croquet. Some mentioned table games like Monopoly and Sorry, but some didn't like games at all.

Perceivers remembered liking creative make-believe play, but always believing they were real people: teachers, moms and dads, doctors, or store owners. They also enjoyed dressing up and putting on plays. Perceivers like typical toys—trucks and trains for boys and dolls and dishes for girls—but are disinterested in nonsensical or whimsical playthings. They want their toys to be miniatures of the real things—cooking sets for girls or tool sets for boys.

In today's world, concerned parents must scrutinize toys to protect their children from the bizarre and occult items now flooding the market. One twelve-year-old girl was alerted to this problem. "I was at a slumber party," she related, "and knew that the Ouija Board game my friend brought out was satanic. I explained why it was and persuaded them to play another game."

We'd like to offer a suggestion from our family's experience. When our boys were still preschool age we instituted a weekly "Family Night." On this special night the boys chose what we had for dinner; afterward we had family devotions, and then they selected the games we'd play together. To avoid arguments David chose the game one week, and Dan the next. They loved it, and we tried to keep the evening free of outside interruptions.

17. The Perceiver and Pets.

Most perceivers love pets. Our survey indicated that most had pets. Those who didn't, however, seemed not to mind. One perceiver wrote, "My brother had a pet, a dog, and I enjoyed it, but I could have gotten along fine without it. I wouldn't have bothered to get one of my own."

Suzanne was very attached to her pet. "One day my mom came to school for a conference with my teacher," she recounted, "and our dog followed her. Some kids formed a circle around him and kept provoking him with sticks, causing him to growl and bark. I was upset and in tears, and insisted that something be done to help him. The teacher finally let us bring him into the classroom while we had our conference."

Assume your perceiver will benefit from having a pet he can cuddle: a dog, a cat, a hamster. Goldfish, turtles, and birds don't qualify, but you could have them in addition to a four-legged animal. We think a pet helps the perceiver develop a well-rounded personality.

18. The Perceiver's Outstanding Qualities and Traits.

Our survey indicated that most perceivers, rating their best childhood qualities, tended to be: 1) sensitive; 2) honest; 3) loyal; 4) responsible.

Perceivers' sensitivity comes from their keen perception and always relates to what is right, or God's will, as though they stand in fear of offending the Lord. They are also defenders of His Word, the Bible. Older perceivers who read the Bible extract its principles, applying them to their daily lives. They are incredibly strict with themselves.

Our perceiver friend Barbara Beck told us, "I didn't compromise when it came to the Bible. If God said it, that was it! I never wanted to do anything that violated His Word."

Number two, honesty, is a big one, too. We could also describe perceivers as truthful, fair, righteous, uncompromising, and full of integrity. Lillis, from

Kamloops, told us, "When I was young I wanted to be popular, part of the 'in group' at school. But they were dabbling in drugs, drinking, and sometimes, wild parties. I knew what they were doing was wrong. I knew the Lord did not want me to be a part of that. So I stood my ground. I could not compromise. I was left out. It was hard sometimes, but I'd do it all over again."

Loyalty is number three. Perceivers are loyal to family, friends, and the groups to which they belong. One perceiver said, "I would stick by my friends through thick and thin, no matter what."

Fourthly, perceivers are responsible, dependable, and reliable. You can count on them, and entrust them with more responsibility than the average child.

Look for, encourage, and cultivate these traits in your perceiver.

19. The Perceiver's General Interests.

Of the variety of childhood interests mentioned by those we surveyed, three stood out: 1) reading; 2) sports; 3) music.

Reading, of course, appeals because perceivers are good students and because it is a loner's activity. Perceivers are extremely philosophical, serious, and introspective, always seeking to know the meaning of life, their purpose, God's plan. Encourage your perceiver to seek, to read, to discover truth, especially about God and our purpose here on this earth. He will likely grow up challenging others to find meaningful relationships with God, and may even be one of the few who will be called to be prophets (according to Ephesians 4:11).

Provide your perceiver with a quiet place where he can read, study, and ponder. His own room is ideal, but if he shares a room, find him a spot to call his own—a corner of the basement, a nook in the attic, a tree house. He needs privacy.

Darryl told us, "When I was old enough to have a room of my own I was delighted. I would 'fix it up' and spend as much time there as possible. It was my haven, my place to read, to think, to pray, or to ponder the great questions of life."

A Christian perceiver usually enjoys reading the Bible, and as he gets older may discipline himself to read it through once a year. This is good, but don't let him fall into the trap some perceivers do: "I *only* read the Bible; I never waste my time on books written by Christians." This shows pride, and contempt for other gifted or inspired writers who could bring perspective and balance to the perceiver's life. He deprives himself of a valuable benefit.

Sports seem to provide the perceiver with a sense of accomplishment through physical effort, without his having to interact with others on a more personal basis. Music, the third interest mentioned, also affords a chance for accomplishment. Sports and music may be important channels for the perceiver's intense energy.

20. The Perceiver's Special Joys.

The greatest joys indicated on the survey were: 1) family activities; 2) being out in nature; 3) being approved.

Confirming our belief in the family unit as the most important factor in a child's life, survey respondents from all seven gift categories overwhelmingly agreed that family activities gave them the most joy in their childhoods. Even though many parents assume that interest in family activities ends in the teenage years, many respondents said they still loved to do things with their families.

Obviously God intended every child to be born into and nurtured by a loving, two-parent family right up to his departure from the family nest. In our country today about half are one-parent families. In some situations nobody is at fault. But increasingly one or both parents are unwilling to be committed to the marriage relationship established by God and affirmed by Jesus in His first miracle at the wedding in Cana. Jesus also told His followers that while Moses had allowed divorce because of hatred that produces hardness of heart, it was not God's plan from the beginning. In many homes parents stay together "for the sake of the children," but hardness of heart still pollutes the home.

Love should permeate every home, providing the atmosphere in which each child can grow with confidence and security. Our hearts have been deeply touched by the hurting responses from within all seven gift categories where this was not so. Wounds and warps caused by unloving parents are carried into adulthood, robbing people of their rightful childhood inheritances.

Perceivers account for about 25 percent of our counselees. Sixty percent are compassion people. The other five gifts make up the remaining fifteen percent.

One reason perceivers need counseling stems from the hurts they have encountered in childhood. Their keen sensitivity, insecurity, and self-image problems combine to make many problems that do not go away with adulthood. Instead they are amplified. Most perceivers do well in counseling because they want what is right, and want God's will to be done.

The exception? The perceiver who was never disciplined enough to bring his stubborn self-will into submission to authority. Allowing pride to pollute his personality, he formed an independent "know-it-all" attitude: "Nobody's going to tell *me* what to do."

One such perceiver husband brought his young compassion wife to me and with prideful contempt said, "Here, fix her! She's the problem in our marriage. Sometimes she dares to refuse to do what I tell her to do. She even has the gall to tell me once in a while that I've done something wrong. I'm never wrong. If you can just get her to submit unconditionally to me our marriage will be okay."

He went on to say he wanted to sit in on the counseling sessions so he could be sure I counseled her correctly. Already she was intimidated and fearful of him, a typically victimized compassion person who dared to speak her mind a few times and was aggressively tromped upon.

When I suggested that *he* might need counseling, too, and that he might be the main problem in the marriage relationship, he quickly exited to find another counselor. If only his parents had disciplined him.

We've worked with several other couples in which the perceiver husband was so polluted he projected all the blame on the wife. Sometimes we made progress, but usually the husband decided he didn't need any more help. Those marriages went from bad to worse.

We tell parents of perceivers that their spirited, strong-willed children are like wild horses needing to be "tamed" and "trained." Without boundaries established through discipline, perceiver children grow into adults who continue to ride roughshod over others.

Perceivers often also need counseling to *understand* their gift. They often grow up frustrated by the forces at work within them, particularly their keen perceptions of others' faults and sins, which can lapse into critical and judgmental attitudes.

A seventy-three-year-old woman came to us just after we'd finished teaching about the gift of perception at one of our seminars. Tears welled up in her eyes and ran down her cheeks as she spoke.

"If only I had heard this fifty years ago," she said. "I have lived all my life with a torturing awareness of what was wrong in people and situations. But I didn't know what to do with it, so I criticized. Then I criticized myself for being critical. All my life I've wanted to be different. Now I see that God has given me perception for a reason—so I could pray for people."

Three weeks later we returned to do another seminar. At the first coffee break this woman came to us with joy written all over her face.

"These three weeks have been the best in my whole life!" she exclaimed. "Every day I'm interceding for the needs God is showing me. It's wonderful; I'm seeing so many answers to prayer. And I like myself now. I'm so glad I learned about my giftedness while I still have some of my life left to live."

You see, perceivers are shown what is wrong so they can intercede according to God's will. Prayer is their main ministry. Perceivers should be slow to speak and quick to pray.

Teach your perceiver child how to pray for others, and as he gets older, how to intercede and do spiritual warfare. You'll be amazed at the results.

We were vacationing by trailer in the Banff area of Canada when our station wagon's engine died. Don pulled over to the side of the road, miles from any sign of civilization, to check under the hood and wiggle wires. Still the car wouldn't start. As he murmured and complained seven-year-old Dan jumped out and laid his hands up against the hood.

"Dear Jesus, please make this car start," he prayed earnestly. "Now you can start it, Dad," he called with innocent confidence.

To appease him Don tried the ignition. It worked. The look on Dan's face said, "I knew it would!" Three more times on our trip the engine quit. Three more times Dan prayed—and we joined him. Three more times it started. We never did figure out the problem.

Have your junior child start a prayer diary, keeping any size notebook and a pencil handy wherever he usually prays. Suggest he draw three columns, a small one on the left side of each page for the date, a medium-sized one on the right side for answers to prayer, leaving a large center column for prayer requests. When he sees an answer to prayer—and we can guarantee he will—he can record it in the right-hand column. This will encourage him and help him to develop a powerful prayer life. Take an interest in this project, but only look at the book if you're given permission. It must remain his personal property.

The second greatest joy, being out in nature, helps perceivers feel close to God and His creation. The third, feeling approved, indicates this as a real need, perhaps because they often aren't approved. Many parents *think* about telling their children they love them and are proud of them, but don't ever get around to it. Perceivers need to hear it!

Remember: Discipline the perceiver child consistently and fairly, give him lots of hugs and verbal affirmation, and guide him into a ministry of prayer.

TRAIN UP YOUR SERVER

9

The server child is one of the easiest to raise. His desire to please and be helpful makes him highly cooperative, steadfastly dependable, and seldom rebellious.

1. The Server's Emotions.

Of the seven groupings of children representing the motivational gifts, only two tend toward shyness: servers and compassion children. Shyness appears in newborns and is manifested clearly in the server's infancy and early childhood.

A current scientific study of shyness in children confirms what we've already observed in servers and compassion children through our survey and in counseling. Psychologists discovered modes of reaction in three-month-old infants, indicators that those children would be shy toddlers, and probably shy adults. They concluded that shyness was an innate characteristic, not a result of environmental conditioning. (The latter, however, can affect the severity of shyness to some degree.)

A server is not shy because he dislikes people. He does like them. But he is cautious about new people, needing to build up a certain trust level before he feels comfortable. This remains true during the growing-up years and even into adulthood.

Don't force your server into new relationships until he's ready. You may find it best to have new babysitters come to visit first, just to get acquainted. When taking your child into a church nursery situation for the first time you may need to stay with him until he feels comfortable with the adults in charge and the new surroundings.

The server's insecurity stems from his fear of the unknown, of new situations or people, and of relating to them. Walk your child through new encounters and situations. You are his security blanket. He may symbolically and literally hang on to your coattails or hide behind you. Be patient. Socialization takes time. On the other hand, don't forgo activities because of your child's shyness. A little trauma now and then is not going to hurt him.

The server is sensitive and emotional. Tears can come easily. Give him lots of hugs and verbal assurances.

He is also easily embarrassed, and won't like being talked about in front of others. Speaking to people may embarrass him. Blushing comes easily. Fill him with positive comments: "You can do it!" "It's okay, you can if you try!" "Just say what you feel!"

While a server is a slow bloomer emotionally, he will develop increasing confidence as you support him with love, positive expectations, and affirmations.

2. Expression: The Server's Communication Skills

The server operates more easily in the feeling realm than in the intellectual. His verbal abilities are less capable than those of children with speaking gifts— perceivers, teachers, exhorters, and administrators. A server expresses himself best through actions. He believes that what he does for someone speaks much more loudly than anything he might say.

A server may do dishes, sweep floors, feed pets, clear the table, carry in packages, or empty the garbage to tell his parents how much he loves them. Parents who do not recognize these signals may not benefit fully from their child's expressions of affection.

One server's parent complained, "She doesn't seem to love me as much as my son does; he always gives me hugs and tells me how much he loves me."

"Not so," I told her. "Your daughter shows her love through her constant helpfulness. Your son's compassion gift enables him to express his feelings more easily."

Psychologists tell us that only a small percentage of communication is verbal. The rest is through body language, facial expression, tone of voice, and actions. Learn to read between the lines and appreciate what your server child does; it will speak volumes.

A server is often quiet, less boisterous than perceivers, less talkative than teachers. But he is not as soft-spoken as a compassion child.

A server is often "seen but not heard," playing quietly nearby as other family members talk and share openly. A server is content with this state of affairs, but a wise parent will make occasional efforts to draw his server into the conversation, to increase his confidence in personal interactions while in the secure atmosphere of his home.

A server's natural shyness carries over into classroom situations. He tends to stay in the background. When the teacher directs a question to the whole class the server is reluctant to raise his hand, though he may know the answer. If called upon, he will usually respond, but not without some embarrassment and insecurity.

At parent conferences a concerned teacher may point out the server's reluctance to speak up in class. Be open to suggestions. Do whatever you can to encourage him in verbalization skills, but realize he will probably not become an extroverted conversationalist. Affirm him when you can; don't criticize his limitations or compare him with others, especially siblings.

3. The Server's Self-image.

Most servers have low self-images. In our competitive culture, verbal skills and achievements are measuring rods of success and acceptance. Even preschool children are often rewarded for their verbal accomplishments, while helpfulness is not necessarily praised. By the time the child enters public school he is caught in its competitiveness and graded by a procedure biased toward extroverts.

No wonder the server feels he doesn't measure up: He's being compared to a standard he cannot meet. How often is a child given an A for volunteering to clean erasers, or for helping a friend with his homework during lunchtime, or for keeping his desk tidy? Obviously there must be some standard for measuring a child's progress through the system. But the server is at a disadvantage, senses it, and consequently thinks less of himself. Separating servers from more competitive children, as we've mentioned before, will improve their self-images and enable them to blossom in abilities.

Give your server the positive reinforcement and approval he desperately needs. He needs to be appreciated for who he is and for what he does to help you. When he makes his bed and hangs up his clothes without being asked to do so, praise him. When he runs errands for you, thank him. The server's natural helpfulness and neatness are automatic and consistent, and parents often take for granted and forget to affirm these lovely qualities.

A server identifies strongly with what he does to help, and cannot easily separate what he does from who he is. When appreciation is not expressed he feels unappreciated. He finds security in doing, and his tireless energy enables him to accomplish much. His expertise will be in manual skills, not academic achievements. Enthusiastically encourage the development of those skills and you will, in the process, help him to develop a better self-image.

4. The Server's Approach to Life.

Servers approach life practically, always evaluating new information by how helpful it will be. Their mechanical and technical abilities, coupled with exceptional manual dexterity and close attention to detail, will make them productive adults. But servers must also learn basic academic skills.

One young server builds heating ducts for homes and businesses. His gift has enabled him to be a highly skilled craftsman. But it is difficult for him to read instructions or to write the necessary reports. His family moved often when he was growing up and he fell behind in school. His parents did not obtain help for his increasing illiteracy; at sixteen he was so discouraged he dropped out of school. His poor reading skills now inhibit occupational advancement.

Be sure your server gets all the tools he needs to work with in his adult life.

5. Imagination, Reality, and the Server.

Servers have natural creative streaks, usually displayed early in life in arts and crafts projects. Servers work well with their hands, are neat, precise, and clean up after themselves!

Provide your server with creative materials at home. Preschoolers like Play-Doh and pre-cut colored paper strips to make chains. Primaries enjoy tempera paints, pastel chalks, or felt-tip pens in a rainbow of colors. They may want to try wood carving, sculpting, or papier-mâché. Junior girls and boys enjoy sewing lessons, knitting, crocheting, and embroidery, and spending time with Dad in his workshop. Music, especially instrumental, will be another creative outlet. Schools usually offer instrumental instruction (and rental instruments) in about the fourth grade. Be sure your server has this opportunity.

Servers are very good at pretending. And whatever they do must always apply practically to their lives. If something is not ultimately useful they will regard it as not worthwhile.

6. The Server's Behavior (and Effective Discipline).

Like all the other respondents, servers recalled being obedient children, and they usually are. They want to please. Fortunately they do not have the perceiver's stubborn self-will. You probably won't have to discipline your server often, but when you do, he will repent quickly and make things right.

7. The Server's Personal Habits and Irritants.

On our survey, servers most consistently reported personal habits like neatness and tidiness. You can count on your server to keep his room neat, to hang up his clothes, and to put his toys and games away after he is through with them. If he doesn't, he either has a strong secondary gift that is interfering or he needs more clear, simple instruction from you.

He may also surprise you by picking up after the rest of the family. He doesn't like clutter, anywhere. This may become an irritant to a sibling who wants things left just where he dropped them.

Servers' helpfulness can also become an irritant. The child who wants to help cook may get in the way of a mother's tight dinnertime schedule. The child who wants to learn how to make things may hinder his father's pet project in the workshop.

While tight schedules sometimes make it impossible to let your server help you, look for times when you *can* allow it. Yes, it will take longer, but this is a part of the training process.

Servers do better with bite-sized chunks of chores. If you give your server a long list of jobs to do on Saturday morning he will be overwhelmed, and may only do one or two before finding excuses to quit. It is much more effective to give him one chore at a time, thank him for doing it, and then ask if he'd like to help you with another. He'll help all day. But don't forget to express appreciation. He needs it to build his self-esteem.

Servers like to work with their hands and are eager to learn to do things on their own. Show your server how to do something once; he'll probably want to do it himself, his way, without interference from his parent. This can be frustrating, but try to welcome his independence.

When our grandson, Jon, was just two we began to see evidence of his server gift. We'd show him how to tie his shoe laces and he'd immediately want to do it himself. "Me do, me do," he'd say, brushing off further assistance.

Our advice? Give your server child clear directions, and turn him loose. Let him ask you if he needs further help.

8. The Server's Friendships.

About 95 percent of the servers we heard from told us they only had one to three friends, usually quiet, sometimes even introverted, kids. If they have an extroverted friend whom they follow rather unquestioningly, it can lead to problems if the friend is a poor influence. Get to know your children's friends. Be aware of influences that are affecting them.

Servers, especially, need to feel they can bring friends home. It's not always convenient, it makes the house noisy, and you'll probably have to feed them, but your server will reap many benefits.

9. The Server's Relationships to Peers and Others.

Our survey indicated that servers' relationships are best with parents, good with teachers and older children, and fairly good with peers.

Servers naturally tend to feel more secure at home and with parents; hence, the "best" rating for child-parent relationships. Servers desire to please, to help, and to be "model children," causing many parents to feel closer to, and spend more quality time with, their servers than with those children who challenge their authority and exhaust their patience. Obviously parents play a big role in shaping the server's character.

Good child-teacher relationships come from servers' desires to please and their willingness to obey authority unreservedly. Since they are seldom discipline problems, they enjoy happy, unbroken relationships with their teachers.

We were surprised so many servers related well to older kids. We think this reflects servers' willingness to follow, eagerness to please, and non-competitiveness. Older children probably enjoy servers' admiration and therefore treat them kindly.

While answers ranged from poor to good in server-peer relationships, about half indicated "fairly good" as their evaluation. Many listed shyness as a major barrier; it seemed to decrease somewhat at older ages. Continue to build up your child's self-esteem. But remember, he will not change into a gregarious child. His friendships will be limited, but they can be deep and rewarding.

10. The Server's Intellectual Endowments.

Almost sixty percent of the respondents called themselves average students, reporting C averages. About 35 percent said they had above-average grades, C+ to B. The remaining five percent was divided between the excellent (A) and very poor (D) extremes.

Servers who bring home C average report cards are usually doing just fine for their gifting. Academics will not particularly fulfill them or direct their lives. Servers want to work with their hands and will, with some exceptions, probably enter trade or specialty schools rather than college.

Don't reward your children's good grades with money, reinforcing the lopsided preferential treatment society gives to high academic achievers, already a contributor to the server's self-image problems. A server usually fails to live up to his parents' unrealistic expectations, and a monetary reward system puts an unnecessary breach between the server, his parents, and his academically high-achiever siblings.

A server who is measuring up to the average performance level of his gift should be rewarded equally with the teacher who brings home straight A's. Take all your children out to their favorite restaurant, or buy tickets to the circus or ice follies just to say, "We're proud of all of you!" If money is tight, make a butcher-paper banner affirming them all, to greet them after school. Follow up with a "we're-proud-of-you" family night with fun, games, and lots of buttered popcorn.

Yes, you can encourage your server to do better in school, but be sensitive to his limitations. Don't push. He may need extra help with his homework, while his self-motivated administrator sibling doesn't need any. Don't compare them. Quietly make time in your schedule to help the server.

Servers probably won't want to obtain four-year college degrees. But they will be interested in specialized training at trade, art, music, beauty, barber, or computer schools. Some prefer to take jobs right after high school graduation, often combined with in-house or on-the-job training.

There are many occupations suitable for the server including: accounting, agricultural worker, architect, assembly line worker, auditor, bank teller, barber, beautician, bookkeeper, builder, bus driver, cashier/checker, carpenter, childcare provider, civil servant, clerk, computer operator, computer programmer, cook, dental hygienist, dock worker, electrician, farmer, firefighter, fisherman, flight attendant, forest ranger, geographer, heavy equipment operator, industrial designer, interior decorator, janitor, landscaper, librarian, licensed practical nurse, mathematician, mechanic, mechanical drawing, metalworker, miner, office worker, pet groomer, plumber, postman, professional housecleaner, receptionist, seamstress/tailor, secretary, shipbuilder, statistician, surgeon (if coupled with a strong secondary gift), surveyor, taxidermist, business education teacher, shop teacher, technician, telephone operator, toolmaker, truck driver, waiter/waitress.

These occupations have similar requirements: a person must be good with his hands, able to pay attention to details, and willing to do tasks repeatedly. Taking secondary gifts and other factors into consideration, there are many other options. For a complete look at the occupational success probabilities see the test charts in chapter 22.

11. The Server: Leader or Follower?

Seventy percent of all servers who responded to our questionnaire said they were followers as children, and remain primarily so in adulthood. Twenty percent said they were sometimes leaders and sometimes followers. Only ten percent felt they were primarily leaders, and they all had strong secondary gifts of perception, teaching, exhorting, or administration to explain their leadership interests and abilities. Those server/perceivers, server/teachers, server/exhorters, and server/administrators probably enjoyed taking leadership, but were constantly tempted to do all the tasks themselves instead of delegating.

Some schoolteachers view the server's helpfulness and hard work as indicators of potential leadership capacity. But forcing the classic server into leadership produces fear and frustration—fear he won't live up to expectations, and frustration in his natural lack of leadership skills. Once deprived of "hands on" tasks and told to lead, he is out of his element. Conscientious and confused, he may come home from school in tears. Dry his tears, listen to his frustration, give him some advice, and tell him to do the best he can. If possible, ask the teacher not to place your server in a position of leadership again. It moves him unnecessarily out of his comfort zone. Let him be the excellent support person that he is.

12. The Server's Scholastic Achievements.

Don't expect your server to be a high academic achiever. Don't push him into college unless he really wants to go. It is tragic when parents project their own desires and goals—based on their own motivational gifts—onto children who are gifted and motivated differently.

One server's parents were both teachers, motivationally and occupationally. They continually talked to their son about entering college to become a teacher, too. Intimidated by their insistence, he complied. But he was constantly frustrated in teaching. He did love his summer job, building houses.

After taking our course and discovering he was a server he decided to go into construction work full time. Now he's happy and fulfilled, loves working with his hands, and has free time to do the interdenominational youth work he enjoys.

Do expect your server to excel in working with his hands and in serving. Your compliments will foster these achievements. Provide opportunities to increase his hand skills. Don't feel bad if you are not equipped to teach such specialties yourself. If a father is uncomfortable with tools or mechanics, perhaps an uncle or neighbor would be willing to teach the server. Local YMCA's and parks' departments offer classes in cooking, sewing, painting, and computers. Enlist grandma's (yours or someone else's) help to instruct in knitting, crocheting, or canning. Grandpa might be a great instructor in wood carving or guitar.

Most junior high and high schools offer electives in home economics and shop. Encourage your server to take them.

13. The Server's School Subject Interests.

From the survey we learned that servers enjoyed the following school subjects most: 1) math; 2) English; 3) history & science; and 4) home economics/shop.

Math and English were close, but math had the edge, requiring, as it does, the servers' natural flair for precision and detail. We've observed that servers have the neatest papers in class. Their penmanship is precise and carefully done. Columns of figures line up perfectly. If they make one mistake they're apt to crumple up the paper and throw it away, starting all over again.

History and science tied for third place as server favorites. Their capacity to pay attention to and remember details plays a role here. Servers memorize dates, names, and places quite easily, and they enjoy science laboratory classes and experiments.

Of all seven gift categories, only servers significantly mentioned home economics and shop. We were not surprised: Servers not only enjoy, but excel in these classes, and parents can expect some A's. Servers love anything practical, and will enjoy sewing, cooking, and family-living courses as well as wood shop and metal shop.

Servers seemed to enjoy spelling, an evidence of their good memories for detail. Art—a "hands on" subject releasing servers' creativity—was also mentioned quite often.

14. The Server's Reading Interests.

On our survey servers listed their favorite books as: 1) adventure; 2) mystery; 3) romance; and 4) historical novels. We were surprised at the first two choices since servers are usually not adventuresome. Then we realized these books provide them with vicarious enjoyment. Romances and historical novels also fill needs not usually met in their real worlds.

Providing your child with books from these categories will develop his reading skills. In addition to adventure classics by Mark Twain and Robert Louis Stevenson, try new ones like Frank Peritti's *Escape from the Island of Aquarius* and *Trapped at the Bottom of the Sea*. *Mandie and the Mysterious Bells* and *Mandie and the Secret Tunnel* are just two in a great mystery story series for juniors, about a turn-of-the-century young girl from the backwoods of North Carolina.

Teenagers enjoy Sir Arthur Doyle's *Adventures of Sherlock Holmes* and *Hound of the Baskervilles*. Girls may like romances like *Exit Betty*, *Spice Box*, or *Crimson Mountain*, by Grace Livingston Hill, or the Canadian West series by Janette Oke. Historical novels with wide appeal include the Pioneer Family Adventure Series for young teens by Sandy Dengler, and the Little House Series by Laura Ingalls Wilder—beginning with *Little House in the Big Woods* and concluding with *These Happy Golden Years*. If your child doesn't enjoy reading (and some servers don't), check to see if he is having reading problems. Read to him and with him to generate his interest, or have him join a reading club or attend storytelling sessions at the library.

Remember: Servers handle tasks better in small amounts. Offer one book at a time instead of checking out a whole pile from the library.

15. The Server and Sports.

About one-third of all servers questioned reported no participation in sports. Those who did participate preferred "just-for-fun" noncompetitive activities. Spontaneous neighborhood softball and basketball games were most popular.

Other servers said they enjoyed volleyball, swimming, roller-skating, bicycling, and track.

Don't push your server into organized sports, unless he has a secondary gift that will give him that desire. And to the athletic parent who yearns for your child to follow in your footsteps we say, "Give the kid a break. He's not going to be the athlete you were. Let him develop his own interests and abilities."

16. Games and Toys for Servers.

At least 95 percent of the female servers we surveyed loved dolls, which provide wonderful creative play opportunities. Mid-elementary age girls may find outlets for their manual skills in sewing doll clothes from a wide variety of available patterns. Female servers also liked playing "house," an indicator of their later love for homemaking.

Male servers reflected only minor interest in trucks and trains but strong liking for building blocks, Legos, Lincoln Logs, and construction sets. Start them out with basic sets and add periodically through Christmas and birthday presents. They will spend hours building marvelous creations, enhancing their manual skills and general knowledge of construction, a field for which they are well-suited, if not professionally, at least practically in the realm of their own homes one day. Male servers also love to build models—store-bought or homemade.

Card games were popular with the respondents, as were puzzles. The usual children's games of Rummy, Fish, and Old Maid seem to challenge them. Later their interests turn to Sorry and Monopoly and myriad table games available today. Puzzles are enjoyed by servers of all ages. They enjoy a progressively more complex challenge until they finally tackle the 500- to 1000-piece challenges. Servers have the patience to work on them for a long time, often leaving them on an otherwise unused table for days, and working in installments. They also love coloring and activity books.

Servers make excellent collectors, with their neatness, manual skills, patience, perseverance, and attention to detail. Stamps, coins, matchbook covers, bottle tops, butterflies, rocks, or whatever catches their interest will be collected patiently and catalogued and filed meticulously.

We stayed recently in a German home where a college-age server showed us a collection of rocks he started in grade school. As a teenager he often bicycled long distances on hearing of a good location for a particular kind of rock. In shop class he built a chest of shallow, compartmented drawers in which each rock could be properly identified and stored. The collection was incredibly neat, and so typical of a server's effort.

If your server does not yet have a collection, consider starting him on one for his birthday. Take him to a hobby store and see what he lingers over.

17. The Server and Pets.

A pet is a must for a server child. Those we questioned made comments like, "I absolutely loved my pets!" "They were my special friends!" "I felt my dog understood me when no one else did." "I don't know what I would have done without my dog's unquestionable love." While eighty percent of servers surveyed had pets, 98 percent said they loved pets, indicating that those who didn't have them (usually because parents didn't want one) wished they had.

Be sure your server has a pet he can hug—one that will respond to him. Dogs and cats are best. Hamsters, guinea pigs, rabbits, and ferrets will do. Birds and fish really won't fill the bill. They don't hug well. But if you're in a rental situation or condo where four-footed animals are not allowed, they're better than nothing. Don't rule out turtles and ant colonies, either. If you live in the country a horse would delight a server, and he'd take good care of it.

18. The Server's Outstanding Qualities and Traits.

Adult servers who responded to this survey question about their best qualities as children indicated they were: 1) helpful; 2) reliable; 3) sensitive; and 4) obedient.

Sixty-five percent listed helpfulness, or doing things for others, as their best trait. We were not surprised. Had we given multiple choice rather than open-ended questions, the results would have been closer to one hundred percent. A server's joy comes from doing helpful things for others.

Let your server be helpful. When you refuse his help he may feel *he* is being rejected—or at least in part.

Various words were used to describe their second-best quality of being reliable: trustworthy, responsible, dependable. "People could always count on me," they told us.

Sensitivity, the third trait mentioned, referred to servers' identification with and consideration for the needs and feelings of others. They were also quick to meet the needs they recognized.

The mention of obedience in this list indicated it as a priority in servers' lives.

Compliment your child on these outstanding qualities whenever you can. He needs to hear what you think and feel about him. Don't assume he knows. Say it! In counseling children we often hear, "My father never says anything good to me. I'm not sure he even loves me." When we talk with the parents we find the love and appreciation present, but uncommunicated. Even if a child is constantly complimented by others, he needs his *parents'* affirmation. No one can do for him what you can!

19. The Server's General Interests.

Of the variety of childhood interests mentioned by servers on our questionnaire, three stood out: 1) handwork; 2) animals; and 3) homemaking or building skills. None of these was a surprise. If we placed each of the gifts in the diagram of a body, servers would be the hands. Remember, hands need to keep busy. Be sure your server has opportunities to work with them.

Servers love animals, as we mentioned in section seventeen. But their interest will extend beyond the home. Take younger servers to the zoo. If there's a special animal petting area, let them spend time there. If possible, visit a farm now and then. It will be a special blessing to them. And when you visit in another home with pets, note how your server migrates to them immediately.

We think servers grow up to be the most domestic husbands and wives. Be sure to give your child the opportunity to practice and learn homemaking, building, and fixing skills in your home. But don't overdo it.

"My parents worked sixteen hours a day," Belinda said, "so I cleaned, and fixed all the meals. I have to admit it upset me when my sisters and brother didn't want to or even offer to help me." Belinda enjoyed helping, but her family took advantage of her.

20. The Server's Special Joys.

The greatest joys servers indicated on the survey were: 1) family activities; 2) appreciation; and 3) serving.

Family activities ranked as the number one joy for all survey respondents, regardless of their gifts. The family unit is God's basic building block for society, but in our country fifty percent of all homes fall apart through divorce. Lack of training in proper parenting passes the problem on to future generations. Programs like Dr. James Dobson's *Focus on the Family* are helping parents to do a better job of parenting and building emotionally healthy families, and we recommend them to you. Put every effort into making your family strong, and spend quality time with your children.

Appreciation ranked second among server joys. Remember, servers must feel others appreciate what they do, since their self-worth is tied to their actions. Everyone needs positive input in his or her life. It's easy to criticize or find fault with someone, but how often do we bother to give compliments or encouragement? Psychologists tell us it takes *four* positive comments to overcome *one* negative comment. As Christians we need to contribute to the building up of our own children in particular and others at every opportunity.

Serving, number three, is a natural joy for servers. They love doing things for others. One family became concerned when their teenage daughter started taking over many domestic chores; the mother, especially, felt threatened to see her duties rapidly disappearing. But the motivational gifts test showed them their daughter was just doing what came naturally. Enjoy your server's help.

Remember, help your server build a better self-image, give him lots of verbal affirmation and appreciation, and guide him in developing his manual skills.

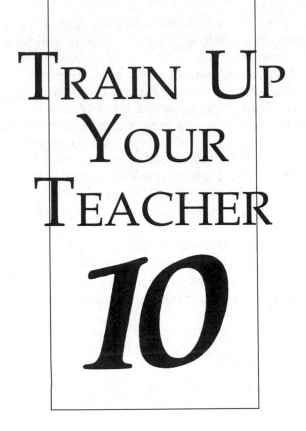

TRAIN UP YOUR TEACHER

10

The teacher is gifted with an unusually sharp mind, ideally suited to follow intellectual pursuits. His life's greatest contributions will be academically oriented.

1. The Teacher's Emotions.

While the perceiver's extreme emotional fluctuations plotted on a graph resemble a roller coaster ride, the teacher's stable emotions look more like the horizon of the Kansas plains—flat and straight. Teachers are calm, cool, and collected. Hardly anything ruffles their reserved personalities.

A sixteen-year-old girl who had just identified her gift of teaching shared how her two older, highly emotional sisters could not stand their parents' constant fighting and left home in their mid-teens. "But I won't have to do that," she explained. "I figure if my parents are dumb enough to fight it's not my problem. I just go in my room when they start in, and read a good book." She was able to detach herself from the marital conflict; her compassion sisters had been so involved emotionally they could not remain in the home's volatile atmosphere.

Characterized by stable dispositions, teachers often appear unemotional, and must learn how to express both positive and negative feelings precisely. Not ones to touch affectionately and spontaneously, they may even have to learn how to

102

hug. Being reserved and detached, they usually feel uneasy at strictly social gatherings.

But even though these children are not enthusiastic huggers, they still need to *be* hugged. The initiation needs to come from you. Your teacher child will learn to respond more and more as you consistently show affection to him.

2. Expression: The Teacher's Communication Skills.

Teachers are naturally good communicators. It's easy for them to verbalize and they are usually exceptionally articulate. Quick learners, they build amazingly extensive vocabularies for their respective ages.

I recall one boy (about eight) who moved into our neighborhood. He used such big words the rest of us couldn't understand what he was saying. We thought he was trying to show off and often avoided him. Now I understand—he was a teacher. I wish I'd understood it then.

Teachers take life quite seriously and their senses of humor are somewhat thwarted. They often look upon joviality and frivolity as a waste of time. Teachers are often responsible for their own isolation. They want to talk—a lot—on matters they deem important or worthwhile, but are not given to chitchat or small talk. They are drawn to adults, older children, or peers who have the same gifting or similar interests.

Your teacher will ask a lot of questions; he respects you and wants to learn from you. Take time to answer him.

3. The Teacher's Self-image.

Almost all teachers have good self-images. This was confirmed by our survey. The only exceptions were those who had been abnormally traumatized in childhood by extensive abuse. Teachers' objectiveness enables them to filter out negative input from their environments. Firm control over their emotions prevents them from being negative reactors.

It probably won't take concerted efforts to build your teacher's self-esteem, but he—like every human being—needs love and affection.

You *will* need to help him avoid what the apostle Paul called "thinking *too highly* of himself." Pride creeps into his life almost automatically, and he may think he is better than his peers. Intellectually he is, but he lacks in other areas. He tends to measure himself on his intellectual ability and accomplishments alone. You can help bring balance to his life. Teach him the value of humility, of recognizing his giftedness as a result of God's grace, and not something to boast about or flaunt before others.

The book of Proverbs has some choice bits of advice concerning the matters of pride and humility:

> When pride comes, then comes disgrace,
> but with humility comes wisdom.
>   Proverbs 11:2, NIV

A man's pride brings him low,
but a man of lowly spirit gains honor.
Proverbs 29:23, NIV

In 1 Corinthians 8:1, Paul says that knowledge puffs up, but love builds up. The greatest qualities a teacher can seek, humility and love, will neutralize the pride problem.

A survey respondent who scored very high on teaching wrote to us: "Throughout my school years I always enjoyed reading and learning new things. I couldn't understand why other kids didn't pursue learning as I did. I thought they were lazy or unmotivated. I'm ashamed to admit this led me to think I was better than most of them. At the seminar I was helped to value the other gifts and the people who so beautifully demonstrate them. I wish I had known this as a child."

Teachers can indeed develop superiority complexes. They must lean on the Holy Spirit, not on human knowledge and reasoning. The teacher's primary tool is his mind, but Proverbs 3:5 warns us not to lean on our own understanding.

Help your child strengthen some of the weaker areas of his personality. Encourage a sense of humor; teach him to laugh at himself and his mistakes. Help him get in touch with, understand, and express his emotions. Encourage him to develop broad social relationships.

4. The Teacher's Approach to Life.

A teacher approaches life realistically. His sharp mind quickly evaluates everything around him, and he deals more in facts than in opinions or feelings. The proverbial searcher after truth, a teacher won't let go until he gets to the bottom of something. He will ferret out a matter until he's explored it thoroughly.

Once your teacher makes up his mind and forms an opinion, it's almost impossible to get him to change it unless you present new evidence, new facts, or information of which he was unaware. He will change it then; his integrity demands it. This resistance to change may appear as stubbornness, but it's not. Your teacher must *know* what is truth, and have a *foundation* for what he believes or proclaims.

The unquestioning obedience you get from a server will not come from your teacher. He's not easily persuaded. Don't say to him, "Don't ask why, just do as I tell you." He *needs* to know why; understanding is the basis for his action. If you're interrupting what he's doing to make a request, say, "Take these to our neighbor right now, *because he's waiting for them*."

Teachers are most apt to ask who, what, where, when, why, and how come? This may come across as rude or impudent.

Friends of ours, Vi and Jim, were living in Munich, Germany, for a few years and invited their fourteen-year-old grandson to live with them for a while and attend a German school. They had not bargained for an adolescent whose motivational gift was teaching, nor did they recognize this as the cause of his incessant questioning.

"He must ask five hundred questions a day," Vi bemoaned. "Some that are none of his business."

"He follows me around asking why I do this and why I do that," Jim said. "And he's learned more German than we have, so he's always correcting us."

When we watched the boy in action, our suspicions were confirmed. He was a teacher.

We shared with Vi and Jim the need to channel, not squelch, this gift, and we gave them some practical suggestions. The simple awareness of their grandson's gift relieved the pressure of the situation.

Teachers are not as idealistic as perceivers, but they want life to be the best it can be. Coupling their idealism with practicality, they try to figure out workable solutions to problems.

5. Imagination, Reality and the Teacher.

The gift of teaching is the least imaginative of all. When the preschool leader says, "I want all of you to pretend you are butterflies; flap your wings, and we'll fly around the room in a circle," the teacher child says to himself, "Butterfly? I'm no butterfly." He will comply grudgingly, while server and compassion children take off on mystic flights of pure delight. But, directed to pretend he's driving a fire engine, he will respond well because it's something really possible to do.

Charades is not the teacher's favorite game. When he does play he sometimes feels embarrassed to act out his assigned role. Yet he enjoys participating in a school drama as long as he plays a real person rather than a pumpkin or a tree.

In artistic endeavors the teacher prefers to draw realistically, finding it hard to do abstract art. I have a strong secondary gift of teaching. When my seventh grade art teacher assigned us the task of drawing an animal and then abstracting it into pieces and textures, I tried, but was frustrated. I hated the idea. When my mom asked me later, "How did your day go?" I burst into tears. I confessed I wanted to draw real things, not something I considered bizarre.

Don't force your teacher to be imaginative; let him find his own creative outlets in the real world.

6. The Teacher's Behavior (and Effective Discipline).

Teachers, like all children, *think* they are obedient, but their independence gets in the way. While the server views himself and his parents as "we," the teacher feels totally other, separated, and autonomous. He's willing to cooperate if it seems reasonable, but his cooperation is not automatic.

As a result the teacher can be argumentative without even realizing it, believing his challenges are justifiable. Parents must strike a balance between tolerating a teacher's individualism and teaching him obedience to their authority.

For a one- or two-year-old who has not yet developed much reasoning capacity, the rod will be the most effective means of establishing parental authority and instilling the rudiments of proper behavior. But as the teacher grows in his ability to reason and understand, firm and serious talks may be increasingly helpful, with the rod remaining a back-up instrument of instruction. If you start early with the rod and move gradually into the use of reason, your teacher child should make a smooth transition into the early grade-school years, becoming increasingly self-disciplined. The rod may no longer be needed.

Retain the child's right to ask questions, but don't let it lapse into argumentativeness, bringing you down to peer level with your child. You are not his peer, you're his parent, and you have the final say. You have the right to cut off the "Yes, buts." Teachers are clever, and will try to manipulate you. Don't let them.

Teachers want to be obedient, and will be with sound, reasonable parental training. But if parents are unreasonable or irrational in their demands (which is often the case with emotionally disturbed or alcoholic parents) it's hard for the child to respect and obey.

7. The Teacher's Personal Habits and Irritants.

Teachers have distinctively good study habits. Self-starting and self-motivating, they seldom need prompting to study, but do it automatically, with an amazing amount of enjoyment. Teachers love to learn, and often do their homework right after school, before going out to play or reading their newest books. This positive, productive personal habit becomes a negative only when studying is all they want to do, neglecting an essential part of childhood—play! At that point parents should encourage recreation and enjoyable social relationships.

Neatness is a common trait, not because teachers hate clutter, but because they want to know where everything is.

Punctuality is a pattern for teachers. They want to arrive *exactly* on time, and are seldom early and seldom late. They may get after other family members who tend to be late. Take this as a blessing, an indicator that some changes need to be made so the whole family can be punctual.

A teacher's most irritating habit is his propensity toward intolerance of those who think and act differently from him. His intellectual pride gets in the way. A teacher figures he's learned what's right and true, abides by it to the best of his ability, and thinks everyone else should, too.

Parents may need to show a teacher how the different motivational gifts make people unique, according to God's plan. If everyone were alike, what a boring world this would be! Help him to see the value in variety, the facets of a diamond that make it shine more brightly, the rainbow fanned out from one light source into seven lustrous colors.

Teachers also rationalize and make excuses. Their sharp minds, proficient reasoning, and ease of verbalization make them natural debaters who enjoy the challenge in making a case for just about anything. Don't let your teacher get by with this in important situations. Help him face his rationalization. Ask pointed questions: "Why are you thinking this way right now?" "Why did you say that?" "What are you trying to get out of?" "Why do you not want to take responsibility for your action?"

You may need to tell him why his explanations are not acceptable, or why he must be accountable for what he's done.

8. The Teacher's Friendships.

About ninety percent of the teachers in our survey said they'd been content with just a few friends—one to three—during their childhood. A few said they were loners, often escaping into a world of books, preferring them to friends. The ten percent with many friends had socially inclined secondary gifts of exhorting, giving, or administrating.

One teacher, remembering his childhood, said, "I had a small circle of friends because most kids my age couldn't understand me or were threatened by my intellect and large vocabulary. I didn't think I was a know-it-all, but I always seemed to have answers for everything."

While most classic teachers will never be gregarious, learning social skills and relational abilities greatly enhances their lives. Since they relate best to other teachers and to more serious or intellectual people, encourage such friendships by suggesting he invite specific friends over to work on projects or study together. Take these friends along on your next camping trip or to a museum. Get your teacher involved in the library's reading club. He may meet new friends with similar interests there.

Also involve him in your church's clubs as early as possible. Awana (Approved Workmen Are Not Ashamed) is designed for children from four to twelve years old. It promotes Scripture memorization (which appeals to teachers). If your church has no programs for children, see what is available in your community— Good News Clubs, Scouts, Camp Fire Girls, YMCA, parks department, or community clubs.

9. The Teacher's Relationships to Peers and Others.

Almost one hundred percent of the survey responses showed teachers relating very well to their parents and, usually, to their teachers. Since children with this gift tend to be a bit more serious, mature, and academically inclined than their peers, such information is consistent with what we might suppose. Actually teachers relate so well with their school instructors that peers are often jealous, calling them "teacher's pets." As we have mentioned, the professional goals of educators cause them to be drawn instinctively to children who love to learn and are spontaneously studious.

One teacher, Phyllis, wrote: "I learned early that I didn't belong to my peer group. Left to make a place for myself among adults who appreciated a child who was an excellent student, perfect in deportment, and confident in discussions, I still missed having friends my own age."

The teacher relates better to older kids than he does to peers, and relates well to younger children as long as he is cast as the boss or instructor. Otherwise, he finds them boring.

Concentrate on helping him develop the few close friends he does have. Open your home for slumber parties and birthday parties and other special occasions. Dad's availability is a special blessing for a boys' campout or hike where friends can be included. Usually by high school the teacher will have enlarged his circle of casual friends.

10. The Teacher's Intellectual Endowments.

As you have surmised by now, this is the most intellectual of all the gifts. In a diagram of the body, teachers would be placed in the mind. They often have the highest IQs, are eager and fast learners, and fit well into our competitive academic system. They learn aggressively, often more than they are asked to, turning in six-page reports when only four pages are required. They love to take advantage of extra credit opportunities and are unhappy with less than straight-A report cards.

Teachers will research and dig into every subject of interest to them. When looking up one subject in the encyclopedia they'll often get waylaid reading about other subjects that catch their attention as they flip through the pages.

Teachers frequently qualify for and enter accelerated classes and honors programs. They become top achievers and are selected for honor societies. Most valedictorians and salutatorians are teachers, as are essay contest and college scholarship winners.

Teachers should definitely go on for higher education. If your teacher doesn't win a scholarship, see that he gets to college anyway. If finances are limited, start him in a junior college and have him transfer later to a four-year school. Many students earn their way these days, working part-time during the school term and full-time in the summer.

Some teachers go to graduate school, with master's degrees and doctorates as common goals. Our older son, Dave, an administrator/teacher combination, is enrolled at Yale University School of Divinity and has always loved to study. Teachers with a call to Christian service should consider attending a Christian college, Bible school (if accredited), or seminary.

Some of the jobs and careers suitable for teachers include: anthropologist, archaeologist, astronomer, biologist, botanist, chemist, chiropractor, college professor, composer, computer programmer, curator, doctor, engineer, geologist, journalist, librarian, market researcher/analyst, mathematician, medical technologist, meteorologist, minister, missionary (linguistics), nutritionist, oceanographer, optometrist, pharmacist, philosopher, physician, physicist, proofreader, psychiatrist, psychologist, reporter, researcher, school administrator, scientist, surgeon, teacher (English, foreign language, history, mathematics, science, special ed.), theologian, or writer. See the charts in chapter 22 for other possibilities.

11. The Teacher: Leader or Follower?

Only some classic teachers are leaders, and that's usually in specialty areas—the debate club, the honor society, or the constitution committee. If a teacher has a strong secondary gift (exhorting, giving, administration) and therefore has more social skills, he will take leadership more often in a greater variety of ways.

A teacher, with his limited number of friendships, is more apt to be appointed to head a committee than to be elected by his peers, who frequently vote according to popularity, not necessarily ability. Helping him to be more friendly will increase his leadership possibilities. Schoolteachers *will* see his leadership potential and want to encourage it.

As a teacher gets older his leadership abilities will blossom, and in adulthood will probably be channeled into the areas of his profession or expertise.

12. The Teacher's Scholastic Achievements.

Teachers are the highest academic achievers. You can expect your child to be a top student with B+ to A grades. He will not feel he has done well if he gets what he considers "just a *B*" in a subject, and will be happiest when he brings home a straight-A report card.

Do affirm his good grades, but don't let him look down on siblings who are not such high achievers. They may excel in areas like popularity, sports, and leadership, in which he does not. Help him learn how to appreciate others' achievements, even in fields in which he shows no interest.

Some scholastically excelling teachers are encouraged to skip grades. They can usually handle it academically, but some may be unable to adjust socially, further separating them from meaningful friendships. Evaluate each case individually.

13. The Teacher's School Subject Interests.

Teachers normally like and excel in all subjects. Our survey revealed the following: 1) history; 2) English and literature; 3) no preference—likes all subjects; 4) math and music.

A liking for history and the tie between English and literature show the teacher's keen interest in reading. Teachers are natural bookworms. They read prolifically.

Our son Dave took a year to work—and to court his wife, Scotti—between college and graduate school. When his job took him out of town during the week he roomed with a co-worker from our church. "I'm amazed at Dave's interest in books," he reported to us. "I'd watch TV all evening and Dave would read books—dozens of them!" We'd seen this trait of his secondary gift in him for a long time.

Response number three is universally true for teachers. Everywhere we meet teachers who tell us how much they enjoyed all their school subjects and learning in general. Survey respondents commented, "I loved every subject in school"; "I got top grades in every subject"; and "I found every subject to be interesting; I had a hard time deciding what I liked most."

While math and music tied for fourth place, almost every other subject was close behind in percentage of preference.

The only challenge we see for a teacher's parents is to help him to narrow his interests enough to pick a field to specialize in at college. School counseling offices offer many tests to help. Our Occupational Success Probabilities Test in chapter 22 may also assist you. A young man told us he took a battery of tests recently to help him determine possible vocations. "It took me three days and cost $800," he said. "Then I took your test that only cost one dollar and took twenty minutes of my time, and it revealed the same vocations."

14. The Teacher's Reading Interests.

Our survey showed teachers preferring to read: 1) everything, prolifically; 2) historical novels; 3) mystery stories; 4) biographies.

From the time a teacher is old enough to sit still while a parent reads a simple story to him, his love for books is evident. A toddler may carry books around with him like other children carry toys, or sit for a long time turning pages and pointing to pictures. Teachers seem quick to learn the alphabet, and often outshine other first graders in reading proficiency. They join summer reading clubs at the library and finish suggested summer quotas by the end of the first two weeks. Teachers want their own bookshelves, and new books will be favorite presents. One family, where five out of seven members had teacher gifts, recalls the best Christmas they ever had, when 35 books were exchanged among them!

A friend of Dave's who seemed husky enough to be the whole right side of their football team quit and went to work. Where? In the school library, of course, so he could be near the books. We thought it was such a shame for the team to lose him, but when we discovered he had a teacher gift we understood.

Teachers enjoy historical novels for their rich plots and historical settings. History, remember, is their favorite school subject. Mystery stories appeal to the natural detective in teachers, an aspect of their love for research and discovery. Biographies of significant people bring more leisurely enjoyment.

Teachers also read nonfiction books for pleasure, or because they are interested in the subjects. One might develop an interest in writing and search the library for how-to-write books. Another may become fascinated with recent archaeological discoveries in the Middle East, and read relevant books on Egypt and Israel.

A set of encyclopedias is a must in a teacher's home. He will use it often, sometimes sitting down to read it just for pleasure.

A teacher may put aside the book he's currently reading to start another. Or, he may read several simultaneously. Josh, still an avid reader as an adult, admits he's never finished reading many of the hundreds of books he owns. "I've got book marks in many," he explains. "But I really mean to finish them!"

Here are a few suggestions for great birthday or Christmas presents for your teacher. A Christian school librarian can give you extensive lists of good books for various ages.

Historical novels: *Little House on the Prairie* by Laura Ingalls Wilder; *Anne of Green Gables* by L. M. Montgomery; *The Robe* by Lloyd C. Douglas.

Mysteries: The Chronicles of Narnia (six books) by C. S. Lewis; The Sugar Creek Gang series, *Treasure Hunt* and *The Indian Cemetery* by Paul Hutchens; *The Secret of the Samurai Sword* by Phyllis Whitney.

Biographies: *The Hiding Place* by Corrie ten Boom; *The Savage My Kinsman* by Elisabeth Elliot; *Twice Pardoned* by Harold Morris.

15. The Teacher and Sports.

Generally speaking, teachers do not take particular interest in sports. If they do, it's usually a rather low priority, unless a secondary gift such as exhorting or administration, is operative. Some teachers prefer watching sports to active participation in them. Others said they'd just as soon read a good book.

Teachers who did mention a sports interest usually listed a recreational activity such as bowling, waterskiing, or swimming that they enjoyed just for the fun of it.

One teacher so disliked participation in sports, "it was like punishment" when her parents insisted. Parents shouldn't push their teachers to become sports-minded, but should encourage reasonably regular activities like swimming, biking, tennis, handball, or bowling—for exercise. Most schools require physical education classes, which will at least offer some exposure to a variety of sports and calisthenics.

16. Games and Toys for Teachers.

Young teachers enjoy the challenge of puzzles, alphabet blocks, and educational toys as well as the traditional dolls, trucks, and trains. Older ones like erector sets, chemistry sets, science kits, and other creative learning tools.

Grade-school-age teachers like challenging table games: Monopoly, Scrabble, Sorry, Canasta, Rook, and Flinch. They also like dominoes and crossword puzzles. Active games requiring some plotting and planning like hide 'n seek, kick-the-can, and capture-the-flag are favorites. Teenagers enjoy Clue, Password, Pictionary, and Outburst. When buying a game remember the teacher's fondness of words, discovery, and learning.

Generally, many survey respondents preferred books to games.

17. The Teacher and Pets.

Generally, teachers seem rather indifferent about pets. If they have them they like them, but not as enthusiastically as servers and compassion children do. If they don't have them they don't feel they're missing out. It would be good to examine your child's particular bent toward animals before getting a pet.

18. The Teacher's Outstanding Qualities and Traits.

Recalling their best qualities from their childhoods, respondents to our survey said they were: 1) intelligent; 2) honest; 3) diligent; and 4) dependable.

Number one is unsurprising, since intelligence is the teacher's greatest endowment. He becomes aware of his intellectual ability early in his school career, and teachers and parents often commend him for it.

Parents, be sure your child is sufficiently challenged in school, or he will become disinterested. Talk to his instructors if you spot signs of boredom, and together plan a more stimulating regimen.

Teachers' honesty shines in their ability to work hard for good grades, without cheating. Honesty also carries over into other parts of their lives.

Diligence is part of a teacher's lifestyle. Teachers work hard, apply themselves well, and keep at the learning process to glean everything they possibly can.

Dependability is important to teachers—a badge of honor. They want to do their best. If a teacher cannot fulfill an obligation he will find a replacement to get the job done. If he cannot finish a term paper on time he will likely consult his teacher, and make arrangements for an extension.

19. The Teacher's General Interests.

While the teachers surveyed mentioned many interests, three appeared most frequently: 1) reading; 2) studying; and 3) the arts. By now we're sure you understand teachers' intense interest in reading. If you want your child to know about a subject, simply buy him a relevant book, and he will be glad to read it.

The interest in studying reflects both teachers' love for learning and for researching. I used to write junior high school curricula for two Sunday school publishers. I'd spend a minimum of twenty hours of research before even beginning to write a one-hour lesson. I wanted to be sure I had learned all I could about that lesson so I'd be confident in what I'd write. In school and college I was the same way—researching extensively, often burning the midnight oil to be sure I'd covered a subject well.

Teachers have an innate interest in fine arts and music in particular, as well as a degree of interest in drama and opera. Take your child on occasional trips to art museums. When we visited Kassel, Germany, last year we were escorted to a large art museum by a man with the gift of teaching. He told us he'd been keenly interested in museums since childhood. Needless to say, he was a well-informed, excellent guide.

Teachers have a great capacity for art appreciation and music. Check out library books on the great masters and spend time exploring these treasures with your teacher. Expose him to tapes or records of great musical masterpieces. Take him to musicals, plays, and even the opera if he's interested. You'll enrich your own life, too, in the process.

20. The Teacher's Special Joys.

The greatest joys mentioned by the teachers surveyed were: 1) family activities; 2) learning; and 3) being accepted. As we've said before, family togetherness and activities are the greatest gifts you can give your child.

Joy in learning is consistent with all we have learned about the teacher. The actual process of learning—attending school, studying, researching, discovering—thrills him. Others endure the process in order to graduate. The teacher enjoys every step along the way. After graduation he looks forward to continued learning, whether formal or informal.

College-age teachers may carry extra heavy academic loads. Don't worry: Studying stimulates them, and the process releases joy and blessing in their lives.

Throughout the learning process teachers love to help others learn, too. During their teenage years teachers often instruct younger children or assist in Sunday school. Our daughter-in-law, Scotti, is an administrator/teacher combination, just like her husband, Dave. Her mother, Jane Hunter, told us, "Scotti would often line up about twenty dolls and stuffed animals on the sofa. She'd pretend they were at Sunday school or Vacation Bible School and teach them a Bible story."

Joy in being accepted reflects the teacher's insecurity. Our teacher friend Vince Hart told us, "While I had a secure home as a child, I often felt uncertain about love and affection. My family was not very expressive, and neither was I. But I longed to be sure they *really* accepted me."

Remember, teachers are not readily accepted by their peers. Yet every person needs and longs for acceptance. Help your teacher—successful in academics but less skilled in interpersonal relationships—to feel good about himself. Look for ways to make him feel accepted for *who* he is rather than for *what* he accomplishes.

Remember: Encourage your teacher's exceptional academic ability, guide him in the development of true humility, and help him develop greater skills in interpersonal relationships.

TRAIN UP YOUR EXHORTER

11

Exhorters are outgoing, fun-loving, and adaptable. They love people—all kinds—and they want everyone to have full, happy, and fulfilled lives. The exhorter is like a coach full of good advice, an enthusiastic cheerleader, and a dedicated team player, all rolled into one.

1. The Exhorter's Emotions.

Exhorters are happy, cheerful, and contented, with habitually bubbly personalities. Yes, they have problems, but their positive attitudes cause them to believe that an answer to every problem exists "out there somewhere." In the meantime, they enjoy life.

Exhorters are sensitive to the needs of others. They care about people; they want to help them, encourage them, and assist them in solving their problems.

Exhorters are balanced in their feelings, able to express a wide range of emotions without letting those emotions affect their lives in a negative way.

An exhorter's anger doesn't usually last long. He is quick to forgive and restore relationships. When things go wrong, he may feel frustrated temporarily, but will look for ways to ease the situation. Like a rubber band stretched the to the limit, he ultimately bounces back, feeling he can learn and grow through trials and tribulations.

2. Expression: The Exhorter's Communication Skills.

When we draw a diagram to indicate what each of the gifts might be in the body, we always show the exhorter as the mouth—open, happy, and talking. Exhorters have well-oiled jaws and are fluid conversationalists, talking constantly.

This talkative trait is evident even in small children. "Margaret, aren't you ever going to stop talking?" we'd kid my young exhorter niece. She'd go right on telling us nonstop why what she was saying was important.

We believe God has endowed exhorters with fluid facility in speech because words can encourage. You won't have any trouble getting your exhorter child to speak. He loves public speaking and jumps at the chance to speak in front of the class. He volunteers quickly to answer the teacher's questions. He loves giving reports and a microphone or tape recorder brings out the ham in him.

You *will* have trouble controlling his verbosity. Just when you settle down for a nice, quiet adult conversation or get lost in a good book, he may bound into the room to tell you all about the wonders of his day or his latest escapade. Help him recognize the parameters within which he is not allowed to articulate. Protected moments where quiet prevails are necessary for family life.

If your exhorter can't stand the silence, give him a piece of paper and ask him to write down what he wanted to say. Either he will save his thoughts for later or he will write them down. One exhorter told us, "If I'd had no voice when I was a kid, I would probably have written prolific letters." Most do that, too.

Another problem is interrupting. Exhorters are so eager to share or toss in opinions they'll jump into conversations while others are still talking. They won't even realize they're interrupting. You may have to point it out many times—right when your exhorter interrupts—before he realizes what he's doing. His teachers may also complain about his interruptiveness.

Exhorters tend to dominate conversations or discussions. They'll often raise a hand in class to answer a question before they've even figured out the answer. Exhorters can turn dialogues into monologues without realizing it. Quieter friends won't mind, but others may ask, "Don't you ever let anyone get a word in edgewise?"

Help your exhorter bring his overtalkativeness under control, or it will mar what is otherwise a very popular personality.

3. The Exhorter's Self-image.

Exhorters usually have good self-images. Their basically happy dispositions, resilience, and optimism enable them to view themselves with a degree of objectivity. They can laugh at themselves and their mistakes, knowing they're not perfect, but in process.

Everyone enjoys the exhorter's positive personality. He has strong faith in himself, in the potential in others, and in God, wholeheartedly believing Romans 8:28, "that God causes all things to work together for good to those who love God, to those who are called according to His purpose" (NAS).

Nonjudgmental, exhorters accept others, and allow them to be themselves. This makes them popular with their peers but also produces a potentially dangerous problem: compromise. Exhorters may go along with the crowd even when the crowd goes against their personal standards. The "live-and-let-live" attitude sounds good, but the flip side can be a lack of conviction and a wishy-washy integrity.

Talk to your exhorter and help him to build strong standards and avoid compromise on important issues.

4. The Exhorter's Approach to Life.

Most exhorters have well-balanced approaches to life. They are idealistic, seeing good in almost everyone, and wanting every person to live up to his full potential. Exhorters who are Christians are convinced that with the Lord's help, anyone can improve. As early as the later grade-school years an exhorter's friends will begin to ask him for advice and help with relational problems. By the time he enters high school he will be known as a reservoir of advice, and may be counseling friends on a regular basis.

But the exhorter is also a realist. Everything he does—even the advice he gives—is practical. If something works for him he knows it can work for others.

He's also creative with words and thoughts, full of ideas, and willing to try just about anything to see if it works. He is not creative with his hands, however, or in art. In fact he will usually rate poorly on manual dexterity.

Exhorters are wonderfully adaptable, able to give and take in relationships. They work around tension or trouble in the family and don't let it get them down.

In one family with two grade-school-age children the father was ill. A side effect of his illness was irritability, resulting in frequent, sudden outbursts of anger. The son, gifted with compassion, took his father's irrational behavior personally, and needed professional counseling in his later teen years. The exhorter daughter determined she'd roll with the punches, ignore as much of the conflict as she could, and go on with her life. She breezed through her teen years nicely, spending much of her time with friends and keeping busy with activities at church and school.

The exhorters' exceptionally well-balanced approach to life provides many good pointers from which we can all learn and benefit.

5. Imagination, Reality, and the Exhorter.

About seventy percent of the exhorters we questioned felt they were highly imaginative as children. We think this shows in their "can do" optimistic outlook. If they don't know how to do something, they try to figure it out. If something looks complex, they imagine how it can be simplified, perhaps even spending two hours figuring out how to make a one-hour task easier. Exhorters think things through and produce a variety of solutions.

Yet in spite of their imaginative capacity exhorters are ultimately practical. They're always thinking, "What good would this do?" or "How will this be helpful to someone?"

Some exhorters admitted to daydreaming, either for enjoyment or as an escape from the reality of difficult circumstances. But they didn't use daydreaming as a permanent escape from the difficulties of life.

Encourage your exhorter to use his imaginative abilities to help others. His creative words can encourage those who are discouraged. His undaunted confidence in others' potential abilities can strengthen and uplift them. His cheerleader-like enthusiasm is contagious, motivating others to succeed.

6. The Exhorter's Behavior (and Effective Discipline).

The majority of the exhorters we surveyed remembered themselves as essentially obedient children, but about 25 percent admitted to being rebellious, mouthy, manipulative, or all three. Exhorters display a degree of independence, and parents may need to use the rod from time to time to bring it into subjection to their authority. Usually exhorters are eager to please, actually appreciating discipline. They may view spankings philosophically: "Oh well, I probably needed that."

Clever with words, the exhorter may try to weasel out of discipline by choosing apologies he knows his parents want to hear. You must discern whether or not he's sincere; don't let him be an escape artist.

He may also try to talk you into letting him do something you really don't want him to do, giving fifteen reasons why he needs to go over to Johnny's house right now. If you need him to set the table, be firm.

An exhorter's mouthiness may get him into trouble. He may be rude and impudent, or make smart-aleck remarks without thinking. Talk with him about taking responsibility for what comes out of his mouth.

Some exhorters admitted to being mischievous to the point of exasperating others. An exhorter usually has a good sense of humor, but may need guidance in expressing it. If it's carried too far, it's too much. My exhorter mother, who was prone to be mischievous as a child, admitted that she initiated a prank that got her in trouble with her father, the principal, and town authorities. She talked her teenage friends into pushing a cow up the stairs and into the belfry of their school. It was funny until the fire department had to be called to lower the cow to safety.

7. The Exhorter's Personal Habits and Irritants.

Exhorters are habitually neat, clean, and tidy. They keep their rooms in order and pick up after themselves, and they don't like clutter.

"My sister and I had a room together. She was a slob, leaving things all over the place and dropping her clothes where she took them off, " one exhorter said. "Junk piled up on the dresser and desk until you could hardly see them. I kept my side of the room neat and griped at her untidiness. It didn't do much good, so when I had friends over I'd clean up her side of the room, too."

Exhorters are also neat because they are *not* savers, and occasionally go through their belongings to see what can be weeded out. They will throw away or give away items that are no longer useful to them.

Like servers, exhorters are helpful. They want to please, and to be considerate.

An exhorter's nonjudgmentalism and acceptance of the potential for good in others are positive traits, but they can make him vulnerable to bad influences in his life. Concerned parents will want to be aware of his companions and certain, if any are of questionable character, that he is influencing them, not vice versa.

Some exhorters have temper problems, usually resulting from a lack of discipline in their lives. Explosions of temper are attempts to get their own way through manipulating and intimidating others. Here's where the authority of the rod works wonders to instill proper behavior. Tempers untamed before the teen years will escalate into other rebellious behavior, and in marriage the spouse will be the unfortunate target.

The interrupting habit mentioned previously remains one of the most irritating, but it can be modified.

8. The Exhorter's Friendships.

It's no surprise that exhorters have the most gregarious of all the gifts. They love all kinds of people and have many friends. You will not need to promote friendships with these children. If anything, they will have more than they can handle, wishing they had more quality time to spend with them.

Exhorters are well-liked because of their sunny dispositions, ease of communication, and open acceptance of others. It's not unusual for them to be very popular at school. But this popularity brings responsibility for the exhorter to influence his peers positively. Many will copy his example thinking, "This is the way to become popular myself." Don't lay too heavy a burden on him, but encourage him to set good examples in his attitudes and behavior.

Occasionally the exhorter's popularity can backfire, becoming a problem especially during the teenage years. "Being well-liked caused jealousy in others when I was in school," a now-mature exhorter said. "This was difficult for me to understand. I just wanted to get along and be friends with everyone. I felt I must be doing something wrong to cause this jealousy, yet I knew of nothing deliberate, and so the inner confusion went on—unanswered until I understood about the motivational gifts."

Remember, your exhorter's desire to be popular makes him vulnerable to compromising his own standards for the sake of friendship. He may adopt a "live and let live" attitude, causing others to believe he approves of his friends' inappropriate behavior when, in fact, he only tolerates it. Such compromise may hurt his Christian witness. Talk to him about it. He may not realize what's happening, and may be open to suggestion or change. The younger child may need you to set and enforce strict standards until he's able to maintain them on his own.

118

Your exhorter is probably a joiner. Most are. Set limits when he's younger, and as he gets older, help him make wise decisions about the extent of his social involvement in groups. Otherwise he'll become over-involved, possibly neglecting his studies.

As a Christian parent, make sure he joins at least some Christian groups. If you start him with your church's groups in grade school, he will probably continue right on through the youth fellowships.

Some parents complain, "That means I have to run him to the meeting every week, then go back again to get him when he's through." Yes, training your child in God's ways takes some sacrifice!

Think about the leaders that prepare and give their time to benefit your child. Why not offer to help once a month or more? Arrange car pools if possible. Maybe you can schedule an adult prayer meeting or Bible study for the same time slot, or take along a good Christian book you've been meaning to read.

If your child joins a secular group like Scouts or Camp Fire Girls, be sure you know something about the leaders' moral values. Make an appointment to meet with them. Ask candid questions. Be sure your child will be in good hands. Sadly, some sick or morally depraved adults take leadership of children's groups, and you certainly don't want your child exposed unnecessarily to them.

If no suitable group is available, you may want to start one through your church or in your neighborhood.

If you live in an isolated place, your exhorter is going to need pre-planned social times with friends. Arrange for a friend to come home with him on the school bus once a week to play, do homework, or even spend the night.

9. The Exhorter's Relationships to Peers and Others.

Exhorters relate well to everyone—younger children, peers, older children, parents, teachers, and adults in general. Good relationships are important to the exhorter; he wants to like people and have them like him. Strained or broken relationships bother him. Quick to forgive and ask forgiveness, he is even willing to take the blame in a deteriorated situation for which he is not responsible, if it will help bridge the gap.

The exhorter's adaptability, positive personality, kindness, and tolerance give him patience with those younger than himself. He wants to encourage them and boost their self-images.

The exhorter respects older kids and is willing to take the subservient role in order to learn from them.

Adults respond to the exhorter's friendliness and positive expectations, and his talkativeness comes across as competent conversational ability. He is normally agreeable and pleasant to be around, and teachers find him easy to work with and quick to respond. His propensity to learn from life's experiences makes him alert and eager to participate.

An exhorter is transparent, quick to admit his faults and shortcomings, knowing he is not perfect but rather "in process." He will reveal his own past mistakes in order to help another avoid them. As a result the exhorter is a natural and excellent counselor to his friends. They are often attracted to him for advice on personal problems. They relate to his openness and can identify and share their own problems without fear of judgment or admonishment.

We have talked with dozens of exhorters who remember other students seeking their counsel during junior and senior high school and college days. It can become time-consuming.

Gwen said, "I had to watch my schedule in college. So many came to me for informal counseling I could get way behind in my homework. I finally had to set limits. It was truly hard for me to say no, sometimes. I yearned to help people, but my folks also expected me to pass my courses."

Encourage this advice-giving inclination. Your exhorter should increase his skills in this area, since it will be a valuable part of his adult life. His advice is often good, and always practical. He will make some mistakes, but will learn from them. Help him to talk with you about them, analyzing and discussing positive alternatives. Be open and transparent with your exhorter, and he will feel free to come to you for advice often.

10. The Exhorter's Intellectual Endowments.

Exhorters are usually above average to excellent students. One-third reported B+ to A averages, one-third reported B to B+ averages, and one-third reported C averages. The range is broader than is evident in other gifts. Secondary gifts may influence their academic achievements, as will the extent to which their sociability hinders studying. Most could be top students if they applied themselves.

Encourage your exhorter to develop good study habits, making homework a priority over socializing. But don't expect him to compete with a teacher, whose whole focus is learning.

Your exhorter will probably be college bound. He could do exceptionally well in the social sciences, or other areas involving working with people. Some of the jobs and careers that would be suitable include: advertising executive, ambassador, auctioneer, guidance counselor, minister, occupational therapist, personnel manager, psychiatrist, psychologist, public relations director, radio/TV announcer or talk show host, realtor, receptionist, recreation director, religious education director, social worker, sociologist, speech therapist, elementary teacher, English teacher, physical education teacher, social studies teacher, special education teacher, travel agent, and writer (especially of biographies and how-to books). For a more comprehensive view see chapter 22.

11. The Exhorter's Scholastic Achievements.

Only one-third of the exhorters surveyed viewed themselves as having sharp intellects, but more than sixty percent reported they were above-average students. It seems their performance exceeds their self-evaluations.

In addition to good (if not always top) academic achievements, expect your exhorter to achieve in student activities, leadership, and sports.

Exhorters' attraction to people draws them into student activities and peer group endeavors. They love being wholeheartedly involved, are effective motivators, and frequently rise to leadership positions.

Exhorters also shine in sports, especially competitive team activities.

Be sure your exhorter has ample opportunity to get involved in activities, leadership, and sports. He will feel fulfilled with whatever level of excellence he achieves in these areas.

When in high school I applied for a particular, sought-after scholarship. I was told I'd be evaluated in four categories: grades, leadership, activities, and need. The donor ranked all of these equally in determining the recipients. A well-rounded personality was more important, in this case, than excellence in just one area. Given ample opportunities to participate, exhorters are usually well-rounded in achievements.

12. The Exhorter: Leader or Follower?

Exhorters are second only to administrators in leadership. Our survey showed seventy percent were involved in leadership at school fifty percent of the time or more. Twenty-seven percent said they were usually followers, leading only occasionally. Seven percent, with secondary gifts lacking leadership orientation, said they were never leaders.

While in leadership style the administrator may resemble a bandmaster marching ahead of his players, the exhorter is more like a coach who gets his committee in a huddle, gives suggestions, and says, "Go to it, team!" Your exhorter always sees himself on the same level as those he leads, but motivating them to action. A good idea person, he's open to others' suggestions and is adaptable to whatever will work for that group. Members of the group will feel close to him and find him easily accessible. Unless his talkativeness interferes, he works well with them.

Affirm your exhorter in his leadership attempts. He motivates and encourages others, but he needs someone to encourage *him*, to tell him he's doing a good job. Lacking your verbal affirmation, he may feel insecure about his leadership ability and turn down future opportunities for lack of confidence.

13. The Exhorter's School Subject Interests.

The exhorters we surveyed chose English as their favorite subject, probably because, as the basis for language, it enables their number one favorite activity—talking! Exhorters also mentioned a number of related subjects: reading, languages, spelling, literature, and composition.

Math and history tied for second place, but art, music, science, and social studies were close behind. Many respondents mentioned they liked most subjects. This general interest in school subjects reflects exhorters' openness, and echoes their acceptance of a wide variety of people.

Your exhorter will not care much about technical information and theoretical supposition but will love subjects that help him understand people. Encourage him to take high school electives like psychology, sociology, and family living. A summer spent as a volunteer or paid counselor in a church or secular camp or community athletic program will help him put his people skills to work. Keep him involved with people; he won't fare well stocking shelves in a warehouse or working on an assembly line.

14. The Exhorter's Reading Interests.

We were not surprised to find people-loving exhorters favoring biographies and autobiographies. Start reading simple biblical biographies to your preschooler and wean him onto them as he's old enough to read to himself. Try the Arch Books, a wonderful series of stories (more than eighty of them now) about Bible characters and events, often in rhyme, with bright, attractive pictures. Our kids adored them from toddler age right up into the early junior years, reading them over and over again. Look for the Lion Bible Stories series (fifty books) and *Precious Moments Stories from the Bible*, too.

For juniors offer *To be a Pilgrim* (John Bunyan) by Joyce Reason, part of the Faith and Flame series; *Young Man in a Hurry* (William Carrey) by Iris Clinton; and *Crusader for Christ* (Billy Graham) by Jean Wilson.

Junior highs will enjoy *The Inn of the Sixth Happiness* by Gladys Aylward; *The Story of My Life* by Helen Keller; and *His Gentle Voice* by Julie Wayner.

For high schoolers consider *Run Baby Run* by Nicky Cruz; *A Step Further* by Joni Eareckson; *Born Again* by Chuck Colson; and *Tested by Fire* by Merrill Womack.

Exhorters' second reading preference was the general category of fiction. Within it they often specified mysteries, like the Agatha Christie books, and romances, like *Going on Seventeen* and *Angel on Skiis* by Betty Cavanna.

Exhorters have little interest in nonfiction reading for pleasure, with the exception of how-to books. Books of facts leave them cold.

15. The Exhorter and Sports.

The vast majority of exhorters love sports in general, and specifically active group sports, informal or organized. Baseball was the number one choice, followed closely by basketball, volleyball, football, soccer, and track. Exhorters like competition, and some even thrive on it.

Get your exhorter involved in a team sport in school, Little League, through the parks' department, YMCA, or your church. When I was Director of Christian Education in a large denominational church we ran a wonderful basketball program for boys (today we'd have it for girls, too) throughout the whole school year. Starting at the fourth grade level, the program continued through junior high as part of a Seattle church league. The coaches also taught our boys' Sunday school classes, making regular attendance a requirement for playing on one of the teams.

An effective evangelistic outreach, the basketball program grew to include more than one hundred boys.

Exhorters also enjoy competitive or recreational individual sports like swimming, hiking, bicycling, skiing, tennis, badminton, and bowling.

16. Games and Toys for the Exhorter.

Exhorters need to be active. Our survey showed they liked skates (both roller and ice), bicycles, energetic group games like kick-the-can and run-sheep-run, climbing trees, and playing ball. Indoors they enjoyed table and card games and creative play activities like "house," "doctor/nurse," or "school." Women respondents almost unanimously reported spending a lot of time playing with dolls, and interacted with them as if they were real people.

Exhorters are seldom happy to play alone, wanting friends to play with nearly all the time. It's true your living or recreation room will be messier as a result, but it's worth it. Scoot them outside when the weather permits. If you have to provide snacks remember popcorn, Kool-Aid, and lemonade are inexpensive.

When the exhorter's mother hears Julie Andrews sing, "The hills are alive with the sound of music," she may superimpose, "My house is alive with the sound of children." Rejoice: They grow up all too soon. Enjoy them while you can.

17. The Exhorter and Pets.

Eighty-five percent of the exhorters surveyed said they had pets when they were children. Almost all liked them, but some commented, "I enjoyed my pet, but I preferred to be with my friends." Exhorters do well with pets but don't need them as much as do servers and children with the gift of compassion.

Actually, the best pet for your exhorter may be a talking parrot! (We're only kidding. . . . Or are we?)

18. The Exhorter's Outstanding Qualities and Traits.

Adult exhorters reflecting on their childhood best qualities said they were: 1) friendly; 2) loving; 3) obedient; and 4) happy.

We already know exhorters are friendly. Their focus on people, broad acceptance of others, adaptability, gregariousness, and positive personalities attract others. Exhorters are greatly loved by young and old alike. They view every person in the world as a potential friend.

This is a charming attribute but it makes younger exhorters vulnerable to morally depraved, abusive strangers. Many schools now warn children about such dangers. Make sure your child understands. Don't squelch his friendliness, but teach him applicable safeguards for your situation and community.

An exhorter's loving quality is second only to the compassion child's ability in this area. He truly loves people and seeks things to like even in the unlovable. His effortless verbalization of his love for others will enhance their self-esteem.

Like children with all other gifts, he views himself as obedient. He usually is. A small streak of independence may appear on occasion, but he wants to please. Peer influence in his teen years may pull him off course. Be firm with him. Teenagers want boundaries even when they say they don't.

Exhorters' happiness is contagious. Their upbeat, positive attitudes and frequent smiles and laughter benefit friends and family alike. Less prone to physical sickness or emotional stress than some, they prove the proverb that a merry heart does good like a medicine (Proverbs 17:22). An exhorter's moodiness or depression is a sure sign he needs to forgive someone. Get him to talk about it, forgive, and make things right, if necessary.

19. The Exhorter's General Interests.

The exhorters surveyed ranked their general interests as: 1) people; 2) outdoor activities; 3) reading. The first and most often mentioned response is obvious: Exhorters are people people, centering their whole lives around interpersonal relationships. They take joy in contributing to others' lives, in encouraging and building up others' self-esteem.

The interest in outdoor activities reflects their propensity toward active, athletic lives. They are kids on the move, involved, with energy to burn. With outdoor activities ranging all the way from organized sports to walking in the woods, they have a special appreciation for nature. Get your exhorter out of doors.

Our church women's group sponsors a summertime activity called "Day at the Park" about every two weeks. Choosing parks with good play equipment and swimming, softball, or hiking opportunities, we print up a schedule ahead of time showing where we'll be from ten in the morning till one in the afternoon. We encourage the moms to car pool, bringing all their children and a picnic lunch. The little ones have a great time on the play equipment, the older ones play games or swim, and the moms enjoy fellowship. We eat lunch at noon so those whose little ones nap can leave. Everyone enjoys fresh air, exercise, strengthened relationships among the families, and the occasion to enjoy God's beautiful creation.

Reading is another way exhorters learn to know about and understand other people. Remember—biographies are their favorite books, and make great birthday and Christmas presents.

20. The Exhorter's Special Joys.

Exhorters mentioned: 1) family activities; 2) making others happy; and 3) being around people as their greatest sources of joy.

Once again we find family activities the strong basis for children's greatest joy. Even though your exhorter craves being with friends, don't neglect quality family time. One recent study showed that the average American father spends only five minutes a week in direct, focused time with each child. What a sad situation! There is no adequate substitute for caring, attentive parents.

I am grateful that Don realized the importance of fatherhood right from the beginning of our marriage. He already had eleven years of experience in raising Linda. I was delighted to see how much time he spent with her, talking, playing games, throwing frisbees, or going fishing. Sometimes he'd take her out to dinner—just the two of them. She felt so special.

When the boys came along Don was equally attentive. And when he was offered a promotion at the Post Office he turned it down. Why? He wanted to be available for the kids, and being a letter carrier meant he arrived home just before they finished school each day. He was also able to attend all their after-school football, basketball, and soccer games, and every track meet. Becoming a postal supervisor would have entailed longer hours and seldom seeing the boys make baskets or touchdowns. We could have used the extra money, but we couldn't buy back the time or opportunities.

Remember, bigger screen televisions, video games, new skis, or the gift of a car on his sixteenth birthday don't communicate love to your child. Your affectionate touches and *time spent with him* say, "I really love you."

Making others happy gives an exhorter a sense of self-worth and accomplishment. The splendid byproduct is joy, for he instinctively knows he is doing what God created him to do. Joy always results from operating in one's motivational gift.

The third item listed, being around people, is to be expected as a source of joy for exhorters.

Remember: Provide your exhorter with adequate opportunities to interact with other children; help him learn to curb his talkativeness when necessary; and direct his energy into helping and encouraging others to overcome their problems.

TRAIN UP YOUR GIVER

12

In some ways the gift of giving has been elusive, the most mysterious of all the seven gifts to identify. Givers are well-rounded people with some similarities to servers and exhorters, but not as wide a range of distinguishing characteristics. Consequently you will recognize some already familiar traits, but will also see the giver's unique features.

1. The Giver's Emotions.

Like exhorters, givers are happy children. They are positive in their outlooks on life and enjoy people. They want to live life to the fullest.

But givers are not always outgoing and sometimes are quite shy, much like servers and children with the gift of compassion. They normally feel secure within their own families but find it difficult to meet new people. A preschool giver may hide behind his parent when a stranger comes into the house, responding to the stranger's "Hello, how are you," by hanging his head or disappearing into the safety of his parent's shadow.

Don't worry about his shyness. You can't force him to be outgoing. When he's little let him sit on your lap or close beside you when you're talking to strangers, so he'll feel more secure, less prone to hide.

With friends a giver is able to identify and express his feelings, but he will not reveal those depths to casual acquaintances. Most survey respondents said their emotions were stable, in control, with no major ups and downs. Some acknowledged occasional moodiness.

Your giver will probably have few difficulties with his emotions, but if he does, help him to talk about and resolve them. If he's moody, find out what he's upset or angry about. Teach him to forgive.

2. Expression: The Giver's Communication Skills.

Responses were split 50/50 on ease of expression. Half said it was difficult for them to speak, especially in front of groups. The other half said they communicated easily. Secondary gifts and degrees of natural extroversion or introversion influence this skill.

If your giver has difficulty in this area, work with him on expressing himself well. He will feel comfortable with you, so ask questions requiring explanations, like, "Why do you think your sister didn't want to play with you this morning?" or, "What do you think will happen if I let go of this balloon?" Let him practice expressing himself without recognizing your deliberate encouragement.

3. The Giver's Self-image.

Once again givers' responses to our question were evenly split. About forty percent said they had good self-images and about forty percent said they didn't. About twenty percent claimed to be average in this area. Most respondents who had difficulty verbalizing also had poor self-images.

You know your giver best. If his self-image is suffering, ask yourself these questions: Are you giving him lots of affection through touching and hugging? Are you verbalizing your love? Are you spending quality time with him? Are you teaching him to express himself better? Do you listen carefully to what he says? Do you affirm his good qualities? Do you discipline him firmly and fairly? Do you urge him to talk about his negative feelings?

Help him to base his self-image on fact, not on presumptions or fears. Tell him who he is in Christ, and how the Lord loves him unconditionally.

Help him to develop a good prayer life. Givers (along with perceivers and compassion people) will eventually be called to be intercessors. (We all intercede from time to time, but are not all *called* to be intercessors.) Teach him how to pray and encourage him to pray for others, especially those who have not yet come to know Jesus Christ personally. Pray with him for special needs and celebrate with him when his prayers are answered. Help him learn to trust in God's help.

4. The Giver's Approach to Life.

Givers scored a three-way tie between practical, realistic, and idealistic approaches to life, again making their gift hard to define. But since they are capable of all three approaches they also are capable of well-rounded, balanced approaches to life.

One giver said, "I feel I was really well-balanced as a child, probably because I was a giver, and had a reasonably good home situation. I was shy and not too sure of myself, and occasionally had some fears, but life for me was quite 'normal,' I think."

Some givers defined themselves as idealistic, but always ready to look at real or practical circumstances and to adjust accordingly.

If your giver is idealistic without the practical balance, he'll need to become more realistic and practical. Upset when circumstances do not measure up to how he'd like life to be, he may become moody or depressed. Help him learn to cope with life as it is, putting his idealism to work in practical ways.

If he is a realist who aims low to avoid failure or disappointment, help him to set higher, yet practical and attainable goals.

If he is a practical person with limited faith, encourage him to trust God in realistic ways.

Whichever approach dominates your giver's personality, he will enter wholeheartedly into life.

5. Imagination, Reality and the Giver.

At least eighty percent of the adult givers who answered our survey said they had good imaginations as children. Adept at pretending, givers "fly around the room like butterflies" almost as enthusiastically as servers. They can throw themselves into role-playing and enjoy it, and do well in dramatic presentations or plays. Encourage this propensity.

The giver is quite creative, displaying original ideas in art class, or, once he grasps the basics, playing a musical instrument with innovative skill. Private art or music lessons could increase his creativity and help overcome his shyness.

6. The Giver's Behavior (and Effective Discipline).

Givers truly desire to be obedient. None of the adult giver respondents said he was rebellious as a child. Some admitted their behavior was only fair to good at times, but most remembered being consistently well-behaved.

Because the giver has one of the three serving-type gifts defined in 1 Peter 4:11, he is a quiet, easy-to-get-along-with child, wanting to please parents, teachers, and even babysitters. He seldom picks fights with siblings or peers and often gives in or gives up to avoid arguing.

Normally your giver will be easy to discipline. A firm word will often be sufficient. Once you've established your authority, the need for the rod will be rare. It's good to have around, however, for those times when he tests the seriousness of your parental role. Remember, consistent discipline produces inner security in your child's life.

7. The Giver's Personal Habits and Irritants.

Givers are both neat and helpful. Their rooms are almost as tidy as servers' rooms and they are quick to help, regularly carrying out household chores without complaint. They don't always spot needs for help like servers do, but once asked, they're eager to assist.

John really loved to help his dad and mom. "But," he said, "I didn't always see what was needed, so I'd ask my parents to tell me when they needed help. It made me feel good when I could do something for them."

Like exhorters, givers want to get along with everyone and are friendly, though often shy in their expressions. Givers are usually introverts, while exhorters are usually extroverts.

Two habits unique to givers are their incredible abilities to make and save money. As soon as they are old enough to understand money's significance they will find ways to increase their financial assets. Born entrepreneurs, givers may open corner Kool-Aid stands or car washes, or deliver homemade "business cards" offering reasonably priced babysitting and lawn-mowing services around the neighborhood.

Even though Chris moved every two or three years during her childhood because her father was in military service, she still found ways to make money. One time she and a friend had a shoe polishing business. Another time they neatly recopied their mothers' recipes and sold them *back* to them.

Givers also learn early to *save* money. My nephew Rex, his brother, and two sisters lived with us for a while. Whenever we gave the children spending money three of them took off immediately for the grocery store to buy candy or ice cream. Not Rex. He'd save his until he had enough to buy something useful. When we gave the children nuts or candy Rex ate one piece and stashed the rest away to eat later. Sometimes when I cleaned the house I found his treasures hidden under an overstuffed chair, behind some cups in the china closet, or under a sofa cushion. I kept his hiding places secret. Today Rex continues to exhibit the characteristics of a giver: He's industrious, makes good money, and invests it carefully.

Let your child venture into the business world in ways suitable to his age. Teach him the value of money and how to be responsible with it. Matthew, a classic giver, wrote, "When I was ten years old I decided to earn my own money for Christmas presents rather than take money from my folks. I worked very hard, and even though I wasn't able to earn as much as my folks usually gave me for presents, I felt good about being able to buy them with what I'd earned."

Givers can become stingy, hoarding money because it's become too important to them. Quell this tendency by presenting money as a tool to be used in God's service, not as an end in itself.

Another potential problem is stealing, not for the giver's own use, but to give away. A giver from Canada who's now in full-time Christian ministry shared his childhood situation.

"My family was very poor. There was no money for gifts, and yet I longed to give them. So I began to shoplift whenever I needed a gift, and had great joy in giving it. There were some twinges of guilt, but the pleasure of being able to give my friends gifts suppressed it. At sixteen I was caught and spent time in a detention home. There I met Jesus. He changed my life and released me from the pollution in my gift."

A poor self-image may hamper your giver's natural inclination to make money, resulting in laziness, lateness, and procrastination. These are clear signals he needs more work to build up his self-confidence. As he likes himself more, his motivation will increase.

8. The Giver and Friendships.

About 95 percent of the givers surveyed reported being comfortable having just a few friendships.

Givers typically choose friends from among the three serving-type gifts—givers, servers, and compassion people—since their quiet and reserved natures mesh well. But other circumstances—proximity, age similarity, isolation, or compatible lifestyles may bond givers with those having speaking-type gifts.

Don't try to push the latter type of friendship, or your giver may be overwhelmed or dominated, increasing his insecurity and decreasing his self-esteem. But if circumstances and mutual interests coincide, let it happen.

Your giver will be very supportive of his friends, developing strong ties of loyalty that will endure into adulthood.

Clubs and groups are not necessarily for your giver. He may enjoy them, however, for fellowship's sake or to stimulate a particular interest. (For instance, a shy giver living on a farm may be drawn into a local 4-H club to learn more about becoming a productive farmer.) But competitive groups will not appeal to him. He'd rather see someone else succeed or win than win himself. A giver is prone to yield to others, to open the door, to let someone slip in line in front of him, even to give away credit due to him if it will help someone else.

Givers do enjoy noncompetitive groups. Church groups like AWANA make it easy for *everyone* to win awards and badges for learning Bible verses, so no one feels left out or thwarted by overeager extroverts. Your giver will prefer a small group to a large one, unless the large one is subdivided into smaller groups some of the time enabling him to feel more at home.

9. The Giver's Relationships to Peers and Others.

Givers, like exhorters, get along well with everyone. Despite their shy, reserved natures, they give and take well, and work conscientiously at their relationships. Givers are not as popular as exhorters, but their willingness to take cooperative, subordinate, and/or supportive roles attracts peers as well as younger and older children.

Although as children givers are often fearful of adults, they gradually learn to relate well to them. Their relationships with their parents are close. Givers respect teachers, other authority figures, and adults in general.

Your child may feel he gives more in relationships than he receives. He's probably right, but don't let him fall into resentment. Remind him God has equipped him to give generously in all aspects of his life. Help him to rejoice in God's gifting, and to be grateful for every opportunity to give.

If, on the other hand, his generous heart overrides his good judgment, or others take advantage of him unnecessarily, you may need to intervene.

"One time my father gave me twenty dollars to spend however I wished," Janice told us. "A young boy came by our house one afternoon wanting a donation so he could go to summer camp. My heart went out to him. I wanted to give him my whole twenty dollars, and would have done so had my dad not stopped me."

Your giver will shine brightest in relating to people when he's involved in making money. Cordial and pleasant, he'll cultivate a "customer-is-always-right" mode, enabling him to succeed in business one day, if it becomes the primary direction in his life.

10. The Giver's Intellectual Endowments.

Givers surveyed rated their childhood intellectual abilities in only three ways: average, above average, and good. Grades were split evenly between average (C) and above average (B), with no one answering poor (D) or excellent (A). Generally givers are C+ to B− students.

It is highly unlikely your giver will be a straight-A student, unless he has a strong secondary gift of teaching or administration. If he is bringing home B's and C's he's working up to his capacity and should be congratulated for his effort. Never compare him to a teacher or administrator sibling who comes by A's easily.

Neither should you accept D's from the giver. Such grades indicate laziness, laxness, or suppressed emotional stresses requiring your attention.

Some givers go on to academic colleges, but more attend business schools. Those who are called into evangelism or other full-time Christian work often enroll in Bible colleges.

Some of the jobs and careers that would be suitable for the giver include: accountant, actor, auditor, bank teller, banker, bookkeeper, business consultant, business owner, buyer, carpenter, clerk, computer operator, computer programmer, contractor, economist, electrician, evangelist, farmer, investment fund manager, landscaper, life insurance agent, manufacturer, mason, mechanic, metalworker, miner, missionary, office worker, paramedic, realtor, retailer, salesman, secretary, business education teacher, technician, toolmaker, travel agent, truck driver, waiter/waitress, welder, or wholesaler.

Many of these jobs require manual skills and business ability. Givers have both. Secondary gifts will extend these job and career options even further. See the complete chart of possibilities in chapter 22.

11. The Giver: Leader or Follower?

About half of the givers surveyed said they were definitely followers. The other half said they took leadership, at least on occasion. Many indicated they felt comfortable with either position.

Givers' secondary gifts play significant roles in this area, tipping the scales toward leadership or followership. Gifts of administration, exhorting, teaching, and perception can add impetus to leadership, while gifts of serving and compassion will incline givers to be followers. Accept your giver as he is, but if you see leadership characteristics he does not recognize, point them out and encourage him to lead from time to time.

12. The Giver's Scholastic Achievements.

Consider B averages fine, normal achievements for classic givers. Once in high school, your giver may get A's in business courses—typing, shorthand, accounting, or business management. He will excel in this area.

Also expect achievements in his part-time or summer jobs. A giver has strong inner motivation to do well in his work, often landing an exceptional job for someone so young. His boss may recognize his natural business ability, increasing his responsibility or promoting him sooner than you'd expect.

Your innovative teen-age giver may wish to start his own business. Encourage him. If he needs financial help to get started, do what you can, or see if a businessman will sponsor and advise him.

Some givers do well in sports; some don't. If your giver is athletic, encourage him, attending games whenever you can. Let him know you're proud of him.

13. The Giver's School Subject Interests.

Our survey showed givers' best subjects to be: 1) English; 2) math; 3) business; and 4) history.

English and math ranked closely. A good grasp of both is essential in order for the giver to succeed in business courses, the third subject mentioned, and in the business world. Givers were the only respondents to mention business courses as their favorites.

We recommend typing for every student, but your giver should learn as early as possible. Encourage him to learn computer skills in school (many teachers introduce them in the third and fourth grades) and at home, if you have a computer available. They will not only help him complete assignments and papers, but will be necessary tools in the business world.

Givers should also take shorthand, business machines, accounting, management, and computer programing. If your high school doesn't offer these classes, consider night school, junior college offerings, or private business schools. Many givers enroll in such classes while still attending high school, or during the summer, and many go on to business college after graduation.

Notice the other major areas of interest: history and geography. Some givers will be called as evangelists or missionaries, traveling the world in their work. Givers not called to go are usually called to support such work. Encourage your giver's early interest in the history and geography of nations, and, if possible, make travel a frequent item on your family agenda.

14. The Giver's Reading Interests.

Givers surveyed ranked their reading interests as follows: 1) a variety of books; 2) fiction; 3) adventure; and 4) animal stories. The first two answers are general because the tallies showed a wide range of reading interests, making it difficult to distinguish categories. Many givers expressed enjoyment in reading a variety of books.

Givers mentioned two particular types of fiction: novels and mystery stories. Some liked novels of all kinds, while others specified historical novels. (Perhaps the latter help givers to "travel" inexpensively, as do adventure stories, their third preference.) One great adventure series for juniors lets young readers create their own stories by choosing alternative plots page-by-page. Look for *The Cereal Box Adventures, Professor IQ's Mysterious Machine,* and *Flight into the Unknown.*

The fourth reading interest reflects givers' deep love of animals. Primaries will enjoy *If Animals Could Talk* by William Coleman, and the Adam Raccoon series by Glen Keane. For older children you can't go wrong with old favorites like *Lassie Come Home* by Eric Knight; *The Yearling* by Marjorie Rawlings; and *Black Beauty* by Anna Sewell.

Givers also enjoy biographies, so you have a wide range of books from which to choose for gifts. Your giver will enjoy reading for pleasure, and will appreciate books all his life.

15. The Giver and Sports.

A majority of givers surveyed said they liked sports, especially group sports. They enjoyed a degree of competitiveness and easily felt team spirit. Only about a quarter reported no interest in sports.

Baseball, basketball, track, and tennis were giver favorites. Skating, biking, football, skiing, soccer, swimming, volleyball, hunting, fishing, horseback riding, and athletic club activities were also listed.

Discover your giver's favorite sports and encourage him to pursue them. Participation in some of the organized sports listed above will extend his normally small circle of friends, and be fun, too.

If your giver does not care for sports, he probably gets enough activity through his physical education classes.

16. Games and Toys for Givers.

According to our survey givers loved spontaneous outdoor games like kick-the-can, softball, or shooting baskets. Building with Legos or construction sets was a second preference, apparently consuming many childhood hours. These toys are available in plastic, wood or metal, suitable for every age level from toddler to teen. Give your child a basic set, and add to it periodically.

Creative make-believe—utilizing their good imaginations to play house or grocery store or dress-up—ranked as a popular giver pastime. Girls reported make-believe with their dolls and paper dolls as well. Givers also liked table games and puzzles.

We suggest focusing on your giver's interest in business. Help him set up a semi-permanent play grocery store. Build shelves and a counter, or use old bookcases and a card table. Provide realistic-looking play money (bills and coins). Open canned goods from the bottom and open boxes carefully, so they can be resealed; eventually your giver will have well-stocked shelves. This type of creative play will enhance his natural business ability.

17. The Giver and Pets.

Most givers reported loving pets, especially dogs and cats. Hamsters, birds, and fish also brought pleasure. While givers enjoyed the pets they had, they also got along without them. Many respondents said they'd rather play with friends than with pets.

All children benefit from having pets. Caregiving, learning to show love, and learning to handle trauma when the pet is hurt, or dies, are all part of growing up. We recommend a pet for your giver, but having one is not vital to his well-being.

18. The Giver's Outstanding Qualities and Traits.

Adult givers surveyed felt that as children they were: 1) industrious; 2) generous; 3) honest; and 4) thrifty.

Givers are hard workers, even as children. Quick to help their parents, they volunteer to work on projects, stay with tasks until they are completed, and take pride in their accomplishments. As they enter the teen years they develop enterprises, often setting up their own businesses and working hard to make them succeed. Innovative and creative in their ideas, they are able to institute them in practical ways. Givers are dependable and responsible.

Givers are generous. Your son may put his whole allowance in the missionary offering, or buy a softball glove for his best friend "just because he needs one." Your daughter may give her new belt or necklace to a friend who admires it. If a giver overhears his parents saying they're short of cash, he's apt to offer them his savings.

Givers also donate their time, talent, and energy to others, helping parents, teachers, friends, or whoever can benefit from their assistance.

Tracy, a formerly misunderstood giver, told us, "My mother often criticized me for allowing my friends to take advantage of me. She thought I gave them too much of my time, efforts, and material possessions."

Honesty is an abiding characteristic; givers' integrity is vital to them, and even small deceptions induce guilt and condemnation. If lying emerges, nip it in the bud. Discuss it with your giver: he'll be quick to repent and bring his conduct into line.

Givers' thriftiness may seem contradictory to their generosity. Not so. Givers are frugal in their personal spending so they will have more to give to others! They save money readily. If your preschooler does not have a piggy bank, get him one. An older primary may even want to start a bank account, to have money available for what he deems "worthwhile" projects—missionaries, starving children, a friend who can't afford to go to camp.

Your giver may also be a careful, deliberate comparison shopper, always looking for the best buy. He doesn't want to waste money unnecessarily. Be patient with him. This special learning process will benefit him throughout his life.

19. The Giver's General Interests.

Givers ranked 1) reading; 2) friends; and 3) making money as their top three interests. We expected making money to be number one, but the survey gave us a broader perspective of the giver.

Givers' interest in making money *is* unique to their giftedness, and is probably a good indicator to spot in your child. Most children prefer presents; your giver is delighted to receive money. Don't earmark it for something you think he'd like. Allow him to decide how to spend it. He may save it, and take his time deciding what to buy.

Humor his money-making endeavors. While he may call on you to provide the lemonade at first, teach him to figure expenses and to understand they must be deducted from his profit. A small loan might help him start a business enterprise. He may borrow the lawn mower, but save up to buy one of his own. Let him: It's good experience.

A giver can become financially independent quite early. Nancy, who now has her own business, said, "When I was eleven I started babysitting to earn my own money, saving to buy my own clothes and Christmas presents for my family. By junior high I was earning enough to provide for most of my extracurricular activities, managing my finances well, and spending my money as I saw fit. It gave me such a feeling of satisfaction and accomplishment."

About half of our survey respondents were not Christians until they reached adulthood and therefore could not relate Christian activities or interests from their childhoods. But those who were Christians as children reported as their greatest interest witnessing to others about their faith in Jesus. They often invited friends to Sunday school, church, or church youth activities, and were bold in talking about Jesus personally.

Jerry Raaf, a Canadian Armed Forces chaplain, told us of his strong, lifelong desire to share the Gospel. Even as a five-year-old he tried to tell his little friends about Jesus, though they didn't always want to hear, and sometimes ran home. Jerry wasn't discouraged. One day his parents missed him but finally located him in the chicken yard. He had locked the gate so the chickens couldn't get away and was preaching his heart out to a captive audience!

You can provide great blessing and early training for your giver by sponsoring a Good News Club (or any type of children's evangelistic outreach) in your home. He will work hard rounding up children to come and will rejoice to introduce them to Jesus. If you can't have it in your home see if there's someone else who can, and let your giver help out. If such a club is already functioning in your neighborhood, get him to it. God usually calls His evangelists from among those with the gift of giving, and childhood experience in leading others to Jesus may prompt obedience to His call. Even if your giver takes the business route, he will support those who do evangelize full-time, and will witness actively to persons within his sphere of activity.

20. The Giver's Special Joys.

The greatest joys givers indicated on the survey were: 1) family activities; 2) helping others; and 3) travel & witnessing.

Respondents from all gift categories consistently listed family activities as their greatest source of joy and blessing. Givers were no exception. They enjoyed them tremendously. And coupled with their interest in travel, family trips and outings brought special pleasure.

Camping trips are wonderful ways to knit family members closer together. We started with an inexpensive nine-by-nine-foot tent when the boys were one and three, and expanded to one with a side room when they got bigger. (Another option is to buy a pup tent for the children.) Summer after summer we explored parks and places of interest from Jasper, Alberta, in Canada, to San Diego, California. Our only expenses beyond food and laundry were for gasoline and modest overnight fees. Sometimes we even went camping by boat in the beautiful San Juan Islands, pitching our tent on one island and exploring coves, inlets, and other islands.

After three straight days of soaking rain in an Oregon park one weekend, we upgraded to a camper for our truck. As the boys grew larger we changed to a small, used travel trailer, and then to a larger one. We sold each unit for the same price we paid for it, so it cost us virtually nothing to use. We developed many family traditions in the process, endless precious memories, and picture albums bursting at the seams. Get-togethers with our grown children now include many refrains of "Do you remember when . . . ?"

Helping others was the number two joy mentioned. Your giver, too, will feel good about helping out. Offer him plenty of occasions to assist you; in the process you will help him to develop a good self-image. When you have company he'll want to help prepare for them and/or serve them. Don't be surprised if he brings a guest a small gift from his possessions. If it's not something he needs to keep, let him give it away.

As we noted in item nineteen, givers who were Christians in childhood placed "leading someone to the Lord" above everything else as their greatest joy.

Remember, help your giver develop confidence in relating to people outside the family; encourage his budding financial and business interests; and make opportunities for him to develop his inclination to witness for the Lord Jesus Christ.

TRAIN UP YOUR ADMINISTRATOR

13

An administrator is a natural leader. Like the Pied Piper, he nearly always commands a string of followers even in early childhood. We chuckle when we see advertisements for seminars that claim to make a leader out of everyone. Learning good leadership principles will not make persons with "follower" gifts into leaders: Children are not clean slates yet to be written upon. They come equipped by their Maker and are entrusted to parents to train up according to their gifts. Your administrator *will* be a leader; it's up to you to help make him a good one.

1. The Administrator's Emotions.

Administrators from reasonably happy homes usually have stable emotions. Their ability to feel is keen but does not vacillate into extremes. They are in charge of their emotions for the most part. Motivated by reason and logic rather than feelings, administrators, like perceivers and teachers, are factually oriented. They can remain objectively detached even in the middle of stressful situations.

Yet administrators are also highly sensitive—to others' feelings, to propriety, and to spiritual climates of individuals or groups. Most administrator respondents surveyed said they had happy childhoods; a few with difficult home circumstances said they were sad or insecure.

Administrators are incredibly confident. The I-can-do-anything-I-set-my-mind-to-do perspective seems to be built into them, and they will tackle jobs others are afraid to handle.

Kathy Alls, an administrator who is a bubbly and accomplished sales motivator, told us the greatest asset to success is enthusiasm. Otherwise calm, cool, and collected, administrators often cut loose with open enthusiasm for their respective projects. This cheerleader role can either make others eager to jump on the bandwagon, or suspicious and leery.

Your administrator probably will not have unusual emotional difficulties, but he needs your loving touch and your time.

2. Expression: The Administrator's Communication Skills.

Twice as many administrator respondents found it easy to express themselves and communicate well as those who found it difficult. Classic administrators apparently have no trouble in this area, but strong secondary gifts of serving, giving, or compassion, may hinder otherwise excellent communication skills.

If you have an administrator with the latter situation, encourage him to draw more on his primary gift. Show your confidence in his ability to speak well even in front of his peers or class. Help him practice his speech or report at home, where you can give suggestions for improvement. But don't discourage him by being too picky. Even the fact that you take an interest in his accomplishments will hearten him.

Administrators express themselves well—clearly and pointedly—at home and usually well with their peers. They know when to talk and when to let others talk; they are good listeners.

3. The Administrator's Self-image.

Again, twice as many administrator respondents reported good self-images during their growing-up years as those who had bad ones. Those with poor self-images were influenced either by difficult home situations or secondary gifts that tend to suggest self-image problems.

Administrators are capable in several areas. They have many friends, and their peers often look up to and willingly follow them. High academic achievers, they excel in our competitive educational system and are stimulated by challenges. These strengths make them feel good about themselves.

Administrators are in danger of thinking too highly of themselves, as Paul warned in Romans 12:3. If administration is your child's bent, help him to rate himself with sound judgment, as Paul admonishes, gratefully seeing his capabilities as God-given for the purpose of serving others. A child taught to have a humble and grateful heart will not be plagued with pride for long.

If self-image problems make your child feel insecure, build him up by pointing out his natural capabilities and encouraging their development. If he has been wounded you can minister to him with the Lord's love and healing, as we point out in chapter 18, "How to Bring Healing to Wounded Children." In the course of our ministry we have discovered there are more people who think "too lowly" of themselves than "too highly." Increasing family instability around the world produces increasingly insecure children.

4. The Administrator's Approach to Life.

Administrators take balanced approaches to life. Many survey respondents listed several or all of the suggested approaches: practical, realistic, idealistic, creative, and systematic. They seemed to feel they could espouse them all.

They're probably right. Administrators face life squarely, realistically. Able to handle one day at a time, their long-range perspective enables them to plan for the future. Their actions always have practical applications. And while they're idealistic about how things should be, they're able to adapt less than perfect circumstances to existing situations.

Capable of creativity, especially in their thinking and planning, administrators are fascinated with graphs, charts, and diagrams as means of communicating concepts and ideas. They approach the making of charts or diagrams systematically, gathering as much information as possible, sorting it, and methodically organizing it.

Administrators want to look at the whole of something, not just the parts. Taking the long-range view, and seeing the over-all picture, both of which are necessary in long-range planning, are natural for administrators. They can hear a variety of viewpoints on a matter and see each one's value in relationship to the whole.

This comprehensive approach is essential to the healthy expression of the gift of administration. If your child lacks breadth in his approaches to life, try to widen his perspective.

5. Imagination, Reality, and the Administrator.

Many administrators surveyed acknowledged both their imaginative and realistic qualities, while in some imagination prevailed and in others reality was paramount. Administrators ultimately use their creativity for practical purposes.

Administrators are visionaries, able to visualize how people can work together to accomplish projects, plans, or proposals. They can see and evaluate alternatives and, applying them to the real situation, come up with the best solution. Administrators can project possibilities, thinking, "If we do this, the result will be that; but if we do it this way, here's what will happen."

Sometimes you may think your administrator is taking too long to look into all the options and figure out how to proceed. Be patient with him; his conclusions are usually far more sound than are those of people who try something without first considering the consequences. If he does struggle too long with a decision, have him write down and/or diagram the possibilities. His sharp visual perception will readily see the best answer.

Your administrator's creativity, as we already alluded, will also be clearly demonstrated in his ability to create visual presentation of ideas and plans: charts, diagrams, flow charts, layouts, and graphs. When I was ten I entered a contest sponsored by a shopping center. Participants were to browse the current issue of the local newspaper and select a Christmas present idea for each member of a hypothetical family. I was only required to make a list, but I thought my entry would be more appealing if it were illustrated with cut-out pictures of the items and people—"mother, father, brother, sister, aunt, uncle," etc. My creative, visual presentation won the prize turkey.

6. The Administrator's Behavior (and Effective Discipline).

Administrators remembered themselves as obedient children. Most are. A few admitted to strong wills, stubbornness and independence, but even more said they were dependable, conscientious, and anxious to please. The latter are more typical, but their inclinations to lead may make them appear bossy and controlling.

One family reported their frustration with an administrator daughter who, from the age of ten, tried to dominate the planning of their annual vacation. "She'd get out maps of surrounding states," her mother said, "and look up places of interest. Then she'd plan an agenda designed to include as many as possible in our allotted vacation time. Bringing us the schedule, and maps with routes neatly marked in red felt pen, she'd say, 'This is what we ought to do next summer.'

"At first we resented her actions, presuming she was impertinently trying to usurp our authority. Even though she included places we'd talked about going, we didn't want our daughter telling us what to do. When we learned about her giftedness we realized she was only trying to be helpful, doing what she loved to do, to plan ahead. Subsequently we'd agree as a family on our general destination, and then turn her loose to plan. She loved it and we benefited from it."

Administrators often begin expressing their leadership abilities within the family context. What better place to learn? But parents must set the boundaries and channel the energies. Your administrator will respect and be glad to work under your authority. Let him know what's allowed and what isn't. He will want to comply. If the garage storage area or sewing room needs to be reorganized, turn him loose. If you're planning a picnic, ask him to make a list of necessary preparations. You'll be amazed at what this gifted child can do.

God provides children as blessings and help for the family. Allowing them to help you also trains them!

7. The Administrator's Personal Habits and Irritants.

Administrators have good habits and bad ones. On the plus side they are studious, seldom having to be told to do homework. They enjoy school and want to do their best; they are conscientious and, for the most part, self-disciplined.

Administrators also plan ahead, living not only for the moment, but for the future. They make lists of things to do and write notes to remind themselves of responsibilities and commitments.

I began making task lists in early grade school. I listed my chores and made a weekly chart to follow: Monday—clear the table, sweep the kitchen, empty garbage; Tuesday—wash dishes, change the litter box, and so on. I had a daily list, also: make bed, brush teeth, feed cat, do homework. I checked off each thing as it was completed.

In junior high school my list was in the front of my notebook, and I referred to it often. I started a new one even before the old one was completed; when it was, I threw it away with a sense of accomplishment. In high school I used a daily planner, and continue to live by one to this day. I don't know what I'd do without it.

My mother used to ask why I couldn't *remember* what to do. I had no answer. I just knew if I didn't make a list I'd forget to do something and feel bad about it.

Our son, David, also an administrator, is a list-maker, too. Don often found several lists around the house and had to track down the owner. He knew if we didn't have our lists we'd accomplish little.

If your administrator is disorganized or forgetful, have him make lists to focus his busy mind—on paper. Today's pre-glued post-it note pads are fun to use, and will help him keep track of his lists. (One administrator confided her secret method: Whenever she did not have paper handy at school for notes, she jotted them on her hands, hoping she'd remember to transfer her notes before she washed up!)

Administrators' bad habits include messiness and procrastination. Administrators are savers, hating to throw away anything because "there might be a use for it some day." So they save and save, until closets and drawers bulge and overflow.

Then procrastination sets in. Administrators always "mean to get at it," but allow other priorities to take precedence because they find the sorting process boring. Step in and make it a priority—on your child's list. Limit his privileges until he gets it done, if you must.

Administrators' messiness and procrastination combine to produce the "stacking" phenomenon. My childhood home had an enclosed stairway leading to my bedroom and my sister's. Whenever I was in a hurry I stacked things on the side of a stair, meaning to take them up to my room later. But I was usually in a hurry and seldom stopped to pick up the items. Each day the stacks rose higher, piling up on other stairs as well. Then my sister rightfully complained, "Mom, make Katie take her stuff to her room; I can hardly get by it."

Under strict orders I'd make half a dozen trips, stacking stuff on my dresser or in a corner, meaning to get at it someday. *I* knew what was in each stack, and could find it when I needed it, so I never got around to putting it away. Finally my mom would discover the situation and ground me from all social activities until the room was neat and clean.

Many other administrators have confessed to the same habit. When we stayed with Vickie King in the Calgary area, where we presented a seminar on motivational gifts, we had fun discussing her gift of administration. At bedtime we started to climb the staircase to our room and *there they were*—eight or ten piles lining the left-hand side of the stairs.

"I've been meaning to take all that up," Vickie apologized, "but I just haven't gotten around to it." I felt right at home!

Teach your child this rule: If it hasn't been used for a year or more, throw it out! If he thinks some things are too good to throw away, have him donate them to a charitable organization, or hold a garage sale.

Your administrator will find housework or yardwork routine or boring. Teach him to do his share, so he'll be a responsible, unselfish adult.

8. The Administrator and Friendships.

Administrators are naturally friendly and gregarious, and usually attract a broad circle of friends. About five to ten will be close friends, and many others who belong to his school and social groups and athletic teams will be casual acquaintances.

You may have to caution your administrator not to spread himself too thin in peer relationships, neglecting special friends while reaching out to make new ones. His tendency to become over-involved in groups and activities also may cut into time available for closer friends who may not be involved in the same groups.

Administrators like large groups better. They're joiners and will even create groups if the type they want to be a part of does not yet exist.

"When I was about seven years old I used to organize my friends into clubs, often a new one every week or so," our daughter-in-law, Scotti, recalls. "I'd put a bird sticker on each one and tell them they were part of the 'bird club' today. Of course I'd be the head of it and tell them what to do or where to go. Next it might be a 'bee club' with bee stickers, or a 'clown club' with clown stickers. I never ran out of ideas."

Your administrator may bring home large numbers of friends—on a regular basis. It was not at all unusual for David to walk in with his whole football team and ask me to make pizza for everyone, effectively scratching my plans for the next few hours. But Don and I agreed early in our marriage to make our home a place where our children would always feel free to bring their friends. So we learned to adapt to such surprises and rejoiced to know our boys' friends felt at home with us.

Do what you can to accommodate your administrator's friends. It will mean a lot to him. These experiences will contribute to his future work in leading and coordinating people and projects.

9. The Administrator's Relationships to Peers and Others.

In a distinctive response, over eighty percent of the administrators surveyed reported good relationships with older children, peers, parents, and teachers. Of about thirteen percent who indicated any poor relationships, some had influential secondary gifts, and some came from insecure home situations.

Administrators, then, tend to have broad relationships as well as good ones. This is preparing them for adulthood, a time when their giftedness will likely lead them to positions in which they must be good at a broad variety of relationships in order to be successful leaders.

Encourage your child's relationships with older kids. He can handle them well. He may even build special friendships with neighbors or a couple at your church or a teacher at school, increasing his understanding of and ability to work with all kinds of people.

10. The Administrator's Intellectual Endowments.

Administrators like to learn, are intelligent, and highly investigative. Twenty-five percent of those surveyed felt they had high IQs, 45 percent felt they were above average, and 25 percent saw themselves as average. Only five percent said they were below average, and these also cited bad home situations and emotional pressures. We would estimate average grades of A −, with some attaining straight As and some closer to a B + average. Administrators' intellectual capacities are consistent with their wide range of capabilities.

Your administrator has the capacity and motivation to enjoy the challenges of higher education, and should attend college. His high school grades may qualify him for scholarships, and his well-rounded personality, leadership experience, and activity involvement will further enhance his chances for such aid. Encourage him to apply. Not all school counselors will spot his qualifications, so investigate the options yourself.

I was fortunate: My counselor saw I was a good prospect for a scholarship, though I thought my A − grade average was not quite high enough. I received a four-year, all-tuition (books included) scholarship in journalism at the University of Washington, a special blessing since my mother was a widow without resources for my college tuition.

Your administrator will be especially successful in any of the following areas that make use of his leadership ability and broad interests and relationships. These jobs and careers include: advertising executive, air traffic controller, airplane pilot, ambassador, business owner, city planner, college professor, music conductor, contractor, department store manager, editor, guidance counselor and/or counseling director, hospital administrator, hotel manager, journalist, judge, lawyer, market researcher/analyst, marketing executive, military officer, minister, personnel manager, physician, politician, public administrator, public relations director, radio/TV producer, recreation director, religious education director, reporter, restaurant manager, salesman, school administrator or principal, teacher (especially physical education), theologian, travel agent, wholesaler, or writer.

Remember: Secondary gifts will color administrators' interests and career choices. See the complete chart of occupational success possibilities in chapter 22.

11. The Administrator: Leader or Follower?

Administrators take great satisfaction in being leaders, and are the most gifted in this area of all with motivational gifts. They will be in leadership positions for all or parts of their lives. Organizing comes naturally to them and they are excellent delegators.

Karen, who scored 92 on the gift of administration, told us, "My gift began showing up at the age of eight. Even though I was raised in a nonreligious home I built 'pews' out of planks and pieces from our wood pile, and organized a 'Sunday school.'

"In my teen years I organized swimming programs for five hundred children for three years. I also organized and led Bible studies for my friends during those years."

Paradoxically, administrators make good followers, too, respecting another leader's authority. But they're not good at co-leadership, unless areas of responsibility are clearly defined. Disliking vagueness, they'd rather be in the more distinct position of either leader or follower. Someone has defined co-leadership as a two-headed monster. Most administrators would agree.

Your child will delegate and organize your family members if given a chance; it comes naturally to him. If he oversteps the boundaries, let him know. When Dave came home from college on weekends he often had things planned for all of us to do in order to accomplish *his* goals.

"Mom, here's my laundry," he'd call as he walked in the door. "Dad, will you fill out these forms for me? Dan, will you call Bob and tell him our basketball get-together is postponed?"

"Whoa! Wait a minute," we'd have to say sometimes. "We're busy with other things right now, Dave."

Encourage your administrator's leadership abilities, even if he is a little unsure of them himself. He will discover a "sixth sense" about working with people and drawing the best out of them, and will be quick to compliment those who follow him on the work they do. A jack-of-all-trades but master-of-none, he will draw naturally on the expertise and abilities of others to guarantee the accomplishment of goals.

Watch out for his tendency to get overinvolved, perhaps as a student-body leader, team captain, and head of a major committee at the same time. Once overloaded, his leadership will suffer and he will be frustrated.

When Dave ran for student-body president in high school he was already busy with extracurricular responsibilities: planning a trip to Haiti, participating in football, basketball, track, and a singing ensemble, and serving as president of his junior class. His opponent's strategy? "Dave's too busy to give his full attention to this job." Dave lost by four votes. At Seattle Pacific University Dave again ran for student-body president and this time it was his main focus. He won by a landslide. (Scotti Hunter was one of his vice-presidents, and he had time to fall in love, too.)

Criticism is an occupational hazard of leadership. There are always those who feel the leader should do things differently, better, not so strongly, not so casually, slower, faster, more cautiously, or more daringly.

If your administrator is in a leadership position, cover him with prayer. He will be bombarded with more than his share of criticism; it won't stop him from pursuing his goals, but it will hurt. Act as a safety valve, by being available to talk with him, pray with him, encourage him, and affirm, "Yes, you *are* doing a good job!"

Without such an outlet irritations, criticisms, and frustrations may build up, causing deep inner problems resulting in depression or ulcers. In addition, he may affect a callous, "so there" attitude, clouding the light of his Christian witness and hindering healthy interpersonal relationships.

12. The Administrator's Scholastic Achievements.

Administrators are top achievers in almost every area, highly motivated and naturally competitive both with others and to better their own records. They enjoy challenges, work better under pressure or deadlines, and are never satisfied with less than the best.

When our son David brought home a report card with four As and one B he was upset because he didn't get all As. When his basketball team won the district tournament but not the state, he was disappointed because they didn't make it to the top. If he made three baskets, he wished he'd made four.

We could almost say administrators are overachievers who sometimes expect too much of themselves. It's hard for them to experience any measure of failure. If this description fits your child, challenge him to do his best, but let him know his honest effort is more important than a top achievement. Don't let him be too hard on himself if he does not live up to his own expectations.

You may need to teach your administrator how to lose gracefully, or how to miss the honor roll by one point and still feel good about himself.

Do expect him to get good grades, mostly Bs and As, and to be chosen for some leadership positions in class, in clubs, and in the student body. He'll probably achieve in athletics, projects, and activities, and in just about everything he does.

Your administrator may be an innovator. When Dave was a junior he felt many of the students in his Christian school were unaware of the problems of people in third-world nations. He was especially interested in the plight of Haitians, and created a way to expose fellow students to their needs. With the help of a teacher and a staff member of World Concern, he arranged for eight students (including himself) and two adults to take a ten-day trip, first to Washington, D.C., to talk with a congressional aide; on to Florida to visit a refugee camp; and finally to Haiti to visit Christian hospitals, schools, churches, and orphanages, and to get acquainted with the people. The trip changed lives, and some of the students are training to return to Haiti as missionaries. The school continues to sponsor a similar trip as an annual event.

13. The Administrator's School Subject Interests.

According to our survey, administrators' best subjects are: 1) English; 2) math; 3) history; and 4) all subjects.

While English and math ranked as favorites, history took a close third. And administrators also expressed likings for science, art, music, social studies, foreign language, geography, literature, business, and physical education. Many wrote an extra note saying they enjoyed all school subjects and found it difficult to pick favorites. These findings are consistent with administrators' wide range of interests.

Your administrator will probably enjoy the variety of subjects he studies throughout grade school. With the advent of junior-high electives, encourage him to try new subjects. He should avoid specializing too early; and later, if he has not yet identified his career goals, he would be wise to spend the first two years of college in general studies. Acquaintance with many subjects will help him as he coordinates and leads.

A few subjects—industrial arts (shop), home economics, shorthand, and others dealing with hand skills—may not appeal to administrators. The pure sciences—chemistry, physics, and calculus—may hold only elementary interest since they do not deal in interpersonal relationships, but administrators may appreciate their intellectual challenge.

14. The Administrator's Reading Interests.

The administrators surveyed rated their reading interest categories as follows: 1) wide range; 2) mystery; 3) biography.

The first response matches administrators' wide range of interests in all of life. They can handle large, epic-sized volumes like Leo Tolstoy's *War and Peace* and Arthur Haley's *Roots*.

The most frequently mentioned type of book was mystery. Who-done-its appeal to administrators' love of challenge. Some found relaxation in reading mysteries. Offer your junior David C. Cook's mystery series, which includes *The Mystery of the Vanishing Present*, *The Mystery of the Tattletale Parrot*, and *The Mystery of the Double Trouble*. Your teenager would like Robert Newman's *The Case of the Baker Street Irregular*, and Betty Cavanna's *Mystery of the Emerald Buddha*.

Administrators' preference for biographies reflects their love of people. Give your junior *Bold and Brave for God* (Gladys Aylward) by Fern Stocker, or *Searcher for God* (Isabel Kuhn) by Joyce Reason. There are many wonderful biographies for teenagers about famous Christians like George Mueller, Brother Andrew, John Wesley, Andrew Murray, and Hudson Taylor.

Also included in administrators' wide range of reading interests were the broad categories of fiction and nonfiction, as well as historical novels, adventure stories, romances (for girls), sports (for boys), classics, and animal stories. Hardly anyone listed fantasy or science fiction, an indication of administrators' lack of interest in make-believe.

Your administrator will be happy to receive books as gifts. He will also enjoy going to the library. Start him early. Some libraries have preschool storytelling programs he'd enjoy, and summer reading projects may interest an older child.

15. The Administrator and Sports.

Almost all administrators love sports, particularly the challenge of individual and group competitive sports. Our survey showed a split right down the middle, with half preferring active individual sports like track or skiing, and half preferring group sports like football, baseball, basketball, and soccer. About fifteen percent expressed no interest in sports, some because of their secondary gifts.

If possible, start your administrator in sports during the mid-grammar school years. If you or your spouse has an athletic leaning, volunteer to coach a team, or assist. Your administrator will be proud to have you involved.

If your child takes no interest in sports, find out why. Does another gift neutralize or minimize his interest? Does he feel afraid? Incapable? Too involved in other things to have the time? If you can, get him into after-school sports at least by junior high age; he has lots of energy to burn, and sports help keep him well-rounded.

16. Games, Toys and the Administrator.

While administrators favored a large variety of toys, games, and activities, three major categories stood out: table games, group games, and creative play.

Table games included old favorites like Monopoly, Scrabble, Life, and Clue, and card games—Animal Rummy, Old Maid, Rook, and Water Works. Since those surveyed were adults looking back on their childhoods, newer games were not mentioned.

The second category, group games, included hide 'n seek, kick-the-can, and neighborhood softball and basketball. Administrators like to be up and running, full steam ahead.

The third category, creative play, centered on group activities like "house," "store," and "dress-up." While a few enjoyed playing alone, the vast majority wanted friends to be part of their creative activities. I recall my love for "dressing up" during the summers when my family moved to our cabin on Puget Sound in a small isolated community of about eight families. With my mother's help I collected two trunks-full of old clothes and costumes. A true administrator, I organized the thirteen children into dressing up and parading up and down the roadway connecting the cabins, so everyone could see us.

I also remember building a clubhouse on the beach. I sent teams in both directions to beachcomb lumber, poles, plastic, and anything else we could use. We spent days straightening nails, sawing boards, and clearing a site. Then the building began. The finished product wasn't beautiful to behold, but all of us could crowd inside for club meetings. Boys and girls claimed possession on alternate nonrainy nights for the adventure of sleeping out overnight and cooking our breakfasts the next morning over an open fire.

Your child will enjoy creative play. Turn your backyard into adventure land. Old wooden boxes, pieces of furniture crates, used curtains and clothes, and a dollar's worth of nails will stimulate his creative juices. Inside toys can be home-made, too. Your preschooler will have more fun with an apple-crate stove and a cardboard box refrigerator she's helped to make than with the fanciest toy store kitchen set.

17. The Administrator and Pets.

About 85 percent of the administrators surveyed had pets when they were children, and most loved their animal friends. About 25 percent expressed in-difference. Several loved their pets but didn't want responsibility for routine care, preferring to play with their friends or do "more adventuresome" things. We often noticed Dave delegating pet care to his younger brother, in typical admin-istrator style.

So while your administrator may want to have a pet, routine care should be a nonnegotiable item on his list of chores. Your child may not need a pet. If you don't have one already, observing your child when you visit a pet-owner's home can help you decide.

18. The Administrator's Outstanding Qualities and Traits.

Adult administrators surveyed, rating their best childhood qualities, said they were: 1) capable; 2) responsible; 3) honest; and 4) gregarious.

Administrators *are* capable in many areas, though not necessarily greatly ac-complished in each one. In leadership and organizational ability, however, they are more capable than children with any of the other gifts.

Administrators *are* responsible. (Other words they used for this quality were dependable, reliable, conscientious, and trustworthy.) Give an administrator a job and he will see it gets done. You can count on him. Administrators can be fun-loving and they have a good sense of humor, but they take responsibility seriously.

Administrators *are* honest, a quality they share with givers and perceivers. Without honesty, administrators cannot lead. Trust is basic to followership.

An interesting aspect of administrators' honesty is a willingness to share credit for what is accomplished. Yes, administrators enjoy pats on the back for work well done, but they prefer to give credit to their co-workers. They see administrative work as a collective venture, requiring the contributions of many people, and sometimes deliberately focus credit along the way on those who have contributed in order to assure a job's successful completion.

Administrators' love for people makes them naturally gregarious. Like exhort-ers, they perpetually focus on people, and are happiest when working or playing with others.

You'll see many other qualities developing in your child: cheerfulness, happiness, intelligence, creativity, love, compassion, consideration, obedience, industry, studiousness, helpfulness, and enthusiasm. Encourage them all; he will need them in the leadership roles he'll fill throughout his life.

19. The Administrator's General Interests.

The number one answer to this survey question was, "I had wide areas of interest." Administrators seem to stand on an invisible platform, constantly surveying everything around them, drinking it all in and reluctant to leave out anything. *Your* child will have great perspective, too.

Administrators ranked doing things with others as their second general interest, again reflecting their people-focus. Whether he's playing, talking, working, leading, singing, or doing something athletic, your child likes and needs to be involved with others.

Number three, reading in a wide area of interest, indicates the importance of administrators' intellectual pursuits. Sports took a close fourth and other interests included music, art, crafts, church activities, outdoor activities, clubs, family activities, learning, animals, and school.

20. The Administrator's Special Joys.

Administrators listed their greatest joys as: 1) family activities; 2) accomplishments; and 3) people.

Again we see the role of family activities in producing joy, this time in administrators' lives. We've already shared ideas for family nights and family camping, but here we'd like to mention family field trips. Since your administrator has such broad interests, help him cultivate them. Take one Saturday a month and explore a local museum or one in a neighboring city. Art, historical, industrial, aeronautical, nautical, scientific, children's, natural history, and wax museums are usually located in larger towns or cities, but rural communities often have specialty museums. The tiny mill town of Port Gamble, Washington (population about 500), boasts a museum detailing its part in the history of logging in the Pacific Northwest. Besides pictures and logging implements, there are several items for children to climb on or operate. In addition, the owner of Port Gamble's old general store has arranged his personal shell collection on a unique, second-floor wrap-around balcony. The display contains some of the most beautiful shells I've ever seen, from all over the world. Our kids loved both attractions, and we returned every two or three years for more in-depth visits.

How about exploring an arboretum, a restored village, a Japanese tea house, a stretch of beach, or a park? What about visiting an ice rink to watch skaters practice for competitions? Sometimes you can get free passes to watch the dress rehearsal of a high school or local theater production. Or set aside a little family-fun fund to save up for circus or ice follies tickets. Find out what's happening in your area and go as a family. You'll enlarge your children's perspectives and build great memories.

Accomplishments are measuring rods for administrators and bring them joy and satisfaction. Be sure to acknowledge your child's accomplishments; he needs to know you appreciate what he's done as important and worthwhile.

Janice, who scored 89 in administration, tells how she used her gift when she was asked to chair the costume committee for the high school play.

"I spent time planning and organizing how I would achieve the goal," she explained. "I thoroughly enjoyed designing the costumes, appointing people to make them, and finally seeing them on all the characters the night the play opened. I was so grateful my parents came to see the result of my efforts. It made all the work worthwhile."

Administrators listed people as their third special joy, a fact that should not surprise us.

Remember: Involve your administrator in worthwhile activities; encourage his leadership ability; and help him develop his wide-ranging interests and capabilities.

Train Up Your Compassion Child

14

Children with the gift of compassion are the most loving and lovable, the gentlest, the most sensitive to others' feelings, and the most creative of all children. At the same time they are the most vulnerable to hurt, the most-often wounded, and the most prone to tears and depression. Raising them is a challenge, wrought with potential problems if this gift is not understood. Your probability of having a compassion child is good, since thirty percent of all children have this gift.

1. The Compassion Child's Emotions.

The compassion child's emotional graph, like the perceiver's, looks like a roller coaster, its giant ups and downs connected by some smoother sections. He is more prone to emotional instability than other children, and is weak in will and logical thinking, basing his decisions on what he *feels* at the moment.

We know. We've had one. Our Linda *was* a challenge, but she's become a beautiful and responsible adult. Don't give up!

When as a teenager Linda wanted to go somewhere with her friends and we disapproved, she'd plead for our permission. Tears would flow. She was sure her friends would reject her if she didn't go with them. We'd offer eight or ten solid, logical reasons why we were saying no. Thinking we'd gotten through to

151

her we'd be surprised at her response. "I don't care," she'd choke out through her sobs, "I want to go with them!" So much for logic. Our communication had not broken through her emotional barrier.

This was especially challenging to me since my administrator/teacher gifts make me highly analytical, logical, and fond of reasoning. Linda was on the *feeling* track and we were worlds apart. I wish I'd known then what I know now about the compassion gift. It would have been so much easier for all of us.

The compassion child needs to express what he feels even if it *is* illogical. His feelings are real and he must cope with them. Your compassion child will talk easily about his good feelings, but have difficulty admitting his negative feelings, let alone discussing them. Encourage him: It's essential for him to bring these deep negatives to the surface, examine them with a loving parent's help, and defuse them through discussion and/or prayer.

Compassion people surveyed consistently described themselves as children as: 1) very emotional; 2) extremely sensitive; and 3) exceptionally shy.

In addition to saying they were emotional, some said they were prone to emotional extremes; others felt they were on the low end of the extremes most of the time. Many frequently felt insecure, and fearfulness often accompanied their negative moods.

The compassion child is the most sensitive child of all, picking up quickly on the emotional needs of others. Greatly concerned for those who hurt, he will do anything he can to relieve their pain.

His sensitivity makes him treat others cautiously; he's wary of hurting anyone by his words or actions. If he inadvertently hurts someone's feelings, he feels terrible, and will quickly try to make amends.

His own feelings are easily hurt. He is so thin-skinned that others often find they have to "treat him with kid gloves" to avoid unintentional offenses. Don't be intimidated; instead, help him learn to modify his super-sensitivity and to stop *looking* for hurtful interpretations of others' comments.

Shyness seemed almost universal among the respondents. They felt insecure about meeting new people and establishing new relationships. As small children compassion people are the last to leave the security of parental protection, sometimes literally hiding behind mom's apron or holding on to her skirt. They are seldom ready for preschool attendance before the age of four, and should *not* be pushed ahead in school. Some do better if held back a year.

Compassion people's shyness is not necessarily going to disappear, but it can be modified. Give your young compassion child lots of affectionate touching and verbal, positive encouragement. Give him as much time as you can; often a few focused minutes of your total attention will supply needed assurance, and he'll be happy to play on his own. Don't allow him to consume your day with unreasonable demands on your time and attention.

Your compassion child will be slow to interact with other children, even as a toddler. He will observe from a safe position for a while before venturing out. Pushing him too fast will increase his insecurity.

Shy as they are, compassion children want good relationships with people, and truly love others. They are more comfortable getting to know one person at a time rather than several.

2. Communication Skills.

About seventy percent of the compassion people surveyed said their ability to express themselves was either difficult or very difficult. Ten percent said their ability was average, and twenty percent found expression easy to very easy. The latter usually had strong secondary speaking gifts of perception, teaching, exhorting, or administration.

Compassion children's communication skills are limited by their shyness and insecurity. The more you can help your compassion child feel secure and loved, the more he will be able to express himself.

Compassion children are reluctant to answer their teachers' verbal questions, or speak in front of the class. When they must, they often communicate haltingly, yet frequently knowing more than they're able to say. They will communicate better on days when they feel good about themselves and about life in general.

Compassion children are usually soft-spoken, occasionally difficult to hear. They often hang their heads and speak to the floor. One second grade teacher who had difficulty getting a compassion boy to speak loud enough came up with an innovative idea: She placed a microphone on his desk. It worked. He got used to hearing his soft voice in greater volume over the loudspeaker and gained confidence to speak louder on his own.

If your child persists in speaking too softly, don't move closer in order to hear him. Instead say, "I can't hear what you're saying, you'll have to speak up." It may take time, but he'll begin to do so rather than to lose your listening ear.

3. The Compassion Child's Self-image.

Children with the gift of compassion have more problems with self-image than do children with other motivational gifts. About seventy percent of those surveyed reported poor to very poor views of themselves. (Note: The identical percentage reported difficulty of expression in section two. The poorer the self-image the poorer the communication, and vice versa.)

We feel low self-images are rampant among compassion children because many parents have not understood their child's gift, and have tried to make him what he's not, sometimes compounding the problem with harsh methods. Divorce greatly damages compassion children, and they are more frequently abused than others—perhaps because they *allow* themselves to be victimized. Children with the other gifts are more prone to defend themselves.

If the prognosis sounds bleak, it is. We do a lot of counseling through our church and as we travel in ministry, and about sixty percent of the people we counsel are compassion people. Their hurts are often so deep and their childhood memories so buried they are not even aware of the causes of their problems. We have devoted chapter 18, "How to Bring Healing to Wounded Children," to this matter.

Fortunately, you can build the ingredients for good self-esteem into your compassion child. Recognize his giftedness as unique and fragile. From birth on give him loving care and affectionate touches. Affirm him: See his potential and nurture it. Be patient with his shyness and tell him often how much you love him. Don't shout at him or defame him.

Your child's insecurity results from basing his life on feelings rather than facts. If his feelings are shaky, his life is, too. He is so subjective he feels responsible for any conflict in the home. When he cannot make it disappear he feels like a failure, often assuming the guilt personally, thinking "If I were just a better child my parents [or siblings] wouldn't fight so much." Talk with him candidly about open or hidden conflict—he senses this anyway—and find out how he feels. Assure him again and again it is *not* his fault.

God wants your compassion child to be a beautiful channel of love and healing to a needy world. But everything within his giftedness that makes him such a potentially great channel also makes him vulnerable to tremendous hurt. Do your best to bolster his self-esteem.

4. The Compassion Child's Approach to Life.

Compassion children usually approach life idealistically, but instead of wanting it to line up with *God's* laws and standards as perceivers do, they want everything to line up with *their* wishes. Their standard is subjective, projecting their desire for everyone to love everyone else in a totally loving, kind, and peaceful environment. They are usually so idealistic that they are unrealistic. They want a world that just doesn't exist.

Brian wrote, "My heart was always for the underdog. I looked for the new person, the non-Christian, the shy or unpopular person, and tried to make sure they felt included. I got upset when others left them out or showed more honor to the popular kids. I thought life wasn't fair."

In addition to being subjective and loving, compassion children are ultimate and undaunted peacemakers. They try hard to get along with siblings, often giving in to avoid a ruckus. At school and with friends they mediate disagreements, patching things up between those who are at "outs" with each other. They may stick their noses in uninvited, and feel hurt when their help is rejected. They may take offence out of sympathy for a hurt friend, but fail to let it go even after others have made amends. They'll attempt to put "Band-Aids of love" on hurt feelings and encourage people to forgive.

Compassion children are often daydreamers. Whenever life is not going to their liking they curl up and dream about how they wish it would be. In school they're apt to be physically present but mentally off in wonderland, prompting occasional complaints from teachers.

While a certain amount of daydreaming is acceptable and predictable for compassion children, don't let it go too far. Your child must learn to live in the real world. Just recently I counseled a young compassion person who was seeking direction for his life. After listening a while to his dreams for the future I said to him, "I have just one word for you."

"What's that?" he asked expectantly.

"It's time to grow up!" I replied. "You're still daydreaming your life away. You're no longer a child. It's time to make decisions based on facts, not wisps of wishful thinking."

At first he was shocked, but my candid honesty cut through to the center of his being and he agreed I was right. He was ready to leave his daydreams.

Don't squelch your child's idealism. It's noble, and one day—when Jesus claims total Lordship over this world—we'll see it come to pass. But Satan is a real enemy, at work in this world whether we recognize it or not. He exists by God's permission and design, so we can have genuine free will to choose between good and evil. Help your child understand and accept living in our presently imperfect world.

While some compassion children acknowledged realistic or practical approaches to life, these viewpoints probably resulted from secondary gifts. Or they may have developed in the older childhood years when idealism proved inconsistent with their experience.

Many also reported approaching life creatively. We'll deal with this under item five.

5. Imagination, Reality, and the Compassion Child.

Compassion people are the most imaginative and creative of all. Many of the world's greatest artists and musicians have been compassion people. Whether they're being the best butterflies in the preschool class or fabulous pianists or painters, they shine!

People with any one of the seven motivational gifts can be endowed with musical and artistic talent. But the *way* they express their talent is influenced by their motivational gifts. A teacher will learn a piano concerto and play it perfectly, exactly the way it's written. A compassion person will add his own feelings and innovations, making it uniquely alive. This dimension of artistic expression will one day extract a standing ovation.

Give your compassion child every possible opportunity to use and develop his creative abilities—music lessons, ballet, or private art lessons. If he's not extremely shy he may want to take part in a children's drama group. Take time to introduce him to the various media through which he can express his creativity. Play records, tapes, or compact disks geared to his age level. If you don't have your own, check them out of the library.

You'll also find art books there for all ages. Teach your child how to make paper chains for the Christmas tree or his original valentines. Spend a Saturday introducing him to acrylic or oil painting. Let him help decorate his own room.

Let him decorate the table for "family night," making the cupboards, attic, and/or basement fair game for props. Let him design a greeting card for a sick friend, or for the neighbors' wedding anniversary. Empty out your fabric scraps container and tune him into the wonderful world of collages. Give him large pieces of tagboard to make big bold posters for his bedroom wall. Ideas to enhance creativity are endless, and he may come up with some of his own.

6. The Compassion Child's Behavior (and Effective Discipline).

Compassion children desperately want to obey, and often just a firm word will check improper actions or attitudes. This does not mean they never need discipline. About one-third of our survey respondents admitted a stubborn streak sometimes led them into rebellious behavior. As one put it, "I tried to get away with as much as I could, but when my parents drew the line, I knew I'd better get into line myself."

Expect your compassion child to be quick to please and generally obedient. But he will need to know what you expect of him in order to comply; his obedience is based less on intrinsic right and wrong than on his subjective awareness of what you say is acceptable or unacceptable. *You* must set good standards for him. If you are lax in your expectations, he will be; if you stand for Christian principles, he will, too.

You'll seldom need to use the rod, but have it available, making sure you've explained its purpose. One compassion person recalled her model behavior slipping in the face of a strong temptation.

"A barn on our farm was loaded with soft, bouncy hay just in from the harvest. My sisters and I had been told jumping in the hay squashed it, rendering it moldy and unfit for the cows to eat.

"One day our desire to jump exceeded our inward restraints. What fun we had—until we were caught, and spanked with the rod. I'll have to admit I knew I deserved it. I didn't repeat the escapade!"

Compassion children are sometimes indecisive, finding choices difficult. They often ask a parent what to do. Since you want your child to learn to make his own decisions as he gets older, don't just tell him what to do; talk with him about it, instead. Explain the alternative choices and their specific consequences. Ask him which he thinks would be best. If he makes a poor choice, continue the discussion until he makes an appropriate one. Your child may be impulsive, making decisions without thinking them through. He is a *now person*, living for the moment, not planning ahead. Training him to take a broader perspective will require time and work, but you'll be investing in his whole future.

He's also apt to crusade for good causes, and will be quick to jump on someone else's bandwagon. He dislikes injustice, unfairness, and unkindness. He can't stand to see someone left out, rejected, or treated poorly.

One man with the gift of compassion recalled a boy from another part of the country, who spoke with a "funny accent," enrolling in his grade school.

"Many teased him and treated him unkindly," he said. "I could tell how much it hurt him, and it made me angry. I gathered several friends who felt the same way and we talked to each classmate individually about his thoughtless behavior. It worked. The boy was accepted."

7. The Compassion Child's Personal Habits and Irritants.

Compassion children are neat, clean, and helpful. They bathe regularly, dress neatly, keep their bedrooms tidy, make their own beds, and can easily learn to dust and clean their rooms. (It's good to make cleaning a regularly scheduled chore, though, or he may forget, doing whatever strikes his interest at the time.) Compassion children and server siblings, equally neat, make great roommates.

Compassion children enjoy working *with* others, rather than alone. They are slow but steady laborers.

One of their most frustrating habits is procrastination. Time seems irrelevant to them. Living for the moment, they are unconcerned about the future. They put off unwanted tasks, full of excuses and unreasonable rationalizations for their nonperformance. A compassion child may *mean* to feed the cat or empty the garbage, but if Johnny comes over to play, his visit suddenly takes priority.

Compassion children are nearly always late, unless a modifying secondary gift is present. They are dawdlers, with one speed: s-l-o-o-o-o-w forward. A preschooler may dress himself well, but seemingly take forever. A daughter may volunteer to dust the living room, but stop to admire or play with figurines in the process. Grammar school compassion children are unorganized about getting ready, taking twice as long to eat their Rice Krispies as other kids, and need a push out the door in order to get to school on time. Even then they're apt to stop and smell the flowers, or pet a puppy along the way. Tardy slips add up until the teacher calls to see what the problem is.

Junior high compassion children, late to class again and again, may come under disciplinary action. Senior highs walk in late to committee meetings so often their peers come to expect it. One wise high school committee chairman said, "We coped with Sally's lateness by telling her the meeting started fifteen minutes earlier than it did. Then when she got there late it was really time to start."

Your compassion child may make the whole family late to church. That must be dealt with. Find out what motivates him most—discipline, a withdrawn privilege, loss of allowance, going off and leaving him (providing he's old enough)—to get his attention, and make Sunday morning punctuality a priority. Waking him twenty minutes earlier or setting the kitchen timer to "ding" five minutes before departure may work.

Compassion children have another bad habit: lying. They may justify it like this: "If I tell the truth I'll get yelled at or punished. I'll just tell a lie this time to protect myself, but I'll try not to be disobedient again." Of course they are, and the pattern persists. Unconfronted, deceitfulness grows. A compassion child caught lying should be punished more severely for his lying than for what he lied about. Explain that to him. Make sure he understands.

8. The Compassion Child and Friendships.

Compassion children usually are contented with two or three close friends. Too many friends would overwhelm them; a lack of friends would make them feel lonely and left out. They see themselves as potential friends of everyone, but build close relationships only to those with whom they share at deep and intimate levels. Many survey respondents said their best friend was another compassion person. "It wasn't so much that we thought alike," one said, "but we *felt* alike.

We were always discussing how we felt about things and were delighted it was nearly always the same."

Not wanting anyone to feel hurt or rejected or left out, compassion children are drawn to the friendless, the outcasts, the misfits, and the hurting. Their love extends unconditionally to those who are in greatest need. Linda used to bring home girls who were obvious misfits, often incredibly shy or deeply hurting. Later we'd ask, "Why did you want to play with that girl?"

"Mom, Dad," she'd reply, wondering why we even needed to ask, "she doesn't have a single friend at school. Somebody needs to be her friend, so I'm going to be."

We believe God created so many compassion people because they're good at reaching out to help the world's hurting millions. The rest of us can learn from their example.

But one aspect of this beautiful trait has a potential barb. This attraction can bond them to people who are "outcasts" because of their misbehavior or rebelliousness. If your compassion child is not strong in his standards, an "outcast" child can influence his life negatively, generating such problems as a rebellious spirit, disrespect for authority, increased lying, stealing, and dabbling in smoking, sexual experimentation, drinking, and/or drugs.

Know your compassion child's friends. Watch for negative influences; if a friend is not good for him, be very careful how you try to disassociate them. Help your child to *want* to terminate the relationship, or you will only drive them closer together. He will see you as unfair or unloving, and will meet secretly with his friend, justifying it as championing a worthy cause.

The Lord may lead you to reach out to your child's questionable friend, who may come from a bad home situation and need a surrogate mom or dad. You have a prime opportunity to show him the love of Christ and lead him to a life-changing salvation experience.

9. The Compassion Child's Relationships to Peers and Others.

The survey results on this item were quite interesting. One-third of our compassion respondents evaluated their relationships with peers and older children as good, one-third as average, and one-third as bad. The influence of secondary gifts and measures of self-esteem and security may explain this wide range. Compassion children have the potential for many good relationships providing their fears and insecurities are overcome, a process accomplished primarily through their parents' love and nurturing.

Fifty percent of the compassion respondents surveyed reported good relationships with adults, parents, and teachers. About 25 percent said those relationships were average, and the same percentage said they were poor. Apparently compassion children relate better to adults than to other children, perhaps because parents and teachers take more initiative in making them feel accepted and loved.

Encourage your child to reach out, to trust people more. If his efforts are not received, assure him he has done the right thing.

We need to mention a couple areas of caution. First, teenagers with the gift of compassion are often drawn to those of the opposite sex with the same gift. Friendship grows into deep caring, and finally blossoms into young love. Because both young people are ruled primarily by feelings, they are in danger of sexual compromise. Talk frankly about this with your child; if necessary set some limitations to keep him from getting into tempting situations.

Secondly, compassion teenagers' loving personalities and helpful counseling of peers poses an ongoing potential problem. If your child counsels the opposite sex, the counselee can easily interpret loving care for personal interest and/or love. During one young man's high school days the girls he tried to counsel always seemed to fall in love with him. He was perplexed; he didn't want to hurt them, but his helping invariably did. Having a third party present and maintaining objectivity would have mitigated chances for misunderstanding.

In our society it is more difficult for a boy to have this gift than for a girl. She is expected to be led by her heart and easily moved to tears. Not so a boy. Social pressures force a boy into the "macho" mold, but a child with the gift of compassion won't fit. He's the peacemaker on the playing field; he'll refuse to fight, and be called a sissy. Talk with your child, and let him know it's all right to be the beautiful, tenderhearted, caring person he is.

Our compassion son-in-law, Don Simms, told us, "I wanted everyone to get along well with everyone. I'd tolerate a certain amount of guff, but when other kids picked on my brothers, even my older ones, I'd stand up for them. I'd even fight for them, if necessary, though I preferred not to fight at all."

10. The Compassion Child's Intellectual Endowments.

Compassion people are the least prone to enjoy academics. They are less gifted intellectually than are children with some other gifts, but their sensitivity and capacity to love are tremendous. Obviously God does not endue individuals with an abundance of every good quality, but purposely limits us so we will need, in some measure, to depend upon each other. The apostle Paul notes this clearly in his introductory remarks about the motivational gifts:

> For as in one physical body we have many
> parts (organs, members) and all of these parts do
> not have the same function or use, so we, nu-
> merous as we are, are one body in Christ, the
> Messiah, and individually we are parts one of
> another—mutually dependent on one another.
> Romans 12:4–5, TAB

Fifty percent of the compassion people surveyed estimated their intellects as average. Hardly anyone said he had a high IQ or a very poor one. About 35 percent considered themselves above average and fifteen percent, below average. These responses, coupled with reported grades (C to C+ averages with a few as high as A or as low as D) represent compassion children as academically average. Yet many show they can do better with some effort, especially in subjects they like.

We think compassion children's focus on feelings and relationships eclipses their ability to perform well in school. Most could probably maintain B averages or better (and some do) if they applied themselves. But to a compassion child time spent with a friend in need is more important than studying for an exam. One related being called to the high school principal's office for skipping his after-lunch class too often.

"I tried to explain I often found someone during lunchtime who was really hurting about something—a broken relationship, difficulty with parents, or rejection. He needed help right then. So I'd stay with him, pray with him, and try to help rather than go to class. The principal just didn't understand."

Compassion children prefer spending time with their friends to studying. Karen admitted, "Hey, I was a social butterfly. My friends meant everything to me. Studying seemed like a drag. Even when we'd get together to study we wasted a lot of time just fooling around."

Help your compassion child to set priorities about doing homework before he takes off with his friends. If he thinks "getting by" is sufficient, look for ways to make a subject more interesting. Your personal interest in what he's studying can increase his. Ultimately, since his own self-discipline to study vacillates, you must set the requirements for study time and accomplishment, as well as limits on socializing. But start early; it's usually to late to begin this at fifteen.

Some of the jobs and careers that would be suitable for the compassion child include: artist, barber/beautician, childcare provider, composer, commercial artist, conservationist, fashion designer, florist, home economist, interior decorator, licensed practical nurse, missionary (especially working with children), model, musician, nurse (RN), nutritionist, occupational therapist, office worker, pet groomer, performing artist, philosopher, photographer, physical therapist, poet, social worker, speech therapist, art teacher, drama teacher, elementary teacher, home economics teacher, music teacher, social studies teacher, special education teacher, telephone operator, waiter/waitress, writer of children's stories, veterinarian, or zoo keeper.

Some of these occupations require college education, but many will necessitate specialized training. College is not for all compassion people. Most of the careers listed involve artistic endeavors, caring about people, or working with animals.

11. The Compassion Child: Leader or Follower?

At least half of the compassion people surveyed said they were followers. About 25 percent reported taking leadership occasionally; the other 25 percent said they were leaders half the time, usually, or always. Most of the latter had secondary speaking gifts, enhancing their leadership potential and skills.

Compassion children are comfortable leading small groups or committees. Don't encourage your child to accept large or high-pressure leadership responsibilities; he'll feel overwhelmed. He might do well as class secretary but be over his head as class president. He might enjoy managing the popcorn stand at the football game but not necessarily the pep assembly. Whatever you do, don't push your child into any leadership position he can't take with confidence and a willing heart.

Compassion children make great committee members—faithful, supportive, caring, able to work well with others. Their slowness and lateness can be problems, but they'll always pitch in and do their part wholeheartedly. They'll shine on committees designed to help the poor, the underprivileged, the forgotten, the elderly, small children, or animals.

12. The Compassion Child's Achievements.

Academically, compassion kids are not usually high achievers. Statistically they tend to have the lowest grade point averages of all seven motivational gifts. But this does not mean that's the best an individual can do.

If compassion children get C's and B's they're usually achieving well for their potential. A's are exceptional and deserve applause, but D's mean they are not working up to par and should be under restriction until improvement is made. Remember, many factors affect achievement levels—secondary gifts, self-images, home influences, and encouraging parents and teachers.

Your compassion child's best achievements will be in interpersonal relationships, and specifically in helping the needy and hurting. He will spend his time, energy, and love reaching out to others, bringing healing and wholeness. His kindness and compassion will offer hope to those whose own inner resources are exhausted, and he will make positive marks on lives others have deemed not worth their time. He will exemplify the love of God more and better than those with other gifts.

He will inspire many, including his parents.

13. The Compassion Child's School Subject Interests.

Our survey showed compassion children's best subjects to be: 1) English; 2) math; 3) art and music; and 4) history.

English was the subject most often mentioned. (Note: English placed first or second in all seven gift categories, perhaps because it figures heavily in our lives and is a continually required subject.) Compassion children excel in creative writing. Their natural creativity and highly charged imaginations enable them to write well and interestingly, especially in fiction. They love writing about fantasy, romance, science fiction, mystery, and animals, and are great poets.

Math took a surprising second. Music and art tied for third, but when added together were more popular than math. History was fourth.

As we mentioned in item five, compassion children can become outstanding artists and musicians because they approach music and art with *feeling*, learning the basics well but adding special depths of expression to make each endeavor unique. Even if they do not pursue careers in these areas their creative abilities draw attention and admiration to their work.

Compassion children love mood-setting music, or music describing action. They enjoy playing in the band or orchestra and may agree to do solo work, especially fun pieces or songs to which they can add their own touches. They may sing in the chorus or choir and enjoy performing solos or duets.

In art they explore various media, and may invent something new. (Who says milk carton creations aren't artistic?) They want their paintings or sculptures to "say something," have an impact, or set a mood. Their styles are individual, often impressionistic. (We think most of the French impressionists would have been compassion people.)

Encourage your child to express himself in art, music, and writing at school. Where special talent buds, line up private lessons. Many compassion children will take advanced training and make powerful contributions in these creative fields.

14. The Compassion Child's Reading Interests.

The compassion children surveyed showed the following reading preferences: 1) romances; 2) mysteries; 3) fairy tales, fantasy, and science fiction; and 4) animal stories.

The first three preferences take compassion children out of reality to some degree and into the world of make-believe. Girls, of course, go for romances, identifying with the heroines and wanting them to live happily ever after. Sad endings are disliked, frequently producing tears.

Both boys and girls enjoy mysteries and science fiction. Compassion children are seldom adventuresome themselves, preferring to experience vicarious thrills. Science fiction answers this need and stimulates their imaginations. They love Jules Verne's *Around the World in Eighty Days, Mysterious Island,* and *Twenty Thousand Leagues Under the Sea.* Young compassion children like fairy tales, and grow into fantasy stories in the grade school years. Be sure they read C. S. Lewis' *Chronicles of Narnia,* J. R. Tolkein's *The Hobbit* (and his other books, as well), and the Dr. Seuss books.

Compassion children enjoy both real and imaginative animal stories at all ages. The classics—*Black Beauty, Bambi,* and the Lassie series—are very special to them, often read and reread. Also try Fred Gipson's *Old Yeller,* Walter Farley's *The Black Stallion,* and Sheila Burnford's *The Incredible Journey.*

Since compassion children have some difficulty handling this world's imperfections, they probably need some degree of escape into the world that could be. As your compassion child grows up, however, he should spend less time in these categories and more in biographies, true-life adventures, and family stories like *Little House on the Prairie.* Introduce more real-life-related books in the older grade school years and certainly by junior high age. If he stays too long in fantasy it's a sign he's not adjusting well to reality.

Books are your compassion child's good friends. He will enjoy them as gifts or as special thank-you's for jobs well done or special accomplishments.

15. The Compassion Child and Sports.

About one-third of the compassion people surveyed said they really didn't care for sports when they were young. They did what they had to for physical education classes, but that was it. About one-third liked individual, noncompetitive sports—swimming, bowling, skiing, tennis, and biking. The last third liked active group sports—baseball, basketball, volleyball and track—but many preferred to play for fun rather than to compete.

Even though sports are low on compassion children's scale of interests, they need to be involved in some physical activity for exercise or fun. Try hiking together as a family. Set up tetherball in the backyard or a basketball hoop near the driveway. Swing sets and visits to parks are enjoyed by little ones and keep them active.

If your child wants to play competitive sports, let him. But don't push, even if Dad *was* a star athlete. Your child's gentle, noncompetitive personality won't make him one, though he will have great team spirit and try hard to cooperate with his teammates. Be there for his games. A cheer for his team is a cheer for him.

16. Games and Toys for Compassion Children.

During their early years compassion children play creatively with trucks, cars, dolls, dollhouses, and coloring books (with crayons or felt-tip markers.) They tend to be rather quiet when they play. In fact, they don't like loud noise and will move their toys to a quieter place. Usually they're content to play near Mom: They like to keep her in sight.

In early grade school compassion children are exceptionally imaginative in their play, pretending to be doctors or nurses, cowboys and Indians, the grocer, or Mom or Dad. Props help a lot. A box of old clothes opens up all kinds of creative ideas and keeps children busy for hours. Girls love paper dolls, often designing and making clothes for them.

Older children seem especially fond of table and card games, old favorites as well as newer, creative group games like Pictionary, Charades, and Outburst.

Take time to play games with your compassion child. If your time is limited, set the kitchen timer, explaining you have to get back to your work when it dings. And don't forget the wonderful times you all can have together on family night.

17. The Compassion Child and Pets.

Like servers, compassion children need pets, definitely ones that can be cuddled, carried, and cared for. Almost every compassion person surveyed remembered a pet, usually a dog or cat. (Hamsters, guinea pigs, rabbits, horses, canaries, and parakeets were also mentioned.) Again and again people expressed how they felt about their pets: "My pet was my special friend"; "I could talk to my dog when no one else would listen"; "I loved taking care of my cat and he loved me back, so much!"; and "I don't know what I would have done without my pet."

Compassion children also bring home stray dogs and cats, wanting to adopt them. (Watch out: Sometimes they're not strays, but a neighbor's!) Your child will adopt a dozen or more if you let him. Decide how many you can handle (check zoning laws if you live in the city—they often set limits) and inform him that your decision is firm.

Donna, a typical compassion child, brought home lots of hurt animals, wanting to make them better. "I'd try to nurse them back to health," she said, "and would weep if they died."

Seeing an animal wounded is traumatic, and can tear at a compassion child's heart. He may grieve for days or weeks over the death of his pet. Help him to work through it as quickly as possible, and replace the pet, if you can, with a new one. These emotional experiences, though difficult, are good training for coping with the real world of life, death, pain, and sorrow.

Allowing your pet to have a litter or two is a wonderful experience for your compassion child, and for all other children, as well.

18. The Compassion Child's Outstanding Qualities and Traits.

In reflecting on the best qualities of their childhoods our survey respondents said they were: 1) loving; 2) caring; 3) helpful; and 4) obedient.

Compassion children are loving. In the diagram of the body they constitute the heart. The more love they expend, the more love fills their hearts. When they've entered into perfect love relationships with Jesus Christ, His love pours through them even more powerfully.

One who loves deeply also has a deep need to be loved. Consequently compassion children who have been deprived of love are deeply scarred. Parents of a compassion child must be sure their home atmosphere supplies the love he needs.

"Caring" is an outgrowth of compassion children's exceptional ability to love. They identify easily with others' needs, wanting to reach out and meet them. Not only do they sympathize and empathize, they are unable to rest if there are hurting people around them.

Let your compassion child reach out to others. If he's concerned about a neighbor who's handicapped and can't get out of the house, let him make a cheery visit. (Accompany him when it's appropriate.) As a schoolmate recovers from surgery, let your child visit in person or spend time on the phone. If he worries about a poor family's lack of food, let him mail them some money or spend his allowance for a bag of groceries.

Compassion children are helpful, not always noticing needs (as servers do), but if asked, delighted to assist. They work better *with* someone, enjoying fellowship, than alone. Your child will be happy to dust if you're vacuuming in the same area. Or, if you're cleaning the garage, he'll enjoy working nearby.

"When I was a teenager I babysat for our neighbors for half price," Julia related. "I knew they both carried heavy loads, and I wanted these tired parents to have a relaxing night out. I knew they couldn't afford the full price.

I did housework and dishes for them, gratis. It gave me great joy to be able to help them."

Obedience was the fourth quality mentioned, and as we've already pointed out, compassion children really try.

19. The Compassion Child's General Interests.

Compassion people have many interests, but three stood out: 1) music and art; 2) reading; and 3) being with friends.

Compassion children's creativity again shows itself in their love for the arts. (We would include poetry, creative writing, and drama in this area of interest.) Actively encourage your child; you may have a budding Beethoven or Cezanne in your home.

The number two interest, reading, reflects compassion children's interest in fiction, not nonfiction. Their imaginations take wing through books on the fanciful, the fantastic, and the future, as we indicated under item fourteen. Don't expect your child to read required books as enthusiastically as he does romances, mysteries, fantasy, and science fiction.

The third response demonstrates compassion children's strong need to have and spend time with friends. Technically there is no such thing as a loner compassion child. He will always reach out to build bridges of love and friendship.

Compassion children also love being outdoors to enjoy God's wonderful creation. Camping, hiking, fishing, beachcombing, and boating hold special places in their hearts.

20. The Compassion Child's Special Joys.

Compassion people's greatest joys included: 1) family activities; 2) friendships; and 3) being appreciated by others.

For the seventh time "doing things with the family" ranked as childhood's greatest joy. How essential for the family to spend time together, share special experiences, and build enduring relationships. If we Christians truly believe in eternal life, then building up our families is the most important task God gives us.

Fathers, your jobs, businesses, and hobbies won't accompany you to heaven. But your children should.

Moms, your super-clean houses, committee work, and careers won't follow you to heaven. But your children should.

Our priorities should be God, family, job, church, and other activities. How sad to see many Christian families placing job, church, and other activities first, and including God and family if there's time. If your family is not first in all your human endeavors, you are out of God's will. Every hour, every minute you spend with your compassion child is an investment in his life, helping God's intentions for him to become realities.

The second most-often-mentioned joy was friendship. Compassion children's loyalty to friends withstands tests and strains, and continues into adulthood.

They never betray friends, nor tell on them, resulting in occasional compromise as they choose friendship over telling the truth. Teach your compassion child the value of truthfulness, and pray he will seldom have to choose between the two.

Compassion children need to be accepted and appreciated for who they are, not for what they do. Though they may try to earn others' love, their hearts cry out, "Love me just as I am." Parental approval and appreciation are foundational to their senses of well-being. (They crave similar responses from friends. Fortunately they usually choose friends who are gentle, loving, and quick to affirm each other.) Praise your child for his positive actions and achievements. Compliment him on jobs well done. Most importantly, tell him—verbally, through affectionate touch, and through time spent with him—you love him just because he is.

Remember: Teach your compassion child how to handle his difficult emotions; channel his beautiful idealism and creativity into the real world; and protect his vulnerable, loving spirit from unnecessary hurt, ministering healing to him when he needs it.

PART
III

PRACTICAL
INSIGHTS

How to Cope with Combination Gifts

15

Only about a third of us have classic gifts, primary gifts so strong compared to secondary gifts that those secondary gifts have little or no impact on the operation of the primary gifts. A person with a classic gift typically exhibits most or all of the characteristics of his gift clearly.

About two-thirds of us have combination gifts, meaning we have one or more strong secondary gifts modifying, to some extent, the operation of our primary gifts.

My primary gift of administration (92 points) is modified somewhat by a strong secondary gift of teaching (82 points). Both gifts constantly influence my life, my interests, my actions, and my approach to situations. The two gifts work together; sometimes they blend and sometimes a characteristic of one or the other takes precedence. During my childhood my administrative gregariousness dominated my teacher's tendency to have just a few friends. I had many, yet I also enjoyed quiet times alone with a good book.

Don's gift of exhortation (89 points) is colored to some extent by his gift of giving (73 points). During high school his desire to help someone with a financial need manifested itself in encouragements to earn what they needed, rather than in gifts of money.

Our daughter Linda's gift of compassion seems to be a classic one. Her score (94 points) stands out far ahead of her other gifts, causing her to operate constantly in a typical compassion mode.

Our sons both have combination gifts: Dave, administrator/teacher, and Dan, perceiver/compassion.

GOD GIVES MULTIPLE GIFTING FOR A PURPOSE

When God creates a child with two motivational gifts of equal or similar strength, be assured he will need both to fulfill God's plans and purposes for his life's work or ministry.

Each combination produces interesting modifications. A child gifted in both perception and compassion will find that the latter gives him special sensitivity to others, causing him to be less blunt and judgmental than a classic perceiver. His gift of perception also modifies his gift of compassion, rendering him more decisive, and able to counsel with reliable objectivity. His compassion gift's tendency to compromise is balanced by his perceiver gift's refusal to compromise, which means he'll compromise only when there is valid reason.

The teacher/exhorter combination produces a child especially suited to becoming a schoolteacher with the ability not only to research the facts, but to present them with colorful, interesting, and life-related anecdotes.

The giver/perceiver combination enables a person to become a powerful evangelist or missionary, with outstanding success in calling people to repentance and salvation.

The administrator/teacher combination produces quality leadership with the ability to back up everything with facts.

The server/giver combination creates a strong, service-oriented person able both to give of himself in person and to offer financial support for others' ministries.

The list goes on and on. If your child has combination gifting, praise God for its unique blend and do everything possible to help him fulfill his potential. Most importantly, teach your child how to ask the Lord what *He* has in mind for his life!

HERE'S HOW TO SCORE

With what you now have learned about the seven motivational gifts, you should be able to recognize and understand the modifying effect a combination of gifts will have in your child's life. In order to help we've prepared comparison scales, one or more for each of the twenty items we've discussed in chapters 8 through 14, plotting the seven gifts in relationship to each other. We've used abbreviations for the gifts: P for perceiver; S for server; T for teacher; E for exhorter; G for giver; A for administrator; and C for compassion child.

Here's how it works: suppose you've discovered your child is an administrator with a close secondary gift of serving. In many ways these are opposite gifts, but the resulting modifications will enable your child to do both meticulous work and overall organization. He will be less gregarious than a classic administrator but more outgoing than a classic server.

Look at the first scale under *EMOTIONS*. Circle the A and the S. The A is three sections to the right of *unemotional*, and the S is four sections to the left of *emotional*.

Therefore your child's combination gift would place him just to the left of the "balanced" position. This near-center position will make him an easy child to handle. The second scale will show similar balanced results: He is neither too social nor too shy.

Proceed to the next scale, labeled *VERBAL EXPRESSION*. Circle the A and S again. The administrator verbalizes easily; the server does not. Again the gifts balance each other, producing about average verbal skills.

Making the same three comparisons for a child who is an administrator/teacher, we see the scores falling on the extreme left. These characteristics, therefore, are further enhanced by this "doubling up" process. Expect this child to be very calm, cool, and collected, quite social, and exceptionally skilled in speech.

Should a child have three strong gifts, circle all three on each comparison scale and observe how they modify each other. A giver/server/compassion combination compared on the first scale lands the child definitely on the emotional side, about where the perceiver places on the scale.

Proceed through all twenty comparison scales with each of your children who have combination gifts and you will gain a more comprehensive picture of each one's personality.

1. EMOTIONS:

| T | — | A | — | E | G | S | P | — | C |

Unemotional   Balanced   Emotional

| E | A | — | T | G | — | P | — | S | C |

Social   Average   Shy

2. VERBAL EXPRESSION:

| E | T–A | P | — | — | G | C | — | S | — |

Easy   Average   Difficult

3. SELF-IMAGE:

| T | A–E | — | — | G | — | — | P | S | C |

Good   Average   Poor

| A | E | T | — | G | S | — | — | C | P |

Self-accepting   Average   Introspective

4. APPROACH TO LIFE:

| P | C | — | E | G | A | — | T | — | S |

Idealistic   Balanced   Practical

| E | T–P | A | — | — | — | — | C | G | S |

Speaker   Balanced   Doer

170

| E | G | S | C | — | A | — | — | P | T |

Adaptable   Balanced   Inflexible

| A | T | P | — | E | G | S | — | — | C |

Systematic   Balanced   Unsystematic

5. REALITY/IMAGINATION:

| T | — | — | A | E | P | — | G | S | C |

Realistic   Balanced   Imaginative

6. BEHAVIOR:

| S | E | C | G | T | A | — | — | — | P |

Most obedient   Average   Most rebellious

| T | — | A | — | G | E | S | — | P | C |

Predictable   Balanced   Impulsive

| C | E | G | — | S | — | A | — | T | P |

Tolerant   Balanced   Judgmental

7. PERSONAL HABITS:

| S | E | C | T | G | P | — | A | — | — |

Neat   Average   Untidy

| T | P | S | G | E | — | A | — | — | C |

Punctual   Average   Late

| S | G | C | — | E | — | P | A | — | T |

Voluntarily helpful   Average   Has to be asked

8. NUMBER OF FRIENDS:

| E | A | — | — | — | C | G | S | T | P |

10+   9   8   7   6   5   4   3   2   1   0

9. BROAD RELATIONSHIPS:

| A E | — | G | C | T | S | — | P | — |

Most   Average   Least

| P | T | — | S | C | A | G | E | — | — |

Prefers adults   Both   Prefers peers

10. INTELLECT:

| T | A | E | P | — | G | S | C | — | — |

Best   Average   Least

| P–T | — | A | — | E | G | — | — | S | C |

Questioning   Average   Accepting

11. SCHOOL GRADES:

| T | A | E | P | G | S | C | — | — | — |
A   A−   B+   B   B−   C+   C   C−   D+   D   D−

12. LEADERSHIP:

| A | E | P | T | — | — | G | — | C | S |
Leader   Balanced   Follower

13. BEST SUBJECTS:

| T | A | P | E | — | G | — | C | — | S |
Academic   Balanced   Nonacademic

14. READING INTEREST:

| T | A | P | G | C | E | — | S | — | — |
Prolific   Average   Minimal
| T | — | P | A | E | G | S | — | — | C |
Nonfiction   Both   Fiction

15. SPORTS INTEREST:

| A | E | G | P | — | — | S | — | C | T |
Most   Average   Least
| E | A | G | — | — | S | C | — | P | T |
Active Group   Balanced   Individual
| A | E | — | G | P | T | — | S | — | C |
Competitive   Balanced   Noncompetitive

16. GAMES & TOYS:

| E | A | — | G | — | T | P | S | — | C |
Active   Balanced   Passive
| P | T | E | S | — | G | — | A | — | C |
Real things   Common toys   Creative play

17. NEED FOR PETS:

| C | S | P | — | G | A | E | — | T | — |
Most   Average   Least

18. QUALITIES:

```
| E | A | — | G | — | T | — | C | S | P |
Outgoing             Balanced                Sensitive
| E | A | — | G | C | T | — | S | P | — |
Extroverted          Balanced                Introverted
| T | P | A | E | — | G | — | S | — | C |
Objective            Balanced                Subjective
| P | T | — | A | G | S | E | — | — | C |
Uncompromising       Balanced                Compromising
```

19. INTERESTS:

```
| A | E | T | C | G | S | — | P | — | — |
Broad                Balanced                Focused
| C | P | — | T | — | A | E | — | G | S |
Artistic             Balanced                Practical
| S | — | C | — | G | E | — | P | T | A |
Domestic                 Both                Nondomestic
```

20. SOURCE OF JOY:

```
| A | T | P | — | G | — | S | — | E | C |
Accomplishments      Balanced                Relationships
| P | — | T | — | C | A | — | E | G | S |
Appreciation/Approval   Balanced             Helping/Serving
```

COPING WITH EXTREMES

Some gift combinations do not present any special problems; some do. The perceiver/compassion combination shapes a more balanced personality, except when this child vacillates from one extreme to the other. One minute he is strong and determined as his perception gift dominates, the next minute his gift of compassion takes over, reducing him to a puddle of tears over life's difficulties.

Many with perceiver/compassion gift combinations told us they experienced this ongoing conflict in their growing up years. They often felt perplexed and had a hard time understanding who they really were. Some felt they had split personalities.

Parents need to recognize this inner conflict and discuss it with their child insofar as he's able to understand. "Johnny, I know you're feeling discouraged and down in the dumps over what happened. Do you realize you're letting your gift of compassion control your feelings? You don't have to allow that. Let's ask Jesus to help you draw on the strengths of your perceiver gift." Then pray together. You'll be amazed at how quickly he will change.

In another situation he may find one of his negative perceiver characteristics controlling his actions. Perhaps you hear him bluntly telling a schoolmate over the phone what he thinks of him. You might say, "Johnny, I heard what you said to that boy. You've allowed your judgmental attitudes to hurt someone again, and you won't have friends if you hurt them with words. Think about how he feels right now. Do you think what you've done to him is right? Is it loving? Is it Christlike?" Let Johnny consider your questions, and insist on answers. His gift of compassion will come to the rescue and he will want to call back and apologize. He doesn't have to approve of everything the boy has done or all that he stands for, but he can let God's love flow through him to build a better relationship.

The administrator/teacher combination can be a problem in the home, since both gifts motivate children to focus outside the home on friends and learning. The administrator/teacher is the least domestic and the least naturally helpful around the house. She won't notice ways she can be helpful and her room may resemble a disaster area. She'll mean to get at it, but homework, the excitement of school activities, and her habitual procrastination of routine or boring tasks hinder accomplishment.

Set guidelines and schedule requirements. "Susan, I know you are a busy and involved person, but there are things you must do regularly, here at home, before you participate in outside activities." Have her write down your requirements on her daily planner, calendar, or schedule.

"On Saturdays I want you to spend at least one hour cleaning out your drawers and closet, and going through all the things you've stuffed under your bed. You're also to clean the upstairs bathroom and dust the living room and dining room. Afterward you're free to take off with your friends.

"Each evening you're to clear the table and stack the dishes before doing your homework. When we have company coming I expect you to be available to help with preparations, unless you have a major event or test. Even so you can schedule some time to help me the night before."

Once on her schedule these requirements are more likely to get done. If she forgets, it's probably because she forgot to look at her schedule. A good antidote for forgetfulness is to add an extra duty. She'll be more apt to remember next time!

Considering your children's combination gifts will yield some interesting revelations. We hope these will foster greater understanding of each child and increase your parenting wisdom. Ask the Lord to give you insight. He will—for He wants to help you in your parenting process, and longs to see His will accomplished in each child's life as well as in yours.

HELP! MY GIFT CONFLICTS WITH MY CHILD'S GIFT!

16

How often have you heard a father say, "My son's a chip off the old block!" Many moms and dads secretly desire (and even expect) to have children who are virtual clones of themselves. The probability of this happening, however, is slim. Even the possibility of having the same motivational gift is only one chance in seven. (The larger the family, the greater the possibility.)

While children commonly have gifts different from those of their parents, conflicts can come with any combination. In other words, some conflicts come because of the similarities in the gifts of parents and child, some because of contrasting differences, and some because of moderate differences. Conflicts are going to emerge in parent-child relationships, and will do so more readily if parents do not understand the differences in the seven motivational gifts. Our goal is to help parents know and appreciate these differences so they can release their children to develop in their full, God-given potential.

HERE'S THE GOODPARENT FAMILY

Let's take a peek into the home of John and Marsha Goodparent and their three lovely children, Tom, Dick, and Mary. John has the gift of administration. He was an all-star athlete in junior and senior high school, and held leadership posts as class president, student-body president, and ways & means committee chairman, to name a few.

175

Marsha is an exhorter. She was voted the most popular girl in school five times, was head cheerleader, and never lacked for dates or activities.

John and Marsha are Christians who want to raise an ideal Christian family, setting a good example for their children to follow and for others to admire.

CONFLICT WITH TOM

Thirteen-year-old Tom, the eldest child, is a teacher child and is a top student. His parents are proud of his academic achievements.

Now tension has arisen between Tom and his dad. John has dreamed of seeing his son on the football field or the basketball court, leading his team to victory. John has even volunteered to act as assistant football coach so he can be right there on the bench to see his son race down the field. Practice for the football team starts two weeks before school, and John has arranged to leave work early two days a week to be on hand to help. He's excited; memories of his own football days flood to his mind. He's been talking to Tom for weeks about what a great team his school is going to have this year with the excellent coaching staff.

Time: the night before practice begins. Place: the Goodparent living room.

"Well, son," John begins, "are you as excited as I am about football practice starting tomorrow?"

"Not really, Dad," Tom replies, not even looking up from a book in which he's engrossed.

"Oh?" John asks, "Why not?"

"I'm really not interested in football. I'm excited because I'll be able to join the debate team this year."

"What!" John exclaims, suddenly realizing his son is not saying what he'd expected him to say. "You *are* turning out for the team, aren't you?"

"Uh, no, Dad. I hadn't planned to."

"But we've been talking about it all week, Tom."

"No, Dad, *you've* been talking about it. I've been listening. You've never asked me how *I* felt about it."

"B–but," John stammers, "I assumed you'd want to be part of the team. You know I love football. I was sure you'd want to make me proud of you!"

"Dad, I'm not *you*. I'm *me*. I don't care for sports like you do. There are things I want to do this year—debate team—chemistry club—the volunteer library staff. I can't handle any more."

"Library! Chemistry club! Those are for sissies!" John's voice is a mixture of shock and anger. "What kind of son are you? You know I've arranged to take off work to help with the team. Why would I do that if I didn't want you there?"

"Please, Dad, don't try to make me what you were. I'm not. You know I've never cared for sports."

"But you were younger then. You're going to be in junior high now. It's time you started acting like a man. It's a tough world out there. You have got to learn to be a fighter, a winner!"

"Football's not everything. A lot of the guys aren't turning out. I'm not the only one."

"But you're *my* son! I've looked forward to the day when we could be involved in football together. I want you there tomorrow. In fact, if you don't show up there'll be no debate team for you. Do you understand? I won't be embarrassed by your lack of guts. I'll make a man of you yet!"

"But, Dad. . . ."

"No buts! You be there. Right after school."

"You're forcing me!"

"You bet I am. It's for your own good. You'll thank me for it one day. You'll see."

"I don't see!" Tom retorts, slamming his book shut and stomping off to his room.

"You'd better be there," John shouts after him.

Marsha enters.

"What's all the shouting about?" she asks.

"It's your son!"

"Uh, oh," she says. "Whenever Tom doesn't do what you want him to, he's suddenly *my* son."

John explains the situation.

"Maybe you're being too tough on him, dear," she suggests.

"Nonsense. He's got to grow up. Besides, his being on the team is so important to me. I don't want a son who's a failure. He doesn't even want to try."

What should Marsha do?

A) Try to talk some sense into Tom?
B) Tell Tom he must obey his father?
C) Put Tom on restriction until he complies?
D) Sympathize with John over the situation?
E) Assume this is a normal father/son conflict?
F) Tell John he's wrong and should get off Tom's back?

Believe it or not, any one of these "solutions" will only make matters worse. To solve this conflict:

1) Marsha is caught in the middle and should not make a snap decision to side with either party. If she sides with her husband she will contribute to the pressure on Tom. If she sides with Tom, her husband will be angry at her. She's in a no-win situation and needs to bring new information into the conflict.

2) John and Marsha need to know about the motivational gifts. If each of them took the adult test, and if they gave Tom the youth test, they'd understand each other better.

3) John needs to realize his expectations of Tom are unrealistic. His demands are driving a wedge between the two of them, and he's setting up the scenario for Tom to develop frustration, resentment, and (possibly) rebellion.

4) John also needs to realize his pride is driving him to push Tom into athletics, and setting him up for failure.

5) John and Marsha's parenting role is not to make Tom into something *they'd*

like him to be, but to help him develop his unique giftedness so he can become all *God* means for him to be.

6) John needs to apologize to Tom for trying to push him into something he's not geared to do.

7) John needs to: a) stay in his coaching position and enjoy the boys who do love football; or, b) give up the coaching position and take time off to attend Tom's debates.

CONFLICT WITH DICK

Take a look at the next scene. Dick, the middle child—age ten and a classic compassion child—comes home after school with a bloody nose and a variety of bruises. Marsha greets him at the door.

"What happened to you?"

Dick can't hold back the tears any longer. "Some kids beat me up after school," he sobs.

"That really makes me angry. Who were they?"

"Just some guys, Mom."

"What are their names? I'm going to call their parents. We can't let this kind of thing go on."

Silence.

"I said, what are their names?"

"I can't tell you," Dick says.

"Why not?" Marsha demands.

Another silence. Then Dick explains, "They're not all that bad, Mom. I've been trying to be their friend. They come from an unhappy home and they just, well . . . they just don't know how to get along with the other kids very well. Nobody wants to play with them and I thought I'd offer. But I guess they didn't want to. If you call their parents I'll never be able to help them. It'll only make matters worse."

Two hours later, John gets home. Marsha tells him what's happened and he goes to Dick's room.

"What's this I hear about you? Are you okay?"

"Sure, Dad, I'm okay."

"What about the other guys?"

"What do you mean?"

"Well, I hope you landed a few punches, too."

"Gosh, no, Dad. You know I'm not a fighter."

"But this is different, Dick. They hit you first. You have a right to hit back!"

"I don't want to do that."

"What are you, some kind of coward? Are we going to have to start sending you to school in dresses?"

Dick starts to cry. The ridicule hurts. He wants to please his dad but his peacemaker tendency conflicts with his dad's expectations. He tries to explain.

"I'm trying to help them, Dad. They don't have any friends at school. Nobody else seems to care. I do."

"Young man, if you can't learn to defend yourself, you leave those boys alone. I forbid you even to talk to them. I'm not going to put up with a lot of doctor bills if you keep on getting hurt."

"But Dad, what if I was always left out, and nobody cared enough to be my friend?"

"Well, that's not the case. Now stop all this idealistic talk. You have to face facts. I don't want you to talk to those boys again!"

Dick begins to cry again.

"And stop that sniveling!" John barks.

Hearing things are not going well between father and son, Marsha comes into the room.

What should she do?

A) Take sides with Dick?

B) Tell her husband he shouldn't speak harshly to Dick?

C) Comfort Dick?

D) Tell Dick he must listen to his father?

E) Agree with her husband's demands?

F) Ask John to come into the other room for a few minutes?

The last answer is correct. A wife should not oppose her husband in front of a child. They should discuss their differences of opinion privately. When they come to a solution they should stand together in it.

Here are some further suggestions for both parents:

1) John needs to understand the special challenges facing a boy with the gift of compassion. He doesn't fit the macho image at all. He's tenderhearted, willing to sacrifice to reach out to the hurting and the misfits. He's a perpetual peacemaker, not a fighter, unless it's for a good cause.

2) Marsha needs to understand a compassion child's keen loyalty to his peers. He does not want to tell on them or get them into trouble. In this case Dick does not want his mom to call and complain to the offending boy's parents because it would ruin his efforts to befriend them.

3) John and Marsha would do well, however, to caution Dick about pursuing this goal right now. The boys in question probably won't relate to his personality type, and his genuine efforts are being treated like the "casting of pearls before swine." Dick's parents need to encourage him to target someone more likely to respond to his care and help.

4) John and Marsha both need to relieve the pressure they've put on Dick. John, especially, should apologize for belittling his son, and look for qualities in Dick he can commend—his sensitivity to others' needs, his helpfulness around the house, his ability to look for the good in people even when bad characteristics predominate. Dick will need verbal affirmations to overcome the inner hurt his father's words caused.

5) John and Marsha need to affirm their son's right to cry, essential for all but especially for the compassion child. Labeling his tears unmanly and pressuring him to suppress his emotions weakens his self-esteem. Tearful emotions *will* come from time to time, and unless Dick is freed to be himself, he will begin to believe they are further evidence of his failure to please his father.

CONFLICT WITH MARY

Now for scene three. The main character is Mary, a bubbly eight-year-old who's an exhorter, like her mother. It's Saturday morning and Mary has just returned from staying overnight at her best friend's house. She's had a wonderful time and can hardly wait to tell her mother.

"Mom, Mom!" Mary yells as she bursts in the kitchen door. "Nancy and I had the greatest time last night! I've got to tell you all about it."

"Shhhhh, be quiet!" Marsha says, covering the telephone mouthpiece momentarily. "I'm on the phone."

"Oh, please hurry so I can tell you," Mary pleads excitedly, jumping up and down.

Marsha winds down the conversation, but not as quickly as Mary would like.

"Hurry up, hurry up," Mary continues, pacing back and forth making impatient faces and gestures at her mother.

By now Marsha is irritated, but hangs up and turns to face her impetuous child. "Okay, tell me about it."

"Well," Mary starts, taking a big breath, "Nancy had such a neat birthday party. She had ten kids—can you imagine, Mom, ten kids for her party? And we had hamburgers and potato chips and red fruit jello and punch and cake, and, oh, you should have seen the cake, it was so beautiful; her mom made it and surprised her and it was all covered with chocolate chips and stuff that looked like confetti in all different kinds of colors. And we had ice cream, too, and her mom said we could have seconds, and even thirds if we wanted and so I did, Mom, I even had thirds, and it was so good but I think I ate too much 'cause I didn't feel very good afterward but then it was okay later and I felt better. It was a good thing too 'cause she had a lot of party games where we had to run relays and stuff, you know, we had to carry peanuts on knives from one end of the room to the other without dropping them and I made it, Mom, in fact my team won and we got these really neat prizes that looked like. . . ."

Realizing this is going to be another of her talkative daughter's painfully detailed reports, Marsha gets up and starts clearing off the breakfast dishes and loading the dishwasher.

"Mom, you're not listening to me," Mary complains.

"I can hear you, Mary," Marsha assures her.

"Well, where was I? Oh, yes, the prizes were really neat. I have mine right here, Mom, please stop and look at it. . . . Isn't it neat, Mom? A real honest-to-goodness weaving kit, and all of us on our team got one and I can make pot holders with it and I can make some for Aunt Betty and Aunt Jane and for my friends and for you, Mom, and Nancy said I can get refills for the kit, Mom, and they're not very expensive and I think it will be great to be able to make presents for birthdays and for Christmas and sometimes just to do something nice for someone. Do you think we can get a refill kit next time we go to the store? . . . Or maybe I'd better see how many I can make first. Oh, and, Nancy liked my present, too, and I think she liked it the best of everything she got, but she sure got a lot of nice stuff and I hope I can have a party like hers for my birthday. It was so neat, Mom, and we all slept in Nancy's room and I got the place nearest the heat vent and I got too hot in my sleeping bag but we didn't get much sleep anyway because everyone was telling stories and jokes and all that stuff and we laughed and laughed until I thought my sides would split. Every one was so funny and everything anybody said just got us laughing again and we just couldn't stop. . . ."

"I want *you* to stop right now, young lady," Marsha snaps. "Enough is enough. I'm glad you had a good time but I don't need to hear all the details. You talk too much, anyway. Why can't you learn to say something without going on and on? And one more thing: I don't want you interrupting me again when I'm on the phone."

Mary looks hurt. She suddenly feels unwanted, rejected. She heads for her room mumbling under her breath, "See if I ever tell you anything again." She slams the door, hard.

What should Marsha do?

A) Let Mary pout until she gets over it?

B) Put her on restrictions for slamming the door?

C) Tell John about it and ask him to discipline her?

D) Ask herself why Mary's talkativeness irritates her so much?

E) Ask for John's advice about the situation?

F) Talk to Mary and apologize for being curt?

The last three answers are all good ones. Here are some additional insights.

1) If Marsha's learned about the motivational gifts she will recognize Mary's overtalkativeness as a mirror of her own, still a problem even in adulthood. Mother and daughter are so much alike their problem areas seem magnified since they strike a resonating chord inside. A little self-examination is always helpful when irritations pop out. If Marsha's really honest with herself she will realize she overreacted and was unkind to her daughter, throwing a wet blanket on her enthusiasm.

2) If Marsha discusses the situation with her husband he's likely to see what Marsha does not readily see. She's too close to the trees to see the forest. John may say, "Look, Mary's just like you; you both go on and on about things. You both interrupt without realizing it. Maybe you need to apologize to her."

3) If Marsha apologizes quickly, Mary will forget the hurt quickly. Exhorters are good at bouncing back. Marsha can explain her irritation to Mary and admit they both have to work on their talkativeness.

4) Marsha should also set some ground rules for Mary. Whenever Mary chatters too long Marsha can signal to her—an index finger over her mouth, or the "time out" signal made with one hand *T*'d over the other. Marsha needs to give Mary her undivided attention sometimes, but perhaps with the stove timer set for five minutes, after which she must get back to work. Interruptiveness should be discussed and discouraged by constant reminders, until Mary has it under control.

All combination gift conflicts can be worked out with a little effort on the parents' part. They must take the initiative to set standards and limitations, to show love and forgiveness, and to bring understanding of these God-given gifts to their children.

CHART OUT YOUR PARENT/CHILD CONFLICTS

The following chart will help you look objectively at the various conflicts you are experiencing with each of your children. Fill in each one's name, his primary motivational gift and yours, and secondary gifts if they are strong. Then indicate the conflicts you've noticed or anticipate. Ask the Lord to help you see how and why these conflicts have developed. Realize how your gifts and your child's might typically lead to misunderstandings, tensions, or frustrations.

Prayerfully consider possible solutions. What changes of attitude are necessary? What disciplinary approach should you alter? What apologies need to be offered? What additional expressions of love could you practice? Write down your solutions as specific goals to work on. Discuss them with your mate. Talk to the Lord about them and ask for His grace to help you to improve your parent/child relationships.

POSSIBLE CONFLICTS BETWEEN GIFTS

To help you identify some possible, even probable, conflicts we have listed the 49 gift combinations between parent and child, including having the same gift. We only present one typical area of conflict; obviously there are many more, and various factors enter into each relationship to make it unique. But we hope this abbreviated list will alert you to these conflicts so you're ready to seek appropriate solutions.

In each case the parent's gift is listed first and the child's second. Both parties may feel tensions or conflicts, which may be exacerbated by age differences, gender, or any number of circumstantial factors.

PERCEIVER/PERCEIVER
  Judgmentalism and unforgiveness develop both ways.
PERCEIVER/SERVER
  Bossiness causes child to feel like servant, causing resentment.
PERCEIVER/TEACHER
  Argumentativeness causes conflict both ways.
PERCEIVER/EXHORTER
  Expresses irritation and unkind comments over child's talkativeness.
PERCEIVER/GIVER
  Intolerance of other ideas causes money use conflicts.
PERCEIVER/ADMINISTRATOR
  Quick judgments and opinions frustrate child's broad viewpoints.
PERCEIVER/COMPASSION
  Anger at child's compromising causes further wounding.

Help! My Gift Conflicts with My Child's Gift!

FATHER		MOTHER
primary gift:		primary gift:
secondary gift:		secondary gift:

1st child:	2nd child	3rd child	4th child
primary gift:	primary gift:	primary gift:	primary gift:
secondary gift:	secondary gift:	secondary gift:	secondary gift:
conflicts with father:	conflicts with father:	conflicts with father:	conflicts with father:
solutions:	solutions:	solutions:	solutions:
conflicts with mother:	conflicts with mother:	conflicts with mother:	conflicts with mother:
solutions:	solutions:	solutions:	solutions:

SERVER/PERCEIVER
Overwhelmed with child's stubbornness, adult loses control.
SERVER/SERVER
Each tries to outdo the other at serving, becoming competitive.
SERVER/TEACHER
Frustration over child's lack of helpfulness.
SERVER/EXHORTER
Feels child is too precocious and bold in relationships.
SERVER/GIVER
Insecurities both ways since each needs to help and to feel appreciated.
SERVER/ADMINISTRATOR
Feels threatened by child's organizational ability.
SERVER/COMPASSION
High energy level conflicts with slowness and tardiness.

TEACHER/PERCEIVER
Frustration over child's indecisiveness and emotional swings.
TEACHER/SERVER
Intellectual emphasis makes child feel overwhelmed and unaccepted.
TEACHER/TEACHER
Arguments over opinions can prevent resolution of differences.
TEACHER/EXHORTER
Disagreements over how truth is arrived at can cause friction.
TEACHER/GIVER
Differences over how time, energy, and money should be spent.
TEACHER/ADMINISTRATOR
Adult can get upset with child's procrastination and clutter.
TEACHER/COMPASSION
Frustration with child's illogical and irrational behavior.

EXHORTER/PERCEIVER
Lacks understanding of child's moodiness and poor self-image.
EXHORTER/SERVER
Talkativeness overwhelms timid child, causing further "turtling."
EXHORTER/TEACHER
Overconcern for child's disinterest in social relationships.
EXHORTER/EXHORTER
Competitiveness in getting others' full attention.
EXHORTER/GIVER
Strong opinions can put undue pressure on child's decisions.
EXHORTER/ADMINISTRATOR
Gets upset with child's procrastination, threatened by his leadership.
EXHORTER/COMPASSION
Takes over decision-making, causing feelings of resentment.

GIVER/PERCEIVER
Tendency to spoil backfires in greater loss of control.
GIVER/SERVER
Preference for this child over others causes sibling jealousy.
GIVER/TEACHER
Frustration with child's "know-it-all" attitude.
GIVER/EXHORTER
Feels child's sociability causes lack of productive achievements.
GIVER/GIVER
May feel the child is developing stinginess instead of frugality.
GIVER/ADMINISTRATOR
Gives in to requests too often and begins to feel "used" by child.
GIVER/COMPASSION
Frustrated by child's lack of industriousness and punctuality.

ADMINISTRATOR/PERCEIVER
Upset when child tries to judge parental or sibling actions.
ADMINISTRATOR/SERVER
Requests child to work but neglects expressing appreciation.
ADMINISTRATOR/TEACHER
Concern about child's limited focus on books and learning.
ADMINISTRATOR/EXHORTER
Upset when child throws away potentially useful items.
ADMINISTRATOR/GIVER
Attempts to push child into broader friendships meet resistance.
ADMINISTRATOR/ADMINISTRATOR
Conflicting organizational ideas cause tension.
ADMINISTRATOR/COMPASSION
Perplexity about communicating with emotionally oriented child.

COMPASSION/PERCEIVER
Total frustration results from attempts to control or discipline stubborn child.
COMPASSION/SERVER
Shows preference for this child to the neglect of others.
COMPASSION/TEACHER
Difficulties in communication based on feeling/thinking differences.
COMPASSION/EXHORTER
Feels threatened and pressured by child's decision-making capacity.
COMPASSION/GIVER
Differences in ideas about earning and spending money conflict.
COMPASSION/ADMINISTRATOR
Feels pushed or pressured by child to be more organized.
COMPASSION/COMPASSION
Empathizes and sides with child against other family members.

How to Enhance Your Parenting Style

17

Parenting is the most important responsibility you'll ever have. You are helping to shape lives. You have the opportunity to invest not only in your children's lives, but through them in your grandchildren, great-grandchildren, and untold future generations.

True, some parents fill the role simply because they happen to have children. But this endeavor merits our intense interest and willingness to learn all we can. Take advantage of church-sponsored parenting teachings and seminars. Read good books on the subject. Talk to those who have proven to be successful parents; glean from their experience and advice. Seek advice from your parents, your pastor, and others you admire who have insights to share.

Parenting should be fun as well as challenging. We should delight in each of our children just as God delights in us.

God wants each family unit to be strong, with parents training their children in His ways. In Ephesians 1:11 Paul says, "In him we were also chosen, having been predestined according to the plan of him who works out everything in conformity with the purpose of his will" (NIV). God has chosen us for the privilege of Christian parenting. We need to discover His plan for us as parents and cooperate with it.

God's laws and principles work whether or not we are aware of them. When we violate one we put another into motion: We reap what we sow (Galatians 6:7). Going God's way ultimately produces blessing. Going our own way gets us into trouble as we knowingly or unknowingly break His commandments. The same is true for our children. If we want them to mature into God's ways we need to train them in His ways.

Each family unit will do things a little differently and that is all right. Agreement between a husband and wife, however, about how they want to raise their children is vitally important. Your children notice disunity, and play one parent against the other. We need to be sure we are training our children; otherwise—by default—our children will be training *us*.

We are responsible for how our children behave, both at home and in other places. Someday we will answer to the Lord. According to Romans 14:12, we'll be accountable for how we have trained our offspring: "So then, each of us will give an account of himself to God" (NIV). We won't be able to blame anyone else.

Here are 26 pointers we've found helpful in enhancing our parenting style:

THE ABC'S OF CHRISTIAN PARENTING

A Affirm who your children are in Christ.

While the most important thing we can do for our children is to lead them to a personal knowledge of Jesus Christ, we bear an ongoing responsibility to teach them who they are in Christ. We need to discipline our children in God's ways and in the knowledge of their tremendous inheritance in the Lord. Consider Paul's prayer, "I pray also that the eyes of your heart may be enlightened in order that you may know the hope to which he has called you, the riches of his glorious inheritance in the saints" (Ephesians 1:18, NIV).

Christian children have been made the righteousness of God in Christ just as Christian adults have. Our children need to know God sees them as forgiven, justified, and made righteous because of Jesus' death on the cross. Tell them how much God loves them, how Jesus will never leave or forsake them, how God will treat them like a loving father treats his beloved children. Affirm their ability to do all things through Christ who strengthens them, to forgive because God has forgiven them, to be more than conquerors through Jesus' residing in their hearts.

B Build a foundation of love and trust.

The foundation of a child's life must be love. If he does not feel loved he cannot love and accept himself or others.

Some years ago an extensive study was conducted to determine what children identify as love. The results? Children cited not nice homes, or fancy cars, or the best clothes, or the latest toys. Only two things were identified: 1) affectionate touch; and 2) time spent with them.

Touching, holding, and hugging children are so important. They thrive on such affection, and can build their lives on the love it expresses. Time spent listening to them, playing with them, and doing things together contributes to their feeling of being loved.

From this basis children also build trust—the ability to hold themselves open to life and to others. Usually formed within the first year to year-and-one-half of life, trust is a foundation upon which to build all successive stages of development. Without it, children's lives will have sandy foundations unable to withstand the buffeting of life.

C Communicate openly and often.

Unfortunately, too many teenagers and adults have accepted what we believe is Satan's lie: that there is a generation gap that causes parents not to be able to communicate well with their teenagers. Even though teenagers will naturally rebel to some degree, our children's teenage years can be a blessing to us and a joy to everyone. If we approach life expecting children to be blessings at all ages, they will be. That is one of the reasons God gave them to us. But if we expect them to be trials they will be. They don't need to rebel if we keep communication open and accept their progressive independence.

Children need love, understanding, and listening ears. We must *take time* to listen to them. Fathers and mothers who are too busy for quality communication with their children do them a great injustice. We have them such a short time; we need to make the most of it, enjoying them as much as possible.

We're not saying everything will necessarily run smoothly, but as we pray for our children, ask for wisdom, and stand together in unity, we will all grow spiritually. The end result will be their graceful coping with the individuation process, and eventual ability to face the world as mature Christian adults who in turn train their children well.

Maintain communication with them after they're on their own. Our grown children still ask for our opinions from time to time; we share them, with no strings attached. We know they're old enough to make up their own minds, but they welcome our input.

D Discipline consistently and fairly.

Each child is different, and we need God's wisdom in disciplining each one. As we've seen in Part II, our children's motivational gifts will determine to a significant degree the kind and amount of discipline they need. Perceivers will require a lot; servers will require very little. All children require some, and it should be consistent.

Because children identify guidelines and discipline with security and love, they test us to see if our guidelines are firm, if we care. How would you feel if the Lord said, "I don't care what you do; do whatever you want to"?

It is up to us to decide what type of correction to use, and when. Many times talking firmly to a child is enough; some situations call for more stringent action: application of the rod, or the removal of privileges.

We personally advocate scriptural advice about spanking: "He who spares the rod hates his son, but he who loves him is careful to discipline him" (Proverbs

13:24, NIV). If one parent wants to spank and the other doesn't, come to a unified decision. Discuss it, search the Scriptures, talk with your pastor or others you respect for their parenting skills, and formulate a plan you will follow—together. Working against each other will be counterproductive and confuse your children.

A rod, handled properly, will bring good results quickly. It represents authority, and if used fairly will increase a child's respect for all authority. It should never be used angrily, violently, or abusively. Pleading, bribery, or humiliation of a child are never in order. Sassing should never be allowed.

Remember, you are the authority and you must do what is necessary to achieve positive results. Always explain to your child why he is being disciplined. Work with him on repentance, if necessary. Take time to give him tender-loving care; tell him you love him. Proper discipline is actually training. It should be a helpful learning experience.

If you decide not to discipline while your children are young, we can almost guarantee you'll have problems with them when they're teenagers. The less they are taught about obedience, the harder time they will have following the Lord.

As our children have grown up, they have come to us and thanked us for disciplining them, for giving them guidelines, and for standing firm on what we believed.

E Expect the best of them.

Children will tend to be what we expect them to be. One twelve-year-old boy told his friend he couldn't stay out any later and needed to get home.

"Why don't you stay at least until we finish another line of bowling?" the friend urged. "Your folks won't care.

"But they're expecting me home at nine o'clock," the boy replied. "I need to go." He did not want to disappoint his parents' trust. The other boy's parents were not expecting him home at a given hour, so he had nothing to live up to. We must expect our children to be obedient, to do well in school, to be honest and reliable. Like a magnet, our expectations will draw from them a positive response.

Don't ever say, "I knew you'd be late" or, "I knew you'd get a bad report card" or, "I knew you'd make a fool of yourself." Negative expectations only reinforce negative behavior.

F Forgive frequently.

God allows imperfect parents to raise imperfect children in an imperfect world. We're not perfect; neither are our children. When a child blows it, we must be ready to forgive. If he makes a mistake, we must help him overcome it. If he's disobedient, we must discipline him, but be quick to forgive him, too.

Forgiveness cancels out a debt that, if left as a cloud over a child's life, would hamper his ability to grow. How often we learn our best lessons in life from our mistakes. What if God did not extend forgiveness to us? We'd soon ask, "What's the use of trying?" We'd give up. In like manner we must not overburden our children with unforgiveness. They should be given every opportunity to grow in wisdom and in knowledge of what is right and wrong. Forgiving our children does not mean we approve of what they've done (or left undone); it simply means we're extending love and grace to them so they can do better next time.

G Give unconditional love.

Children need unconditional love, not for what they do or don't do, but just because they are. Children need to know nothing can separate them from the love of their parents any more than anything can separate us from God's love.

> For I am convinced that neither death nor life,
> neither angels nor demons, neither the present
> nor the future, nor any powers, neither height
> nor depth, nor anything else in all creation, will
> be able to separate us from the love of God that
> is in Christ Jesus our Lord.
>
> Romans 8:38–39, NIV

Fathers, while your children are infants, take time to pick them up, hold them. They won't break. From toddler stage through adolescence, give them lots of hugs. As your children grow, the ways you show your love will change. Teenage boys may get embarrassed in front of friends if you're too demonstrative. But continue to let them know you love them. Be there when their teams play. Take time to go to their school activities. Be available whenever they want to talk.

As girls mature they are usually more expressive than boys, but fathers should use wisdom in bestowing loving touches. A girl needs to feel her father adores her, and will always be her protector.

A child who hasn't received unconditional love has a more difficult time relating to his parents, and will find it hard to show love to others throughout his growing up years. He will go into marriage and parenthood emotionally handicapped, and the next generation will suffer, too.

H Help them to grow spiritually.

As parents, we must be committed to our own spiritual growth so we can set an example for our children. A child who sees his parents praying will want to pray. If he sees them reading the Bible he will believe there's valuable information to be learned and want to read it. If he sees church attendance as a parental priority, he will make it one of his. If he hears gratitude for God's blessings, he'll be thankful, too.

We can help our children relate all they learn about God and the Bible to their daily lives. Christianity is practical; it is a living relationship with Jesus Christ, not a set of rules and doctrines. We need to spend time explaining how the Holy Spirit guides us and how we gain spiritual nourishment from the Word. We can't just assume they understand. We need to talk it over with them, encourage them, rejoice with them.

I Invest time in them.

More than anything else, children want quality time—spontaneous or planned—with their parents. This means we should sit down and talk with them. Our family set aside special family nights, scheduled daily family devotions, and planned family-centered holidays and vacation times.

Every child needs individual time alone with each parent. Once or twice a year Don set aside a whole day to take one of the children out, letting him choose what he wanted to do. (If time is limited, an evening or Saturday afternoon would work, also). The time we invest in our children will bring good results.

J Join in the Family Night fun.

On our special family night we'd let one of our boys pick out what he wanted for dinner, we'd sing and have a time of devotions. Usually we'd have a little Scripture memory competition for all of us to see who could memorize the verse first. The boys usually won. Then we played the games they picked out. Even though we sometimes wearied of McDonald's burgers and "Sorry," we loved those evenings with our boys, and they have fond memories of our Friday nights together.

What works well for your family? If you can't find a time for *your* family night, take a serious look at your *schedule*. Are you too busy working to take time for play? According to Ecclesiastes 3 there's a time for everything. Regular family fun is far more important than moonlighting to pay for a new car or overinvolvement in church activities. Check your priorities.

K Keep Christ central in your home.

People talk about what's important to them. Is the conversation in our homes focused on each person's own plans and achievements? Is it encumbered with unkind remarks? Is the Lord's name used in vain, or is swearing allowed? Or do we regularly discuss the Lord's plans and purposes, relating life's circumstances to His will and to how we can please Him more? Is He glorified in praise and song? Do we proclaim His goodness and lovingkindness?

Are our homes identified as Christian homes? One woman, who helped Christians redecorate their homes at minimal cost, always encouraged her clients to establish a small table with an open Bible, a cross, Scripture plaques, or a Christian picture or painting as close to the front door as possible, indicating Christ's centrality in their lives.

L Live what you teach.

No matter what we try to teach our children they will learn most powerfully from what we do. A child who observes a parent drinking or smoking, hitting a spouse, or throwing things in anger will probably model his life after his parent's, even if he's instructed otherwise.

We counseled a thirteen-year-old boy one time who regularly knocked holes in the wall when he was angry. After talking to him for a while we found his father had an identical habit. We wound up counseling the father.

Children will also pick up our good habits and values. Both of our boys have taken great interest in missions. When we asked why, they reminded us they were used to seeing missionaries in our home, and to having us make short missionary trips.

M Make your home atmosphere positive.

Chapter 19, "How to Change a Negative Home Atmosphere," details positive suggestions: 1) Set the example; 2) Watch words; 3) Check attitudes; 4) Lavish love; 5) Listen attentively; 6) Learn to apologize; 7) Forgive frequently; 8) Observe body language; 9) Let music ring; 10) Express thankfulness; 11) Make room for differences; and 12) Teach the Word.

N Notice and commend achievements.

Every child needs an area or two in which to achieve. We need to notice our children's areas and offer compliments. It is not enough for us to *feel* proud; our youngsters need to *hear* our pride. One day we all hope to hear the words, "Well done, thou good and faithful servant!"

Children's different gifts motivate them to excel in different ways. Don't compare your children with one another; focus on those areas where they shine. A server who receives a positive note on his report card about his helpfulness in class should be commended just as much as the teacher who gets straight A's. A perceiver who shows signs of controlling his temper deserves praise as surely as the administrator who's elected class president. The compassion child who prays with a hurting classmate is to be complimented equally with an exhorter who gives an outstanding speech in class or a giver who saves up enough money to buy his own bike.

O Organize family vacations.

One couple struggled with vacation plans for several years. Her idea of the ideal vacation spot was a cottage on a secluded beach where she could swim, sun-bathe, relax, and rest with no pressures at all. His idea of the perfect vacation was to hit every major city and point of interest from New York to Los Angeles, making business contacts along the way. For a time they tried her way one year and his way the next; they only hated their vacations on alternate years.

But once they had children they realized the self-centered nature of their vacation plans, and began exploring alternatives the children would enjoy. A tiny trailer provided comfort for Mom and Dad, while a pup tent set up beside it appealed to the kids' adventuresome spirits. They spent their two weeks of vacation camped near lakes or ocean beaches. Mom relaxed with the kids and enjoyed the natural setting; Dad ventured off to nearby towns to make business contacts. But five of each seven days were dedicated to family fun, bonding their family relationships.

P Pray faithfully.

If we could "see" what happens when we pray for our children we'd pray far more frequently. A prayer diary is a wonderful tool for focusing on important prayer requests concerning each child, and for recording God's answers. A simple three-ring notebook will do. Set up one section for each child, like this:

DATE OF PRAYER	SPECIFIC PRAYER	RESULT OF THAT PRAYER

Spend time *each day* praying for *each child*. Keep the notebook handy. The more specifically you pray the more your prayers will be answered. Involve your children at times, releasing greater power.

> "Again, I tell you that if two of you on earth
> agree about anything you ask for, it will be done
> for you by my Father in heaven."
>
> Matthew 18:19, NIV

Suzanna Wesley, mother of sixteen children, found time to pray for each child. If she couldn't find a quiet place she flipped her apron over her head and entered into her prayer closet.

Q Quote Scripture when appropriate.

Deuteronomy 6:5–7 (NIV) offers good advice:

> Love the Lord your God with all your heart and
> with all your soul and with all your strength.
> These commandments that I give you today are
> to be upon your hearts. Impress them on your
> children. Talk about them when you sit at home
> and when you walk along the road, when you lie
> down and when you get up.

As Christians our talk should be peppered with Scripture, not in a legalistic or holier-than-thou way, but naturally, spontaneously, as the Holy Spirit quickens remembrance of relevant verses. When we join our children at the breakfast table, what more appropriate greeting than "This is the day the Lord has made; let us rejoice and be glad in it" (Psalms 118:24, NIV). Repeating memory verses at bedtime or sharing verses we've been pondering can open up discussions about the application of scriptural principles to daily life.

When a child is struggling with something hard, we can share the affirmation based on Philippians 4:13, "I can do all things through Christ who strengthens me!" As we drive to the grocery store or grandmother's house, we can sing Scripture songs with our children. (These are available in songbooks, and on sheet music, records, or tapes.) Let the Word of God spill out, naturally! It will become a way of life for the whole family.

R Release them as they're ready.

Parents are to help their children become committed, responsible, accountable adults. This doesn't happen overnight, and each stage of growth in our children's lives brings new challenges and blessings.

During the earliest years our children look up to and learn primarily from us. As they approach school age they learn increasingly from other sources as well—Sunday school teachers, school teachers, adult friends, and peers.

By the time children reach adolescence their peer groups take on increasing influence, but if foundational preparations have been sound, and they've been developing good decision-making skills and responsibility, they will maneuver this stage without major problems. By the time they're in high school they should be making most of their own decisions, with parents holding only final veto power. By graduation many young people are ready to be on their own yet continue close relationships with their parents on an adult-to-adult rather than parent-to-child basis.

S Set a good example.

Someone has said, "Faith is caught, not taught." Children hate hypocrisy in parents. If we say, "Tell the truth" but they see us tell "little white lies" or stretch the truth to get out of predicaments, we are really teaching them lying is acceptable, if. . . . When we preach honesty but cheat "just a little bit" on our income taxes "because we need the money more than the government does," they learn honesty is conditional.

Parents set either the best or worst examples ever to impact their children's lives because they have the greatest influence.

T Train them well in the ways of the Lord.

If we do not teach our children obedience and respect for authority, they will have a hard time responding to God's authority and following His ways.

Proverbs 22:6 says we should train up our children in the way they should go. They won't learn automatically, and the secular world won't train them in God's ways. It's *our* responsibility. We need to tell our children what the Lord has done for us, continually teaching and talking about Him. But remember, teaching is not only telling; it also involves demonstrating that truth in our lives.

U Understand their God-given gifts.

In the Amplified Bible Proverbs 22:6 continues ". . . and in keeping with his individual gift or bent. . . ," referring to the motivational gifts. The Psalmist declares:

> For you created my inmost being;
>   you knit me together in my mother's womb.
> I praise you because I am fearfully and wonderfully made;
>   your works are wonderful,
>   I know that full well.
> My frame was not hidden from you
>   when I was made in the secret place.
> When I was woven together in the depths of the earth,
>   your eyes saw my unformed body.
> All the days ordained for me
>   were written in your book
>   before one of them came to be.
>
> Psalm 139:13–16, NIV

We believe God endows each child with motivational gifts at conception. Knowing our children's giftedness and working with the energy God has put within them frees us from pressures to conform them to "super-child" images.

Understanding our children's motivational gifts doesn't mean we have arrived; it simply means we understand in which directions to train them. Each child is an individual and must be treated as such. But we can enjoy helping our youngsters blossom into all God created them to be. The rest of Proverbs 22:6 assures us when our children are old (on their own) they will not depart from the ways in which we've trained them.

V Value each child individually.

Each child is a unique trust from God, placed in our family for a reason. God makes no mistakes: one child may be easier to raise than another, but each is of equal value.

Siblings frequently ask their parents, "Which one of us do you love more?" The answer?

"We love you all the same!"

One child may be more loveable than another. Loving his sibling may require more effort. God loves each of us equally: He does not love Billy Graham more than He loves you, or prefer the apostle Paul over your spouse. He is no respecter of persons, positions, or accomplishments. Each of us can operate only by the gifts and graces He has given us.

It's the same with our children. One child may be talented in art or music, while another may be gifted in communication, and a third exceptionally expressive of love. But parental love for each must be total and complete.

W Welcome creativity.

Having traveled and ministered in foreign lands extensively, we've seen the result of cookie-cutter creativity. In some countries everyone does everything the same: Art styles are similar, music is learned by the book, and blending with the group is esteemed more highly than individualism. Capacity for spontaneous creativity is greatly lacking.

Persons with each of the seven motivational gifts express creativity differently. Be sensitive. One child may create ideas, another, art, another, music. Provide the tools necessary for creative development.

X Explain why, when you say no.

Many times it's necessary to say no. Constant catering to children's demands only encourages self-centeredness. But when a child is old enough to understand, he deserves to be told why. "Just because I said so," skirts the issue and gives the child the impression of dictatorship. Usually a simple explanation will suffice.

"You can't go over to Bob's house because last time you went you stayed longer than I said you could. Your restriction won't be over until next Saturday."

"You may not ride the tricycle now; you've already had it for half an hour and it's Susie's turn."

"I'm glad you want to help me make cookies, but I can't let you right now because I'm in a big hurry, and must work faster than you can go. Next time you can help."

Y Yearn to see them become all they can be.

Cherish a vision for each child. Seek the Lord's guidance in helping them to fulfill His plan for their lives. Discover each child's potential and don't settle for less; challenge him to do his best. My mother used to tell me, "Katie, if something's worth doing, it's worth doing well."

Success seminars often proclaim, "You can be anything you want to be and do anything you want to do." Not so. A shy server is never going to be the executive head of a giant corporation, no matter how many motivational courses he completes. But the administrator may. Our children's visions—which we as parents can inspire—need to be realistic, accomplishable, and in harmony with their motivational gifts.

Z Zero in on Christian values.

Our world is getting darker and darker. Our nation was established on Christian values, but philosophically secular humanism now reigns. In this darkness the light of the Lord shining through dedicated Christians glows brighter and brighter, because our value system contrasts sharply with that of unbelievers.

John announced Jesus as the Light of the world. "In him was life, and that life was the light of men. The light shines in the darkness, but the darkness has not overcome[1] it" (John 1:4, 5, NIV). Peter explains we've been "called . . . out of darkness into his wonderful light" (1 Peter 2:9, NIV).

Paul warned the Ephesians about the darkness of the world in contrast to the Light by which Christians are to live:

> For you were once darkness, but now you are light in the Lord. Live as children of light (for the fruit of the light consists in all goodness, righteousness and truth) and find out what pleases the Lord. Have nothing to do with the fruitless deeds of darkness, but rather expose them. For it is shameful even to mention what the disobedient do in secret.
>
> Ephesians 5:8–12, NIV

---

[1]Alternative reading of the word *understood* in the NIV.

We must encourage our children to stand up for righteousness, teaching them why Christian values are at odds with what others permit themselves to do. How often we had to say, "We don't care what other parents let their kids do. Our family doesn't do that." Then we'd explain why, so they'd understand.

THE ABC's OF CHRISTIAN PARENTING

A Affirm who your children are in Christ.

B Build a foundation of love and trust.

C Communicate openly and often.

D Discipline consistently and fairly.

E Expect the best of them.

F Forgive frequently.

G Give unconditional love.

H Help them to grow spiritually.

I Invest time in them.

J Join in family night fun.

K Keep Christ central in your home.

L Live what you teach.

M Make your home atmosphere positive.

N Notice and commend achievements.

O Organize family vacations.

P Pray for them faithfully.

Q Quote Scripture when appropriate.

R Release them as they're ready.

S Set a good example.

T Train them well in the ways of the Lord.

U Understand their God-given gifts.

V Value each child individually.

W Welcome creativity.

X Explain why when you say no.

Y Yearn to see them become all they can be.

Z Zero in on Christian values.

Note: This is available on parchment-type paper suitable for framing in 9 x 12 inch size. See "Additional Materials Available," p. 293.

How to Bring Healing to Wounded Children

Not all children will be wounded in the same way, to the same extent, and their motivational gifts will determine the differences. The diagram we used in chapter 15 to show the range of self-image status will also give us a birds-eye view of the range of tendency for wounding. Compare the two:

SELF-IMAGE

| T | A–E | — | — | G | — | — | P | S | C |

Good   Average   Poor

TENDENCY FOR WOUNDING

| T | A–E | — | — | G | — | — | P | S | C |

Very little   Average   Very much

WHAT CONTRIBUTES TO WOUNDING

Many factors contribute to a child's wounding. Here are the main ones.

1. The child's vulnerability to wounding is dependent on his motivational gifting.

The more a child is motivated by his feelings, the more vulnerable he is to wounding. The more he is motivated by his thinking and analytical ability, the less vulnerable he is to wounding. Our extensive study of the motivational gifts yields the following estimated percentages of those with each gift—indicated in the center column—who are likely to be wounded enough during childhood to affect their self-images negatively.

GIFT	WOUNDED	%OF COUNSELEES
Perceiver	70%	25%
Server	50%	6%
Teacher	10%	2%
Exhorter	5%	1%
Giver	30%	4%
Administrator	10%	2%
Compassion	100%	60%

Note: All compassion children are wounded to some degree. Even when raised in the most loving Christian homes, they sometimes *feel* wounded even when they're not, and their beliefs are as real to them as actual hurt. The negative results are the same.

A compassion child's mother may tell him not to go across the street to play: It's almost dinner time, she is busy, and he's not allowed to cross the street by himself. No hurt is intended. But he may *feel* hurt because he does not get his way at the moment, or because he feels his mother doesn't love him enough to stop what she's doing to take him across the street, or because he feels she said no in too firm a voice.

An exhorter would shrug, "Oh, well, I'll do something else for now. "A teacher would think, "I wanted to look at a book anyway." An administrator would plan to ask again after dinner, or maybe tomorrow. None of these would feel hurt.

About two-thirds (70%) of perceivers are wounded to some degree, some of it self-inflicted. When the perceiver's built-in desire to be "right" conflicts with his imperfect conduct, he often gets angry with himself, judging and thus wounding himself.

Servers want to please and feel bad when they don't, or when they are not appreciated for their efforts.

Givers have an average, middle-of-the-road self-image carrying some degree of vulnerability to wounding (about 30%). But their adaptability keeps them balanced.

Teachers, exhorters, and administrators take rational and objective approaches to life, and are significantly less vulnerable to wounding. (See chart.) These three types of children are usually wounded by overt situations like bad homes with one or more abusive parent.

We counsel frequently, and nearly always test the counselee for motivational gifts, so we've observed an interesting pattern. Sixty or more percent of our counselees are compassion people, often deeply wounded enough in childhood to incapacitate their adult lives. While thirty percent of the world's population have the gift of compassion, they are also quicker to realize their need for help and are willing to seek counseling.

Sometimes the wounding has been so harsh and extensive we've wondered how the person has made it to adulthood. Since the nature of the compassion child is gentle and submissive he is an easy prey, often victimized or abused repeatedly.

Compassion children are also good candidates for healing, being eager to recover, cooperative, and willing to forgive.

Perceivers comprise our next largest category of counselees (about 25%). Their biggest breakthrough often comes in discovering their giftedness and realizing they are not necessarily terrible people. Once a perceiver grasps God's call on his life as intercession, healing is on its way. Most perceivers readily follow the preliminary steps of repentance necessary to reordering their lives. But if there is pride in a perceiver's life it remains an impregnable barrier to healing.

We see a few servers and givers. Many more are wounded, but they are either reluctant to seek help or they find ways to endure or help themselves.

We seldom see persons with the other three gifts. They are all better equipped to work through their own hurts and get on with life. Some could use help, but their priorities keep them focused on accomplishments and they choose not to let hurts hold them back. Those who do seek help usually have a major hurt or two, rather than an ongoing series of hurts over many years, as is the case with compassion people and perceivers.

2. Rejection.

A child's greatest hurt is rejection. If he is not wanted—because he was conceived out of wedlock, because he arrives before his parents want a child, or because he's not wanted at all—studies show he feels rejection *in the womb*. His tender spirit is deeply wounded, setting him up for ongoing rejections throughout his life unless the hurt of rejection is healed somewhere along the line.

While mothers release babies for adoption for many valid reasons, these children still experience rejection. Bonding between a mother and her baby both in the womb and at first sight is very real. Separation causes wounding. Adoptive parents need to pray for healing in the lives of their new children.

Divorce devastates a child at any age, but usually the earlier it occurs the deeper are the feelings of rejection, and the deeper the wound. A parent is leaving his partner, but the child feels he is being rejected, too. The compassion child is especially hurt, mistakenly assuming it is somehow his fault.

Children innately know God intended for them to have two loving, responsible, faithful parents, and they are keenly aware when divorce robs them of their rightful inheritance. God hates divorce because it hurts everyone. Yet because hardness of heart (Matthew 19:8) is the cause of divorce, parents who remain together "for the sake of the children" but fail to improve their relationship still wound their youngsters.

A child may feel rejected because she thinks she is the wrong gender—her father wanted a boy but got a girl, or vice versa. A handicapped child may experience rejection, even though his parents don't express it. Or a child may feel rejected when he cannot live up to real or imagined expectations:

"Four As and one B? Why didn't you get straight As?"

With blended families now common, there is tremendous potential for neglect, favoritism, or even more blatant step-parental abuse.

Many children, unfortunately, are wounded by overt forms of rejection. "I wish you'd never been born," or "Why can't you be like your brother?" or, "If we didn't have you we wouldn't have so many problems," can cause nearly-irreparable damage.

Feelings of rejection do not usually fade away. They must be confronted, defused, and healed.

3. Lack of love.

A child is created to be loved. He thrives on love. He hurts when it is not there.

Spending time with a child and showing him physical affection are a parent's best options for communicating love. Time spent talking, listening, working, playing, and doing things together is time invested in a child's life. No one can do for him what a loving parent can do.

A child ignored is a hurting child. A child unhugged for days is a hurting child. A child brushed aside is a hurting child.

4. Negative treatment by parent(s).

Negative treatment by parents ranges all the way from angry words or impatient reactions to damaging and debilitating physical neglect and abuse.

Statistics indicate one out of every four girls is sexually abused by her father or other close relative, and by the turn of the century scientists project the percentage will be one out of every three. I see many sexually abused counselees who were mistreated as preschoolers, and sometimes even in the crib. Shocking? Yes! The results are devastating, but such terrible hurts can be completely healed.

We counsel both men and women who were physically abused as children and now abuse their own children. We see people whose parents were alcoholics and who desperately need freedom from the hurts of those traumatic years. Christian counseling can help them receive healing and freedom through Jesus' love.

5. Negative treatment by siblings or close relatives.

Older brothers or sisters can hurt younger siblings by unkind words or treatment, by ostracizing them, or by physically abusive treatment or incest.

I counseled a woman who was so depressed she could hardly make it through a day at work. With the Lord's help we uncovered the fact that her older brother had started forcing her to have sex with him when she was only twelve years old. He continued doing so until at sixteen she left home to live with other relatives. She hated him for what he did, but was too timid to tell her parents or to stop him. After working through her anger, hatred, and hurt, and receiving healing from Jesus, she was even able to visit him and establish a new relationship.

6. Traumatic experiences.

The death of a parent, brother, sister, or other close relative or friend can cause deep trauma and hurt. I speak from my own personal experience—my father committed suicide when I was three years old. My earliest memory is of hearing the shot and watching all the other family members (I was the youngest) panic and run to the outbuilding from where it came. I remember standing all alone, frightened and crying, not knowing what was happening but sensing it was bad.

I pushed the hurt deep down inside me. About ten years ago I finally faced it, forgave my father for taking his life (I'd perceived it as abandonment), and submitted my pain to Jesus' healing love.

Other traumatic childhood experiences include divorce, separation from a parent, serious injury of a child or his parent, a house fire, loss of a pet, moving and leaving friends, reoccurring nightmares, severe frights, a parent's incarceration, and circumstances hurtful to a loved one.

7. Other people.

The people closest to us can hurt us most deeply, but others can, too. A child may be hurt by an unkind or thoughtless school or Sunday school teacher, an irritable neighbor, or the school bully. Maybe the Scout leader plays favorites, the babysitter is poorly qualified, or the coach barks too loudly at mistakes. Potentially anyone can hurt a child.

WHAT BRINGS HEALING?

God and His Son, Jesus Christ, are the Sources of healing, as affirmed by many verses in the Bible:

> "I am the Lord who heals you."
> Exodus 15:26, NIV

> He restores my soul.
> Psalm 23:3, NIV

> He sent forth his word and healed them.
> Psalm 107:20, NIV

> He heals the brokenhearted and binds up their wounds.
> Psalm 147:3 NIV

> Heal me, O Lord, and I will be healed.
> Jeremiah 17:14, NIV

> And the people all tried to touch him, because power was coming from him and healing them all.
> Luke 6:19, NIV

> He welcomed them and spoke to them about the kingdom of God, and healed those who needed healing.
> Luke 9:11, NIV

If your child has experienced wounding of any kind, you can bring healing to him with God's help. The steps are simple, yet powerful. If you are not comfortable ministering to him yourself, have someone else do it—a friend, a counselor, your pastor. But we find it especially meaningful for the parent to be the catalyst for the child's healing.

1. Surround the child with love and acceptance.

Create a loving atmosphere in which healing can take place. If you cannot love and accept your child *as he is*, despite problems, anger, even obnoxious behavior, you cannot help him be healed. You need not approve of his unacceptable *behavior*, but you must accept *him* in spite of it.

A child will sense judgmentalism or condemnation, and will clam up. Be neutral. Let him sense you want to help him.

Expect healing; he needs to feel there is hope. Hurt, or feelings of guilt over his negative reactions to hurt, may overwhelm a child so he feels his situation is hopeless. Remain optimistic and positive.

2. Teach him to forgive.

Forgiveness opens the door to healing. An unforgiving heart traps anger within. But often a child cannot identify who or what he's angry with. Ask gentle but probing questions about his feelings. Remember, even feelings not based on fact are real feelings, and do real damage.

Open anger, disobedience, temper, hatred, aggressiveness, violence, and/or antisocial behavior are signs of hurt from rejection or physical harm. Children who stuff their feelings inside manifest the hurt or rejection differently: in self-rejection, self-pity, fears, pouting, withdrawal, bouts of unexplainable crying, headaches, nervousness, moodiness, self-hatred, depression, and even suicidal thoughts.

Jesus taught us a tree is known by its fruit. Bad fruit in a child's life signifies the presence of a root of bitterness. Left to grow, it will not only continue to hurt the child, but others around him as well.

> See to it that no one misses the grace of God
> and that no bitter root grows up to cause trouble
> and defile many.
>
> Hebrews 12:15, NIV

If the child cannot remember who has hurt him, pray together and ask Jesus to reveal this information to him or to you. This often yields an immediate answer.

Then explain to your child how Jesus taught us to forgive those who have hurt us. Otherwise our anger keeps us imprisoned, and we will never be free of the hurt. "I tell you the truth, you will not get out until you have paid the last penny" (Matthew 5:26, NIV).

Explain forgiveness as a choice, not a feeling. We can forgive out of obedience to the Lord's command even when we do not feel forgiveness for the persons who hurt us. When we take that step, God's grace is released in our lives and the feeling will follow.

> Then Peter came to Jesus and asked, "Lord,
> how many times shall I forgive my brother when
> he sins against me? Up to seven times?" Jesus
> answered, "I tell you, not seven times, but [sev-
> enty times seven]."
>
> Matthew 18:21–22, NIV

That's 490 times! What is Jesus saying? Forgiveness is a lifestyle for Christians. We must forgive again and again.

Forgiveness is like peeling an onion. Take off one layer, and there's another. When we forgive to the degree we are able, God's grace comes to our aid, and we can forgive more—at a deeper level.

Once your child understands the importance of forgiveness he will want to start the process in his own life. Sometimes a child can forgive completely the first time. Other times he may need to work at the resentment until it is all gone. Have him pray out loud: There is power in the spoken word. If he needs help in forming the prayer of forgiveness, assist him with something like the following:

Dear Jesus, I want to do what You said to do: I want to forgive. Help me to do it with my whole heart. I choose to forgive my sister right now for the mean way she's treated me. She's not perfect, but neither am I. I let go of the anger I've felt toward her, and forgive her completely. Help me to love her the way You want me to. Amen.

3. Ask Jesus to heal him.

Now the child is a candidate for healing. He has done his part, and Jesus is free to act. He's been in the healing business for two thousand years, and He will continue to heal all who *ask* Him to do so, providing they have forgiven others. The day Jesus announced His ministry in His home-town synagogue, He let everyone know He came to heal the hurting.

> "The Spirit of the Lord is on me, because he has anointed me to preach good news to the poor. He has sent me to proclaim freedom for the prisoners and recovery of sight for the blind, to release the oppressed, to proclaim the year of the Lord's favor." Then he rolled up the scroll, gave it back to the attendant and sat down. The eyes of everyone in the synagogue were fastened on him, and he began by saying to them, "Today this scripture is fulfilled in your hearing."
>
> Luke 4:18–21, NIV

Jesus had read Isaiah 61:1–2, a passage everyone knew referred to the Messiah. He was talking less about monetarily poor people than about those who were poor in their knowledge of God's love and grace. He was talking less about actual incarcerated prisoners than He was about people imprisoned by their own unforgiveness. He was talking less about physically blind people (though He did heal those, too) than about people who were spiritually blind to God's divine principles. He was talking less about the physically oppressed than about humans oppressed by Satan because of unconfessed sin in their lives.

Jesus longs to heal us, but He won't force us to receive His healing against our God-given free wills. He waits for us to *ask!*

We have seen children immediately healed by Jesus as we have had them turn to Him. A simple prayer is sufficient. "Jesus, please heal me now of all my hurts." Have the children wait in prayerful expectancy to experience Jesus' love. It is not unusual for them to receive an inner vision of His outstretched arms welcoming them to His embrace. They often go to Him, rejoicing, and report how wonderful His healing love is. Some simply feel it. But even those who experience nothing at the time are healed.

We often have the child thank Jesus for what He's done. Gratitude flows easily from a child after he's been healed, and is *evidence* of his healing. One who is not healed cannot feel grateful.

4. Pray for deliverance.

A wounded child may or may not need prayer for deliverance, depending on the particular situation. Deliverance prayer—taking authority, in Jesus' name, over any spirit or oppressive force influencing the child's life—can enter into the healing process at any one of several points, as the Lord leads.

Jesus gave us power and authority over all the works of Satan and his demonic forces (Matthew 10:1). Jesus in us is greater and more powerful than anything Satan tries to do (1 John 4:4). We have the authority to bind and loose in Jesus' name and to set others free (Matthew 16:19).

Deliverance prayer is a command in the power of Jesus' name. It is not *asking* Jesus to do something: He's already defeated Satan. It's *taking authority* over whatever is hampering the child's ability to conduct his life in a Christlike way.

When a person harbors anger in his heart he gives Satan a foothold—an opportunity to impact his life (Ephesians 4:26–27). But forgiveness clears the way for deliverance, and deliverance clears the way for a person to forgive wholeheartedly. Deliverance can be as simple as:

"In Jesus' name I bind the anger controlling this child and command it to go right now!"

You should see immediate results—a sense of relief, of new freedom, an ability to forgive more deeply, a new joy, or peace within.

5. Teach him to walk with the Lord.

Children do not know automatically how to walk with the Lord. We are commanded to train them up in the way they should go (Proverbs 22:6). We are to teach our children to know and understand the purposes for God's laws and principles: to keep them out of trouble, to guide them into spiritual growth, and to enable them to obey and please our Heavenly Father.

Paul warned Christians, "Fathers, do not exasperate your children; instead, bring them up in the training and instruction of the Lord" (Ephesians 6:4, NIV).

Training and instruction demand an investment of time with our children. But nothing is more important, for we not only benefit their lives, but invest in eternity. Our businesses, leisure activities, and possessions can't accompany us to heaven, but if we've led our children to the Lord, they'll join us in reigning together with Jesus. What a goal!

How to Change a Negative Home Atmosphere

The prevailing atmospheres in many homes, even "Christian" homes, could use fine tuning, if not major redesign.

MANY HOMES NEED IMPROVEMENT

Again and again in counseling sessions clients tell us about childhoods and home situations so bad we wonder how they survived into adulthood. Severe problems and wounded emotions evidence the damage done by devastating home atmospheres.

Some homes are not drastically dysfunctional, but negative enough to influence a child's self-esteem. Other homes yoyo between positive and negative atmospheres, leaving children insecure and perplexed by vacillating messages. Still other homes are sound with only occasional dips into negativism.

Even if your home has been blessed with two positive parents who consistently contribute to an ongoing positive home atmosphere, remember: "Into each life a little rain must fall." Circumstances change. New pressures develop. We can face them or run away. A challenge or two may be on your horizon, and a few of the following suggestions may come in handy.

PRACTICAL SUGGESTIONS FOR IMPROVING HOME ATMOSPHERES

Parents can choose to create positive atmospheres in which their children can grow healthily and happily. Try to:

1. Set the example.

What we teach our children by example they will, in time, teach their children—our grandchildren. Setting the example, not telling them what to do, holds tremendous potential for good—or bad—results.

Perhaps you have one face you show at church and at work, but not at home. Your children will model themselves after your "at home" behavior, and will either adopt hypocrisy as an acceptable way of life or find it a parental trait they despise.

If you yell and shout at your children, they will, years later, yell and shout at theirs. If you hit your wife, your son's subconscious will record your action as normal marital interaction, or he will judge you and wind up reaping the same judgment he's sown (Matthew 7:1–2). If you throw things at your husband in anger, or refuse to talk to him for days, your daughter probably will respond in a similar manner to her husband.

We need to pass blessings on to our children, not curses. This usually involves sacrificing our own likes and desires and putting God's Word into action. In turn, we grow and learn more of Him.

> For we are God's workmanship, created in Christ Jesus to do good works, which God prepared in advance for us to do.
>
> Ephesians 2:10, NIV

2. Watch your words.

My mother's homespun philosophy, "If you can't say anything nice about someone, don't say anything at all," guided my life far more than she ever imagined it would. I was careful with my mouth as a child and in the years that followed, avoiding negative comments and trying to be generous with positive ones. I wasn't always successful, but Mom's words stayed with me.

As a child I little realized Mom was teaching me a scriptural principle contributory to a positive atmosphere in the home my husband and I would establish one day. Ultimately, it would also spare me a lot of accounting.

> "But I tell you that men will have to give account on the day of judgment for every careless word they have spoken."
>
> Matthew 12:36, NIV

Whenever I rattled on too much my older sister Barbara used to say, "Katie, it's better to appear a fool than to open your mouth and remove all doubt!" I'm sure her remark was designed to keep me quiet, but it also made me realize what I said revealed a lot about what I was like, inside. This sobering thought, once again, mirrored scriptural truth.

> "The good man brings good things out of the good stored up in his heart, and the evil man brings evil things out of the evil stored up in his heart. For out of the overflow of his heart his mouth speaks."
>
> Luke 6:45, NIV

"Sticks and stones will break my bones, but words will never hurt me," children often taunt each other. Memorizing the old adage may help them save face, but it's untrue. Unkind or thoughtless words *do* hurt. Hurled from parent to child, they not only bruise feelings as they're spoken, but penetrate the child's mind and bury themselves in his subconscious, causing ongoing negative and destructive effects even into and throughout adulthood.

One study has shown it takes *four* positive comments to overcome *one* negative comment. Imagine for a moment a child with outstretched arms, each hand holding a bucket. One is marked "negative comments" and the other "positive comments." When one of his parents says, "You stupid kid, why did you do that?" a four-pound rock plunks into the negative bucket. If and when the repentant parent later says, "I'm sorry I said that; you're not stupid at all," a one-pound rock goes into his positive bucket. He's still three pounds too heavy on the negative side. It will take three more positive affirmations by a parent or others to balance the situation, and a parent who wants to build up his child's self-image must send five or more constructive comments his way.

If parents only realized the potentially destructive power of the spoken word they would watch what they say more carefully. We learned the hard way. When our son Dan was about six he was somewhat uncoordinated, often knocking over his milk or spilling things on the floor. Impatient with him, Don would say, "Dan, I knew you were going to do that!" or, "Why can't you be careful?"

I'd watch Dan tuck his chin to his chest, his lower lip trembling, tears filling his eyes and spilling over. Later, alone, I'd ask Don if he wasn't being too hard on Dan, but he'd insist Dan had to learn to be more careful.

After a few months we noticed Dan was putting on weight. This continued for a couple of years, bringing ridicule from other children, but we couldn't convince him to cut his food intake. Then the Lord showed Don his words were making Dan overeat, to compensate for the hurt his dad's critical remarks caused. So when Dan spilled his milk Don would say, "Don't worry, son, I used to do the same thing myself. I'll just clean it up and get you some more." Dan started losing weight.

"I didn't realize how much pressure I was putting on our son," Don admits. "I expected him to be as coordinated as his older brother, but he wasn't, yet. I began telling Dan more often how proud I was of him, and how much I loved him. He began to blossom, becoming all the good things I said about him. What a tremendous impact our words have on our children! We can either help or hinder them. I decided to fill our children's positive buckets as frequently as possible."

3. Check your attitudes.

Even if we *say* the right things, our poor attitudes will affect the home atmosphere. One perceiver father took an extremely critical attitude toward church and society, an everyone-else-is-wrong-and-I-alone-am-right perspective. Little by little his three sons adopted his attitude, though their motivational gifts differed from his. The boys had difficulty respecting authority in school, at church, and later in their jobs. Their father's negative attitude leavened the whole lump.

Many parents train their children into negative attitudes without realizing it. Statements like, "I knew you couldn't do it," "I wouldn't expect you to win," undermine their confidence. Parents who complain, "Everything bad always happens to me," or, "I wish I hadn't gotten out of bed today," teach their children self-pity, instead of instilling the belief they can do all things through Christ Jesus (Philippians 4:13).

Children fulfill our negative expectations and attitudes. If we want positive children we have to train them positively. Parents need to agree on the home atmosphere they want and pray about it together, asking the Lord to help them break negative attitude patterns. With His help positive, scripturally based attitudes and expectations surface, children change, and relationships to God grow stronger.

4. Lavish your love.

God designed children to respond to love from the moment of birth. You can't love a child too much; like a thirsty sponge, he'll absorb all you give him.

While ministering in Germany last year we spent ten days with the Noetzelmans, a missionary family from our church. Christina was only two weeks old when we arrived, and her mom, dad, and three older siblings constantly showered her with love. They vied for the opportunity to hold her when she was awake, and stopped by her bassinet as she napped to kiss her and express their love. I had to "get in line" to hold her, and even then at least one of the children usually stood by, saying "Are you through yet? I'm next."

What an inheritance! We wish every child were treated this way by his family!

Bringing two Old Testament passages, Deuteronomy 6:5 and Leviticus 19:18, together, Jesus taught us love is central to life:

> " 'Love the Lord your God with all your heart and with all your soul and with all your mind and with all your strength.' The second is this: 'Love your neighbor as yourself.' There is no commandment greater than these."
>
> Mark 12:30–31, NIV

A child must feel loved by others—parents, siblings, aunts, uncles, cousins, grandparents, and friends—before he can love himself. Just as we love with agape love because God *first* loved us with agape love (1 John 4:19), so a child learns human love from human example.

If a child receives love and loves and accepts himself, he can also love others and God. If the foundational love is lacking, he cannot love God or anyone, but is trapped in his own internal prison of insecurity, fear, and self-centeredness. For without love we are nothing, as 1 Corinthians 13 states so eloquently.

Lavishing your love on a child does not mean spoiling him. It does mean showing your love through affectionate touch and time spent with him, and telling your love through verbal affirmations of his worth as a person.

5. Listen attentively.

The pressures and responsibilities of our adult world sometimes keep us so preoccupied we only half listen when our children talk to us. Children know when we're not really interested in what they're saying. We communicate a clear message: "Your thoughts are of no importance to me."

After my first child arrived my mother delivered one of her well-timed exhortations. "Katie," she said, "when your son is old enough to talk he will want your attention. Stop what you're doing and listen to him with both ears. What he says may not sound important to you, but it is to him. And when he's old enough to talk about a problem, pay attention. The problem may seem insignificant to you, but it is a mountain to him, and he'll need your help."

I am grateful for an exhorter mother who always took time to listen to *me* when I was growing up; I know I always felt she cared. Her advice stuck with me through the years, and benefited my children as well.

6. Learn to apologize.

Young children think their parents are infallible, but they're not. We all make mistakes. We are all subject to sin. Yes, we are made new creatures in Christ when we accept Him as Savior and Lord, but we have to grow in grace and the ability to walk in God's ways.

Our children see us as authority figures, and need to obey us. But they also need to know that as fellow human beings we're not perfect. Transparent parents maintain open relationships with their children, and apologies build strong bridges of communication.

At times you'll need to apologize for something you've said or done to your child. Don't be embarrassed; you are training him to apologize, too. If you've lost your temper, be quick to say, "Forgive me, I didn't mean to say that." When impatience rules your emotions, tell him, "I was wrong to be impatient, I'm sorry." If you forget a promise, admit it, ask his forgiveness, and assure him you'll follow through as soon as possible. Set a good example for him to follow.

7. Forgive frequently.

Forgiving a child for something does not mean you condone his actions. Discipline him first, if necessary. Make sure he is sorry for his action or misdeed.

Then forgive, clearing the slate, so no cloud of unforgiveness hangs over the household.

How many times should you forgive? Peter asked Jesus and got a surprising answer: seventy times seven. Jesus' point? Forgiveness is a lifestyle, an ongoing matter of choice.

8. Observe your body language.

A parent can set the home atmosphere without even opening his mouth. One study has shown only ten to fifteen percent of all communication is verbal. The rest is body language, consisting of bodily postures and eye and facial expressions.

Bodily postures reveal much. Arms folded in front over the chest say, "You're going to get it!" or "I'm not going to let you get too close to me." Fists held upward imply, "I'd like to hit you." Leaning away from someone shows disinterest; leaning slightly toward a person says, "I really care about what you're saying." Whenever my mom put her hands on her hips all of us ran and hid. She was angry. Fingers thumped on the table signaled impatience. A stomping foot meant she was counting to ten and ready to explode.

Arms extended say, "Come here, I want to give you a hug." An arm around the waist or shoulder affirms, "You are very special to me." A kiss on the cheek says, "I love you!"

Literature and tradition contain many references to the influence of eye expressions, including, "The eye is the window of the soul," and "Looks can kill." While a look cannot harm physically it can damage relationships or set a mood. Anger can shoot from the eyes like fiery darts. An impatient look accompanied by a sigh communicates, "I wish you'd hurry up and get lost." A calculated stare can say, "Do that one more time, and I'll hit you." Parents refusing to meet each other's eyes reveal to their children, "Our parents are fighting again."

On the positive side an adoring look says, "I'm so proud to be your parent," and eyes fixed on the child after a command is given let him know, "I expect you to do what I said, right now!"

Facial expressions have an even broader range of communication. Scientific studies have shown positive expressions strengthen a person, while negative ones weaken him. Perhaps the composer of the song, "Put on a Happy Face," was aware of this. It takes more muscles and energy to frown than to smile, a tidbit we used to mention to our children when they were down in the dumps.

A smile affirms, "I like you," or, "I like what you're saying"; a frown shouts disapproval. A pleased look says, "A job well done"; a disgusted look proclaims displeasure.

Greg White, a good counselor friend, has drawn a chart of facial expressions (next page). Stare at one of the faces for about twenty seconds and pay close attention to your feelings. Try another, one of the negative ones. It's amazing how much a line drawing of a facial expression impacts our emotions.

While some negative expressions are inevitable in the normal course of family life, parents can deliberately use body language to create positive home atmospheres.

Content	Delighted	Disappointed	Disgusted	Distant	Doleful	Distasteful
Ecstatic	Enraged	Envious	Exasperated	Exhausted	Forgiving	Friendly
Frightened	Frustrated	Glad	Guilty	Happy	Horrified	Hungover
Hurt	Hysterical	Indifferent	Impish	Innocent	Interested	Lonely
Lovesick	Meditative	Mischievous	Miserable	Ornery	Optimistic	Pained
Paranoid	Patient	Peaceful	Perplexed	Prudish	Puzzled	Regretful
Relieved	Sad	Satisfied	Sheepish	Shocked	Smug	Surly
Surprised	Suspicious	Sympathetic	Thoughtful	Tired	Undecided	Withdrawn

9. Let the music ring.

Music was God's idea. He created it and gave us the capacity to enjoy it. Paul writes:

> Do not get drunk on wine, which leads to debauchery. Instead, be filled with the Spirit. Speak to one another with psalms, hymns and spiritual songs. Sing and make music in your heart to the Lord.
>
> Ephesians 5:18–19, NIV

A Christian home should be filled with joy, laughter, and songs of praise. Good Christian music is available on records, tapes, and on the radio. Fill your house with it, and also introduce inspiring classical or semiclassical music. Music indeed sets the mood.

Take time for family devotions and include plenty of singing. Choose familiar songs to suit your children's ages, but also introduce pieces they will hear in church.

Expose your children to a wide variety of songs. Contemporary praise songs, based on Scripture portions, like "I Will Bless the Lord at All Times" (Psalm 34:1–4) and "This Is the Day That the Lord Hath Made" (Psalm 118:24) will enhance their biblical knowledge and understanding of worship. The great hymns of the ages (like "Amazing Grace" and "Holy, Holy, Holy") and "spiritual songs" (including beautiful Negro spirituals like "Swing Low, Sweet Chariot," today's praise music, and spontaneous singing under the Holy Spirit's anointing) will broaden their appreciation for the diverse ways in which God meets His people's needs. Talk about their meanings. Look up information about their composers or their backgrounds. It's often fascinating.

Encourage sing-alongs as you travel. Sing while you cook dinner or clean the garage. Whistle while you work. Spontaneous praise is contagious: Your children will catch on.

Christian parents must realize a vast amount of today's popular secular music counters every Christian value and moral standard. We sometimes hear parents say, "Oh, well, my child likes it, so I let him have it in his own room."

But day after day that child's mind is bombarded with persuasion to enter into a lifestyle of rebellion, disrespect for authority, sexual promiscuity, and violence. Contrast this message, blasting into his subconscious mind four or five hours a day, with the Christian message, heard a few hours a week at most, and guess what will prevail.

We drew the line firmly on this matter with our boys and explained why we were doing so. They accepted our view, and even found such music to be obnoxious when they heard it elsewhere. If you doubt the negative effects of the music popular with today's teens, check out the excellent exposé books and tapes on this subject available at your local Christian bookstore.

10. Express thankfulness.

Thankfulness in the heart, expressed verbally, blesses both the speaker and everyone around him. While attending seminary in Boston I stayed one weekend in the home of an elderly couple, members of a church where I worked part-time. Grace at mealtime was no routine prayer, for both husband and wife overflowed with thankfulness for all of God's blessings. Their conversations were peppered with thankful remarks: "Isn't the Lord good to us?" or "We have so much to be grateful for!"

These comments registered distinctly because I thought they had so *little* for which to be grateful. Their house was humble, their furniture was worn out, their car no longer worked, their income was sparse, and their health was failing. But thankfulness was a way of life for them, and I longed to enter into it, as well.

> Always giving thanks to God the Father for
> everything, in the name of our Lord Jesus Christ.
> Ephesians 5:20, NIV

Openly and naturally express your thanksgiving to God in front of your children. Like praise, thankfulness is contagious.

Be generous in your thanksgiving to one another. Children need to see moms and dads thanking each other. They need to be thanked for the chores they do, even if they are expected to do them. Express your appreciation for their spontaneous acts—homemade gifts, branches of pussy willows or bunches of dandelions for the table, or hugs that say you're the best Mom or Dad in the whole world.

11. Make room for differences.

Since members of our families probably have a variety of motivational gifts, we need to make room for their differences. They won't all like the same things, nor will they want to do things the same way. Siblings need to give and take, not putting each other down for being different. An accepting atmosphere is a healthy one, allowing each child to grow according to his bent without feeling he has to conform to others' modes of operation.

Take the matter of family vacations. A server may collect rocks, wanting to stop at every interesting outcropping to pick up specimens. But an exhorter may consider his sibling's hobby a waste of time, wanting to get to each campsite early so he can find kids his own age to play with. These differences could produce real tension if their parents fail to consider both children's interests, discussing their valid disparities and the "give and take" necessary to accommodate both. The server's rock stops may need to be limited to three a day instead of five, and the arrival time might need to be four o'clock instead of three.

The opportunity for making allowances out of Christian love for each other is beautifully expressed in Ephesians 5:21: "Submit to one another out of reverence for Christ" (NIV).

12. Teach the Word.

Faith comes by hearing the Word of God. Read it aloud every day in your home. Select small, pertinent passages, gearing them to your children's ages.

We used to keep Scripture cards in a container shaped like a loaf of bread. It sat on the breakfast table and as the boys ate their cereal they took turns choosing and reading a Scripture. Then we'd talk about it. They loved this routine, and looked forward to it each day. (Children enjoy memorizing verses, also.)

Families in which there are wide age differences between children may need to share the Word with them individually. Read one verse to a toddler at bedtime (preferably from an easily understandable version) and apply it to his daily life. His ten-year-old sister, however, is ready for more complex concepts.

Remember, setting the atmosphere for your home is both a privilege and a responsibility. Only you can do it.

How to Eliminate Negative Generational Influences

20

New parents (and their assorted relatives) routinely play an age-old game: "Whom does the baby resemble?" Grandpa's dimple, Mom's red hair, and Dad's round face are easy to identify. As the early months of life pass, however, the game sometimes loses its zest; Grandpa's stubbornness, Mom's phobias, and Dad's short temper are less welcome in Junior's character make-up than their physical attributes were in his appearance.

Two Old Testament passages clearly illuminate a scriptural principle too many Christian parents ignore: Our obedience to God's laws—or lack of it—will strongly and specifically affect our children and their descendants.

GOD PROMISES POSITIVE GENERATIONAL INFLUENCES . . .

Moses made this very clear prior to the revealing of the Ten Commandments when He related God's special promise concerning children.

> Know, recognize and understand therefore
> this day, and turn your [mind and] heart to it,
> that the Lord is God in the heavens above, and
> upon the earth beneath; there is no other. There-
> fore you shall keep His statutes and His com-
> mandments, which I command you this day, *that*

> *it may go well with you and your children after you,*
> and that you may prolong your days in the land
> which the Lord your God gives you for ever.
> Deuteronomy 4:39–40 TAB (italics ours)

God gave us His laws not to make life difficult, but so we could know His will, stay on His pathway—a safe, protected place in which we can walk and abide—and receive His blessings. We get into trouble when we "do our own thing."

Besides, how can we, as believers, say we love God and refuse to keep His laws? In 1 John 5:3 we read, "This is love for God: to obey his commands. And his commands are not burdensome" (NIV).

We want our children and their descendants to have good lives, and we can provide positive generational influences by our behavior.

. . . AND THE ALTERNATIVES

When Moses quotes God in the first of the Ten Commandments (listed in both Exodus 20 and Deuteronomy 5) we hear a startling pronouncement about the alternative generational influences:

> "You shall have no other gods before Me. You
> shall not make for yourself an idol, or any like-
> ness of what is in heaven above or on the earth
> beneath or in the water under the earth. You shall
> not worship them or serve them; for I, the Lord
> your God, am a jealous God, visiting the iniquity
> of the fathers on the children, on the third and
> the fourth generations of those who hate Me, but
> showing lovingkindness to thousands, to those
> who love Me and keep My commandments."
> Exodus 20:3–6, NAS

Our disobedience to God's laws will negatively affect our children, grandchildren, great-grandchildren, and great-great-grandchildren. It will take four generations to neutralize the influence of our sin.

But look at the last part of verse six. God's mercy and love is released perpetually—for a thousand generations—into the lives of our children and all their descendants for twenty thousand years if we obey God's commandments. What a promise!

WE MUST CHOOSE

Which option do you choose for your family? Just prior to Joshua's death he assembled all the tribes of Israel at Shechem and spoke to the elders, leaders, judges, and officials. Challenging them to make a clear decision, he said,

"But if serving the Lord seems undesirable to you, then choose for yourselves this day whom you will serve, whether the gods your forefathers served beyond the River, or the gods of the Amorites, in whose land you are living. But as for me and my household, we will serve the Lord."

Joshua 24:15, NIV

The people said they, too, wanted to serve the Lord, though Joshua stressed the difficulties inherent in their choice, and the serious consequences of breaking their commitment. They affirmed their decision three times.

Each of us must make an independent decision about serving the Lord. He does not force us to serve Him and walk in His ways, but we will be held accountable for what we do. The blessings are great—to a thousand generations. The alternative sends a rippling negative effect through four generations.

NEGATIVE GENERATIONAL INFLUENCE

Is a negative influence launched by a past generation affecting you and your family now? How should you deal with it? Can it be eliminated?

The possibility of change is one of the most beautiful qualities of the Christian life. Yes, a negative generational influence may operate in your family if no one has ever neutralized it. But you can deal with and eliminate it completely, turning the tide for yourself, your children, and, in some cases, for your living parents or grandparents.

Take these two steps:

1. Decide to live by God's laws, seeking His grace and help through the power of the indwelling Christ.

2. Break generational influences (operating much like curses) by taking authority over specific ones you recognize in the name (power) of Jesus Christ.

1. Live by God's laws.

We've already discussed the first step, but if you have never received Jesus Christ as Savior and Lord of your life, you need to do so. Only by having Christ *in us* can we live by His laws. "For we are God's workmanship, created in Christ Jesus to do good works, which God prepared in advance for us to do" (Ephesians 2:10, NIV).

2. Break the generational influences.

Breaking generational influences is one step on the way to becoming overcomers through the authority and power the completed work of Christ gives to each Christian. We have the same amount of authority—God's power and authority—Paul and Peter had, and we have the right to use it (Ephesians 1:18–21). We are seated with Christ in heavenly places (Ephesians 2:6). Satan and all his negative influences have been placed legally under Christ's feet and our feet (Ephesians 1:22). We are stronger than he is, and have greater authority than he does. But we must appropriate it experientially in our specific situations.

Our spoken words in the name of Jesus carry power. As we identify generational influences we can cancel their power over ourselves and future generations.

Suppose you recognize obesity as a long-standing generational problem on both sides of your family, resulting in your own weight problem. Here's how to pray:

"In the name of Jesus I break the generational influence of obesity from my mother's side of the family. And in Jesus' name I break the generational influence of obesity from my father's side of the family. I declare its power null and void in my life, in my children's lives, and in all future generations. I now place the blood of Jesus between me and past generations, choosing to let the power of the Holy Spirit renew my life and enable me to walk with God in this matter."

Your life is now freed from the generational influence of obesity. But don't continue undisciplined eating habits, consuming everything in sight. Take steps to learn about good nutrition; discover the differences between live food and dead food, between useful calories and empty ones. Change your shopping habits. If a special food tempts you, don't bring it home. Find a dieting plan that works for you and follow it. Eat to live, don't live to eat.

Perhaps you've tried to make changes before but were unsuccessful. Try again. You no longer have an unseen but real generational influence standing in your way.

EXAMINE THE INFLUENCES

To help you identify negative generational influences possibly impacting your life, we've prepared a chart (opposite page), based on the research of our counselor friend Linda Pender, and used with her permission. Fill in the names of your family members. Then look at the list of possible negative generational influences on page 223 and write them under the names of relatives who have experienced those problems.

You may be unaware of some family history; ask for more information or work with what you have. As patterns develop you'll see matters for overcoming prayer.

We've arranged the list under seven major categories; some items could fall under more than one. The list is not exhaustive, and you may think of additional influences affecting your family. Include these on the chart as well.

TRACING YOUR FAMILY'S GENERATIONAL INFLUENCES

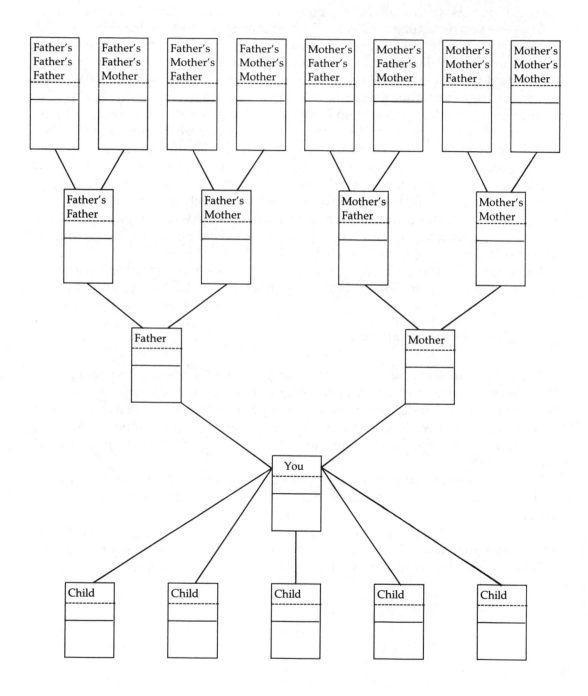

POSSIBLE NEGATIVE GENERATIONAL INFLUENCES

1. SPIRITUAL

atheism
cults
controlling spirits
occult practices
witchcraft

2. PHYSICAL

anorexia
bulimia
diseases
infirmities

3. MENTAL

covetousness
depression
greed
insanity
legalism
mental disorders
pride

4. EMOTIONAL

anxiety
fear of men
fear of women
fearfulness
fears (phobias)
excessive grief
rejection
self-hatred
self-pity
self-rejection

5. IRRESPONSIBILITY

abandonment
alcoholism
compulsiveness
deceitfulness
divorce
financial problems
obesity
poverty
rebellion
thievery

6. VIOLENT/ABUSIVE

abortion
anger
drug abuse
hatefulness
hatred of men/women
murder
physical abuse
rape
sexual abuse
suicide
temper
verbal abuse

7. SEXUAL/IMMORAL

adultery
conception out of
  wedlock
fornication
frigidity/impotency
homosexuality/
lesbianism
illegitimate child
incest
masturbation
pornography
promiscuity
prostitution

HOW ARE THE GIFTS AFFECTED?

The motivational gifts are affected to some degree by generational sins and influences. The farther removed the person with the negative influence, the less the effect. An alcoholic father will have more negative influence on a child than will his alcoholic grandfather. The generational effect from a father who lives away from home (or is deceased) is less than from one in the home. A person who openly practices a sin will be more influential than one who hides it.

Persons with some motivational gifts do experience more negative effects than others. Generational sins impact servers, givers, and compassion persons most severely, with compassion persons usually hit the hardest. Remember, persons with these three gifts are sensitive, subjective, and more easily disillusioned or hurt than are persons with other gifts. They care deeply and often want to help the relative who has the problem.

The giver will try to be forgiving, extending help if he can. If he has a financially irresponsible alcoholic father, he may determine to be a financial success in order to provide adequately for his mother.

The server may try to compensate for an alcoholic father's irresponsibility by taking on more adult tasks. He often winds up losing out on his childhood, and battling with inner resentment.

The compassion child may feel responsible for his alcoholic father's erratic behavior, and especially for his parents' emotional conflicts. He may try to fill the impossible role of peacemaker in this situation, feeling guilty when he's unsuccessful. The most likely candidate for abuse, tolerating it beyond all reason, he doggedly hopes—often unrealistically—for change in the offending individual.

Teachers, exhorters, and administrators are more resistant to negative influences, deciding independently what they will tolerate and what they won't. They are more adaptable to difficult situations, more objective about problems, and better able to bounce back to normalcy when hurt.

A perceiver is in a category all by himself. Quick to take a stand against anything he deems improper, he is also apt to judge a sinning relative, eventually falling prey to the same sin himself. He is objective to a point, but may allow anger and unforgiveness to take over. He will rebel at unfairness and injustice, refusing the authority of an offending parent. Unfortunately his rebellion robs him of the discipline he needs to bring his gift into godly subjection to authority.

PRAY FOR YOUR CHILDREN

If you see influences affecting your children who are still at home, pray with them. Let them talk about and face their deepest feelings. Teach them to forgive the offending relative, but not to tolerate abuse, or approve of improper actions.

If some or all of your children are grown, show them the chart, and try to discuss it with them. Ask their forgiveness if you have passed on negative influences. If possible, pray for them in person, taking authority over generational influences. If distance separates you, mail a copy of the chart to them, and pray with them by phone. If they are not open to prayer, intercede for them privately.

Christian counseling, often available through a church or Christian organization, may help you and/or your children to work through the consequences of negative generational influences. (Carefully selected secular counseling can also help.)

How to Minister to Your Child

21

Knowing a child's motivational gift enables a parent to minister effectively to him. Pollution in the gift may explain his difficulties. His gift may conflict with someone else's, or cause competition with someone who has the same gift. Ministry necessary for a person having one type of gift may differ markedly from ministry necessary for another.

Sometimes the nature of a child's problem is an indicator of his gift. A girl who constantly feels crushed by her father's stern ways may be a compassion person. A child who cannot meet his high expectations for academic performance may be a server. A child who asks his mother nonstop questions from sunrise to sunset may be a teacher.

Sometimes parents can gain insight on a new problem by pulling out the child's completed motivational gifts test and reviewing his responses to particular characteristics. Taking special note of the problem areas of his test will usually provide immediate perspective.

No one can minister to your child as effectively and consistently as you can. Parents are the ultimate authority in a child's life, and up until about junior high age he believes whatever his parent says is right. Use your position to minister to his special needs and help him overcome his problems.

In this chapter we will look briefly at each motivational gift, defining the typical problems. Then we will examine four goals to achieve, consider guidelines to help the child, look at ways to pray with and for him, and explore methods of reinforcing acceptable behavior with positive affirmations. Ask the Lord for other insights on how to help your child. Develop your own additional goals, guidelines, prayers, and affirmations.

Written goals and guidelines help some children. Remember, we only share examples. Personalize them for your child, write your own, or have your child write them in his own words. You may want to post them somewhere. For younger children, place stars or stickers on the list to show accomplishments, affirming and reinforcing desirable attitudes and behavior. We have included a sample chart, "Goals & Guidelines for Ministry," at the end of this chapter. You may order additional copies.

Make prayer times as natural as possible. Use the suggested prayers as examples, altering them with language appropriate to your child's age. A younger child may need coaching, or may wish to repeat the prayer after you. An older child may draw up a prayer list to be sure he covers the essentials. Set specific prayer times, but be alert to opportunities for spontaneous prayer or ministry.

Remember, God has positioned you uniquely to minister to each of your children. Always point them to the Lord and His will for their lives, teaching them to draw upon His love, strength, and help.

THE PERCEIVER'S TYPICAL PROBLEM AREAS

Perceivers are often: strong-willed, judgmental, blunt, opinionated, intolerant, too idealistic, critical, prideful, domineering, controlling, pushy, unforgiving, tattletales, loners, and plagued with poor self-images.

1. Goals.

a) First, teach your perceiver to respect authority and obey spontaneously. Otherwise he will become increasingly rebellious and difficult to handle.

b) Channel his idealism, keen perception, and judgmentalism into the ministry of prayer. God wants him to become an anointed intercessor.

c) Build up his drooping self-image. He's sometimes too hard on himself, and needs to relax his rigid self-expectations.

d) Encourage him to build better relationships in general, and at least one or two close friendships. He will never be the most popular child on the block, but he can improve his interpersonal relations.

2. Guidelines.

a) Establish your authority, and joint authority if you are married. Set and enforce rules and restrictions. Your perceiver needs boundaries; without them he'll never learn to respect authority.

b) Set regular prayer times to suit your situation. Teach him to pray; he will learn to love it. When you hear him criticizing someone, call him on it and suggest he substitute prayer, instead.

c) Set aside times for serious discussions about your child's self-image and life views. Share relevant Scriptures (like the whole book of Ephesians) about who he is in Christ. Let him know you do not expect him to be perfect—you love him for who he is, not for what he does or doesn't do.

d) Observe his relationships with others. Make a list of ways he could improve his behavior, words, and attitudes. Discuss these with him privately, never in front of his brothers or sisters. Correction is always hard to take, even when it's given in love, and it is embarrassing in front of others.

3. Prayers.

a) Lord, help me to want to obey You and my parents. I know I'm stubborn at times, and I'm sorry. I really want to do what is right, and I know it's right to respect my parents' authority. Help me to do what they say, knowing they won't ask anything outside Your will for my life. I trust them.

b) Lord, I realize You've given me a gift for perceiving what others are doing wrong. Help me not to criticize or judge them, but to pray for them, instead. You love them, just like You love me, so I want to love them, too, even if I don't like what they're doing.

c) Lord, I get angry at myself too often. I want to do what's right and when I don't I'm upset with myself. Help me to remember I'm Your child, I'm not perfect, and You love me even when I blow it. With Your help I'll try to do my best. Help me to accept myself as I am and to keep growing in Your love.

d) Lord, sometimes my gift gets in my way. I want to make friends but my bluntness doesn't help. Cause me to think before I speak. Help me to look for the good in others and to appreciate them for who they are, not expecting them to act like me, but rejoicing in their differentness. Help me to be more considerate, more helpful, and more loving to everyone. Help me to find a special friend.

4. Affirmations.

a) Praise your perceiver whenever he obeys you. Express your pride when he drops everything to come when you call. Commend him when he does what you ask without arguing.

b) Thank him when he prays for you or for a prayer request you've given him. Tell him you are pleased when he catches himself in the midst of criticizing and prays, instead. If you observe an answer to prayer he hasn't noticed, tell him about it and thank the Lord together.

c) Commend him when he laughs at himself instead of getting angry at himself. Verbally acknowledge his positive efforts to be all he can be as a young Christian. Continue to tell him he is special to you and to God.

d) Notice when he relates positively to another child, and praise him for it later. Affirm any kindnesses he extends to his peers.

THE SERVER'S TYPICAL PROBLEM AREAS

Servers are often: easily embarrassed, overly shy, perfectionists, critical, interfering, and overly dependent on appreciation.

1. Goals.

a) Help your server overcome some of his shyness. He is not likely to become an extrovert, but he can learn to relate better to others.

b) Perfectionism has merits, but it can enslave a child's life and irritate others. Help your server to eliminate extreme perfectionism.

c) A server sometimes criticizes people who fail to help as he thinks they should. Make him aware of others' differing motivational gifts and forms of service.

d) Encourage him to look to the Lord—not people—for appreciation.

2. Guidelines.

a) Make sure your server spends time with other children, learning to relate better. Take him with you when you visit adults, providing him additional experience in being around people.

b) Let him know a job reasonably well done is appreciated as much as a job perfectly done. Show him he does not have to overaccomplish in order to receive praise.

c) Set limits on critical attitudes and words. When you hear him criticize someone, ask him to stop and think how that person may be serving or helping in another way.

d) Talk regularly to your child about how the Lord appreciates his helpfulness. Direct his focus to pleasing God, not people.

3. Prayers.

a) Lord, help me to be friendlier; I find it hard. I think I'm scared of people, unsure they will like me. Maybe they're scared of me, too. But I know You love me, Lord; You made me who I am. Help me to reach out to others, especially ones who are shy like I am.

b) Lord, please help me not to be such a perfectionist. I feel better when I do something just right, but not everyone thinks it's necessary. I know I bug my sister when I take too long doing something. Help me to know when to stop, and when to keep on working.

c) Lord, please forgive me for criticizing Johnny when he didn't help me pick up the papers blowing around on the playground. I realize now he was busy talking to Steve, trying to help him with a problem.

d) Lord, I'm glad I was able to help the teacher during recess today by cleaning blackboards. Even though she didn't show much appreciation, I know You saw and appreciated what I did. I want to please You in all I do; please continue to show me how to help.

4. Affirmations.

a) Notice when your server makes an effort to be friendly. Tell him—and the Lord—you are proud of him.

b) When your server's perfectionism causes him to spend too long on a task, let him know it will be satisfactory if he finishes up quickly. Compliment him on less-than-perfect jobs.

c) Commend your server for catching himself before or in the middle of a criticism.

d) Remember, this child needs appreciation often. Take time to give it, even for little things, and remind him of the Lord's appreciation, as well.

THE TEACHER'S TYPICAL PROBLEM AREAS

Teachers are often: prideful, intolerant, legalistic, dogmatic, opinionated, unfriendly, and aloof, with know-it-all attitudes.

1. Goals.

a) Humility in the midst of tremendous mental capability is a goal for which the teacher should strive. He knows he's smart in comparison to his peers, but don't let it go to his head. Help him to recognize his intelligence as a gift from God.

b) Your teacher has an opinion about everything and is often intolerant of differing viewpoints. Remind him there are two sides to every issue, and help him recognize the possible validity of others' opinions.

c) This child is often aloof or unfriendly, and must learn to warm up to his peers. He needs to expand his ability to relate to persons with different gifts.

d) The teacher's know-it-all attitude can make him unteachable at home and school and unpopular with his peers. Help him to realize nobody knows everything.

2. Guidelines.

a) The Scriptures tell us to humble ourselves: If we don't do it, God will. Talk with your child about this. The more he stands in awe of God, the more he'll see himself in proper perspective.

b) Establish all opinions in your household as worthy of consideration, not put-downs.

c) Encourage the development of friendships. Be sure your child feels free to bring friends home. Entertain families with children his age.

d) Set a house rule prohibiting know-it-all attitudes, and enforce it kindly but firmly. Discuss alternative attitudes.

3. Prayers.

a) Lord, thank You for my gift of teaching; I realize I have a responsibility to use it well. Help me not to think I'm better than anyone else; without Your help I am nothing. I choose to banish pride from my life and humble myself before You.

b) Lord, I'm quick to form opinions, and lots of times You help me to form good ones. But I know I shouldn't assume my opinion is better than everyone else's. Help me to listen for what is good and helpful in others' opinions, to take time to judge fairly, and to learn from what other people think.

c) Lord, You know how difficult it is for me to make friends. Sometimes I'd rather read a good book than spend time with people who don't interest me. But I need to learn to get along with other types of people, so please help me to show interest in what they like, and to reach out to someone every day.

d) Lord, please keep me from being a know-it-all. You know I enjoy learning, and want to share what I've learned with others. But help me to do it simply, gently, and without boasting.

4. Affirmations.

a) Commend your teacher whenever he humbles himself, continuing to teach him the value of true humility.

b) Appreciate his opinions and search out their value. But tell him he's on the right track when he listens to and/or accepts the opinions of others as valuable, too.

c) Express your pleasure with his honest attempts at developing friendships.

d) When you see him sharing knowledge with the right attitude, commend him.

THE EXHORTER'S TYPICAL PROBLEM AREAS

Exhorters are often: opinionated, interruptive, compromising, overtalkative, pushy, exaggerators, and liable to give unsolicited advice.

1. Goals.

a) Help your exhorter overcome his most irritating characteristic—his overtalkativeness.

b) In his eagerness to talk and share opinions the exhorter interrupts others. Help him to recognize and eliminate this tendency.

c) Talk with him and help him to avoid stretching the truth in little matters as well as big ones.

d) Your exhorter is full of advice. Teach him to channel it appropriately so he won't offend others.

2. Guidelines.

a) If necessary, limit his talking, letting him know you will stop him if he gets carried away. Tell him you have ten minutes to hear about his day at school, and then you must get back to work. He will learn to condense what he has to say instead of telling every detail.

b) Make a house rule permitting family members to call your exhorter on interrupting them. He probably doesn't realize he's doing it so frequently.

c) Challenge your exhorter when he manipulates the truth in order to make a point. Have him restate what he said in simple, honest terms, and don't allow exaggerations.

d) When your exhorter offers unsolicited advice, say kindly, "Did I ask for your advice just now?" When he responds "No—but," remind him you will ask for his advice when you want it. Define interference in other people's affairs as bad manners.

3. Prayers.

a) Lord, please help me to keep my mouth shut. Sometimes I talk on and on, and even think out loud. But others don't always like to hear me. Cause me to think before I speak, to sort out what is important to say. Help me to make what I say count.

b) Lord, I have a bad habit of interrupting. I didn't realize how much I do it until my family started letting me know. I don't mean to, Lord. Make me more sensitive to people and what they are saying, so I'll let them finish before I jump in with both feet.

c) Lord, sometimes I get carried away when I'm telling what happened, and I stretch the truth—yes, I lie. I want to be honest. Help me not to color the truth or to exaggerate. Please check me, Lord.

d) Lord, You know I love to help people by giving advice, no matter what their problem. But when I offer unrequested advice, I'm sticking my nose into someone else's business. Forgive me. Help me to see when my advice is wanted, and when it isn't.

4. Affirmations.

a) Commend your exhorter for any efforts to suppress his talkativeness. When he rambles, affirm the value of his comments, but tell him he's saying too much.

b) Also commend his efforts not to interrupt; your praise will spur him on to do even better.

c) Compliment him for telling a story well, without exaggerations.

d) When you can tell he's longed to jump in and give advice but has purposely held back, congratulate him. Continue to affirm the value of his advice, and his wisdom in waiting until it is requested.

THE GIVER'S TYPICAL PROBLEM AREAS

Givers are often: stingy, too focused on money, tempted to steal, too frugal, manipulative, overworking, and too generous.

1. Goals.

a) The giver is usually generous, but stinginess may rear its head, especially in his relationships with his brothers and sisters. If they have not seemed to appreciate what he's given them before, he may quit sharing with them. Help him learn to give even to those who do not appreciate it.

b) At the opposite end of the scale is the giver's tendency to be too generous. He may give away the expensive toy or game you just bought him for his birthday. He may offer his whole allowance to a worthy cause and have nothing left to operate on. Don't stifle his generosity, but help him bring it into proper balance.

c) Money can become too important—even an idol—to your giver. Help him to keep God the center of his life, not money. Define it as a means to an end, but not an end in itself.

d) A giver—even one who is a Christian—can be tempted to steal, not for his own use, but because he gets joy out of giving to others. Be sure this is not a problem for your giver.

2. Guidelines.

a) Talk to your giver if he's showing signs of stinginess. Be sure to let him air his feelings.

b) Establish guidelines about what things are acceptable to give away and what should be considered permanently his. Explain why. ("If you give away something Grandma gave you, it might hurt her feelings.")

c) If your giver begins to place too much importance on money, talk with him about his feelings of trust for the Lord, and His provision for our needs. Use Scripture to show him the fleeting nature of monetary satisfaction.

d) Should you discover any stealing or shoplifting, confront it immediately. Make him accountable.

3. Prayers.

a) Lord, help me to give without any strings attached. Even if my brothers and sisters don't appreciate what I give them, help me to know You appreciate my generosity. I want to give for the joy of giving, not for the thanks I might get.

b) Lord, I know I got a little carried away in my giving. I didn't think how Grandma would feel when I gave her gift to my best friend. I can't get it back now, but help me to think before I act, next time. You know I want to be wisely generous and helpful, both with my time and my possessions.

c) Lord, forgive me for thinking more about money than You. I want to put You first in my life, always! I know money is just a means to an end here on this earth; help me to keep it in right perspective. Help me to see how I can give of my time, energy, and help, as well as money.

d) Lord, You know how much I love to give. Help me to remember the monetary value of the gift is less important than the act of giving itself. Let me give what I can happily, and as You bless me, I'll enjoy being able to give even more.

4. Affirmations.

a) When you see your child checking his stinginess, express your pleasure.

b) Continue to affirm his generosity and his willingness to learn what's acceptable to give and what isn't.

c) Applaud his efforts to put the Lord first in his life, and to handle money with a correct spiritual perspective.

d) If your child has stolen something, but made it right, let him know you are proud of him. If he's learned to modify his tendency to place too much importance on the monetary value of a gift, commend him.

THE ADMINISTRATOR'S TYPICAL PROBLEM AREAS

Administrators are often: bossy, domineering, insensitive, callous, procrastinating, forgetful, messy, overzealous, overextended, and neglectful of routine work.

1. Goals.

a) Your administrator loves to lead and to tell others what to do. But unless he's been asked to take charge, he's out of order. Teach him how to use his gift without getting bossy.

b) Administrators routinely procrastinate jobs they deem insignificant or boring to concentrate on their own areas of interest. Nip this early or it will get worse. Train your child to take responsibility for all he needs to do, not just for what he wants to do.

c) Your administrator's room will be a mess most of the time, unless he has an "important" reason to clean it up. Establish an important reason—because you say so.

d) Administrators love involvement, but often overextend themselves, burning the candle at both ends until they're literally worn out. Help your child set reasonable limitations.

2. Guidelines.

To preclude bossiness, set clear limitations on your administrator's leadership in the family, and on the use of his organizational abilities. It may be fine for him to organize a family picnic, but not his brother's birthday party, unless his brother asks him to.

b) Your administrator thrives on check-off lists, but he won't put on the list the things he doesn't like to do. Insist he include certain tasks, or do it for him. A chore chart can work wonders if you monitor its use.

c) Set a regular timetable by which your child must put his things away at least once a month, or more often, and hold room inspection. If necessary, ground him until he completes the job.

d) You may need to limit the number of organizations he joins, or at least the number in which he takes leadership or specific responsibilities. If he appears overloaded, insist he drop one activity temporarily, but let him choose which one.

3. Prayers.

a) Lord, forgive me for telling my brother to feed the cat when it was my responsibility. Help me to recognize when I have authority to organize people and when I don't. Increase my sensitivity to others as people, and not simply as means to an end.

b) Lord, I know I procrastinate. Forgive me for putting things off. Help me to organize my time better, and to do the things I dislike first, so I can enjoy doing the things I like to do.

c) Lord, I don't mind living in a mess—I know where everything is! But my parents are right: I do need to keep my room neater. Help me to know what to *throw* away so I won't have so much stuff to *put* away. Remind me to spend ten minutes a day cleaning my room to prevent chaos.

d) Lord, I'm overextended again. Show me what I should give up for now. Help me use my time wisely to accomplish more each day. Show me what I can delegate to others, and help me to do first things first.

4. Affirmations.

a) When your administrator quits delegating jobs to his brother, commend him for shouldering his own responsibilities. When he refrains from bossiness, let him know you're proud of him.

b) As he uses his chart to get chores done on schedule, reward him with a "Well done!"

c) When his room passes inspection, express your pleasure. If he keeps it neat, celebrate!

d) When he drops an activity to get his life in order, assure him he's doing the right thing. When he refuses an additional responsibility because he's already too busy, pat him on the back.

THE COMPASSION CHILD'S TYPICAL PROBLEM AREAS

Compassion children are often: easily wounded, overemotional, compromising, indecisive, undependable, late, unrealistic, illogical, and overly empathetic.

1. Goals.

a) Your compassion child is both more emotional and less in control of his emotions than other children. This potentially explosive situation can lead to numerous problems. Help him to gain proper emotional control.

b) Your compassion child may place caring for people and building good relationships ahead of moral, ethical, and spiritual standards, preferring compromise to hurting or losing a friend. Such caring is admirable, but compromising works against his commitment to the Lord.

c) It's hard for him to make decisions: He'd prefer to have others make them for him. But decision-making is part of life, and he must learn. Help him learn to make smaller decisions, then move on to bigger ones. It will be a process.

d) The compassion child has one speed: slow forward. Seemingly unconcerned about time, he is repeatedly late, despite promises to the contrary. Unless he learns to deal with time realistically, this habit will follow him throughout life, to the frustration of everyone around him. Set goals to help him achieve success in this area.

2. Guidelines.

a) Don't allow yourself to be manipulated by your compassion child's emotionalism. Help him to control his emotional reactions and to use reason and logic more.

b) Be sure he understands your family standards and their biblical foundations. Show him why it is more important to please God than his friends. If he has difficulty in a particular area, discuss a plan of action to overcome it.

c) Make a list of decisions he should be old enough to make. Give him decision-making guidelines and discuss alternatives and their consequences. As he matures increase the list to include more important matters. Again discuss guidelines, alternatives, and consequences. Sometimes just knowing the alternatives and their consequences will build his confidence. If he errs, go over the procedure again.

d) Discuss punctuality with your child, and have him work first at the most crucial deadlines: Making the whole family late to church is far worse than being late to meet a friend. Show him how to plan backward, starting with departure time, figuring how long each stage of preparation will take, and arriving at a time to start getting ready. Be realistic. Allow more time rather than less. Extend this plan to all schedule-related areas of his life.

3. Prayers.

a) Lord, please help me to gain control over these strong emotions You have given me. Sometimes it's hard for me to think instead of feel. Help me to understand my feelings, and to react appropriately. Assist me in looking at and accepting my negative emotions, rather than suppressing them.

b) Lord, I sometimes give in to my friends, doing what I think they want me to do. Please teach me to do what's right in Your sight, no matter what others say. I don't want to compromise when it comes to Your will, but I need Your strength and guidance in all I do. Forgive my past compromises, and guide me in the future.

c) Lord, I want to make good decisions, and I appreciate my parents' assistance in learning how. I need Your help, too. Please lead, inspire, and direct me. Sometimes I'm scared, but together we can do it.

d) Lord, I'm sorry I'm always late. But that's going to change. I want to learn to be on time. Help me to think and plan ahead more, and to remember that my lateness imposes on others.

4. Affirmations.

a) As your compassion child works to control his emotions, praise him: He needs continued encouragement. Free him to air his negative feelings in your presence, and don't criticize him for what he feels. Help him to resolve his feelings through prayer and forgiveness.

b) Commend him each time he stands for what he knows is right and refuses to compromise. Remind him the Lord rejoices in him, too.

c) Affirm every good decision he makes. If he makes a poor, but minor, decision, let it go and let him learn from it. If a major decision is off base, ask him to rethink it, and offer any needed guidance.

d) When he's on time, celebrate. Thank him for his effort. Assure him he can continue to have victory over lateness. Recording his successes on a chart with stars or stickers, and perhaps offering a small, non-monetary reward, will encourage him to keep working.

In this chapter we've outlined ways in which you can minister personally to your child. Praying *for* him and *with* him, as well as guiding him in praying, will be exceedingly helpful. We also recommend frequently laying hands on your child's head or shoulders in blessing. Jesus stopped and blessed children. We should, too, especially our own.

If a problem seems unmanageable, call on your pastor or youth leader for help or suggestions. Take advantage of resources available through your church and Christian organizations.

The form at the end of this chapter is designed to help you minister to your children. Design your own specific goals, guidelines, prayers, and affirmations for each child as well as drawing upon our suggestions. Remember, there's no one more important for you to minister to than *your* children!

Six extra copies of the following form are available in the "Forms & Charts Packet" described at the end of the book.

GOALS & GUIDELINES FOR MINISTERING TO YOUR CHILD

CHILD: _____ PRIMARY GIFT: _____ SECONDARY:_____

	A	B	C	D
PROBLEMS:				
1. Goals				
2. Guidelines				
3. Prayers				
4. Affirmations				

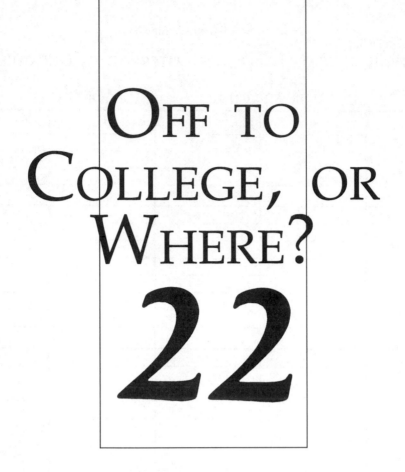

OFF TO COLLEGE, OR WHERE?

22

These days everyone from your insurance agent to your mother-in-law urges you to put away money for your child's college education. But, you wonder, how do I know if my child is college-bound?

We can't predict accurately which of your children will be in college five, ten, or fifteen years from now. But we do know enough about the motivational gifts to tell you some will benefit from advanced academic studies and some won't. Some will pursue technical or professional training. So start your education fund: Regardless of your child's particular bent, it may come in handy.

EIGHT BASIC ROUTES

Young people today follow eight basic routes after graduation from high school.

1. Academic or liberal arts college
2. Business college
3. Fine arts college
4. Bible college
5. Trade, technical, and/or vocational school
6. On-the-job training
7. Military training
8. Homemaking

1. Academic or liberal arts college

Teachers, administrators, perceivers, and exhorters are especially suited to academic life. Some givers and compassion persons pursue academic studies, especially in business administration and areas of social service like nursing. Servers usually are not interested in academic training unless they have as strong secondary gifts one of the four mentioned above.

Teachers and administrators are most prone to seek graduate degrees.

High school guidance counseling offices ordinarily offer a stockpile of catalogues portraying the endless opportunities for study at colleges and universities both here and abroad. These publications explain the differences between standard four-year colleges, two-year community colleges, extension colleges (some offering night and/or correspondence courses), universities (several colleges clustered under one sponsoring umbrella), and smaller, more specialized institutions. State universities and community colleges are sometimes less expensive than private ones. Heavy endowments and generous scholarships at private schools may, however, offset the difference.

Your church or denomination may sponsor or recommend colleges, as well.

2. Business college

Business colleges abound, offering everything from specialized three-month crash courses to four-year bachelor's or master's degrees in business administration. Some have 18- to 24-month associate degrees or 12-month diploma programs.

Servers and givers excel in business colleges, where courses fall under the headings of business or technical training. The former includes accounting, bookkeeping, business administration, computer programming, data entry, financial management, international business, marketing, office administration, secretarial, travel and tourism, and word processing. The latter includes computer repair, correctional officer, dental assisting, electronics technology, medical assisting, robotics, security officer, and veterinary assisting.

Servers and givers are exceptionally gifted in areas requiring good dexterity, a willingness to serve, and a penchant for detail. Givers will do better in the field of business than will persons with any of the other gifts. Administrators may pursue degrees in business administration, and some exhorters or compassion persons may enjoy these fields provided they also involve relating to people.

3. Fine arts college

Compassion persons have capacities for deep feelings and creativity particularly suited to the arts. Still, persons with all seven motivational gifts may be artistically talented. Perceivers will probably outnumber persons with other gifts in drama school. Servers' dexterity equips them to succeed as keyboard musicians.

Some fine arts colleges include the studies of art, music, drama, and dance. Others specialize in just one area. One art institute offers commercial art, commercial photography, fashion merchandising, interior design, music, video business, three-dimensional design, and visual communications. Four fine arts colleges in the United States offer both the performing and visual arts under one roof. One, located in Seattle, offers four-year accredited bachelor of fine arts degrees in art, design, dance, music, theater, and performance production. Entrance requirements include an audition or portfolio review. While about a year of general studies is required, three years are spent on the student's specific field of interest. The admissions director told me the school is not training students to *do* art, but to *be* artists.

4. Bible college

Some time ago the director of a midwestern Bible school called to request enough of our adult testing sets to give to each student. I suggested he would probably find his students to be perceivers, teachers, exhorters, administrators, and givers. "I think you're right," he replied. "We've already tested our teaching staff and they all have the first four gifts you mentioned."

Some servers and compassion persons may attend Bible school intending to enter support ministries, but they usually take technical or trade school training as well. And some young people enroll simply to further their biblical knowledge or to expand their social relationships.

Bible colleges range all the way from simple, nonaccredited courses of study attached to a local church to large, four-year accredited schools. Some are designed to train people specifically for working within a particular denomination; others are intentionally interdenominational. Some focus on training future church leaders; others focus on equipping people for the mission field.

5. Trade, technical, and/or vocational school

Servers, givers, and persons with the gift of compassion are often drawn to trade, technical and/or vocational schools. These institutions offer courses in the fields of applied technology, barbering, hair styling, broadcasting, computer training, construction, cooking, deep sea diving, electronics, floral design, insurance, interior design, iron working, language, modeling, nautical, shorthand, real estate, teller training, and travel. Often listed in the pages of your local telephone directory, these range all the way from crash sessions, ten to twelve weeks in length, to training programs lasting several years. All involve hands-on experience.

A new breed of vocational school has appeared in recent years to offer intensive short-term training, usually eight hours a day or four hours a night for ten to twelve weeks. These courses are extremely practical, often covering business, medical assistance, office automation, or computer skills, and even assist to some degree in job placement. The administrator of such a school told me, "We exist primarily for people in distress situations—the young person who has to find a job quickly or the older adult forced back into the work force by death, divorce, or the loss of another job."

6. On-the-job training

Many businesses prefer to train their own people, thus ensuring employees who do things the company's way. Some firms expect employees to demonstrate basic skills like typing or word processing, or require previous technical or business school training. Persons with any of the gifts could benefit from or succeed in on-the-job training situations.

Aspiring electricians or plumbers must serve as apprentices for two to four years under an electrician or plumber already certified by the state. After completing this requirement they must pass a certification test given by the state's Department of Labor and Industry. Apprenticing is not required for would-be contractors, but on-the-job training is recommended.

Servers, with their tremendous dexterity, do very well in these fields, and so do givers. Administrators who enter these fields usually aim for supervisory or administrative positions.

7. Military training

Exceptional opportunities for a broad spectrum of occupational training await men and women of every motivational gifting in the military. As opposed to civilian sector experiences, these are free, except for a time commitment of three to eight years, depending on the program. As one recruiter said, "This is a wonderful way for young people to get training and to mature quickly as well. The pay is equal to or better than pay for comparable civilian jobs, and the benefits are exceptional."

Another recruiter pointed to the possibility of college attendance during military service, at a college extension on base, at a local college, or by correspondence.

"Depending on the program, the service pays up to 75 percent of the tuition and in some cases even more," he explained. "And various versions of the GI Bill assist with college education after the term of service. The Reserve Program also makes provision for funding college educations."

Military travel options also broaden and mature service personnel as well as enabling them to see the world. Our niece Sharon ran Navy Exchanges in such diverse places as Japan, Washington, DC, Guam, and Bermuda.

Inquire through the recruiting offices of the Army, Navy, Air Force, Marines, and National Guard.

8. Homemaking

Women servers, compassion women, and some who are givers and exhorters often find complete fulfillment in homemaking. But women with gifts of perception, teaching, and administration almost always feel the need for additional stimulation beyond their home responsibilities. That's fine, provided parenting responsibilities are not neglected. No one can do for a child what his own mother and father can. Our greatest investments of time, love, and energy should be in our children.

Since we live in an era when young couples often need more than one income to make ends meet, a young woman should have some marketable skills, developed during high school, in evening classes, or through some of the routes mentioned earlier in this chapter. Our daughter, Linda, assembled pigtails for trailers at home, while embarking into motherhood. Another young mother earned enough before marriage to buy a home computer. Now she types college papers and manuscripts to supplement her husband's income. Several women in our church do home childcare while their own children are young.

In my own case (administrator/teacher) I found my life more fulfilled when I worked part-time at home while the boys were small. For three years I wrote Sunday school curricula for two publishers, the boys playing at my feet as I pounded the typewriter. I had a creative outlet, *and* consistent time with our children.

Not until our youngest went into first grade did I begin working a six-hour day, right in our own garage. The *Aglow Magazine* birthed on our dining room table had expanded to a volunteer staff of 25 women. I walked fifty feet to work after Dan and Dave left for school. I was finished and in the kitchen to greet them when they returned.

Even when the job demanded my full-time attention we'd moved the publications office to a new house on the other side of our cul-de-sac, so my walk was only a hundred feet. I could slip home to feed the kids after-school snacks and listen to their accounts of the day's activities. Don came home about the same time, so I could go back and finish up the day's work.

When the office moved a mile away it was more difficult. I missed the time with Don and the boys, and eventually decided to resign my job. I'm glad I did. I wouldn't have missed those years at home for anything. I was able to put my writing skills to work at home again, enjoy our teenage boys, and attend all their after-school sports events. I was there to feed the whole football team if it dropped in. It was as important to be there for our boys then as when they were small.

MOTIVATIONAL GIFTS & JOBS

Teenagers and young adults frequently ask us, "How do I relate my motivational gift scores to a potential career or job choice?" The remainder of this chapter relates the gifts to 180 of the most common careers and jobs. If your son or daughter does not find his special interest on the list, he can probably find similar ones and draw appropriate conclusions from the comparison. But first, let's look at some general guidelines for determining how likely he is to succeed and find fulfillment in a potential—or presently held—job or career. Give this material to your son or daughter to read and fill out.

YOUR BUILT-IN TRAITS

God's motivational gifting has endowed you with certain built-in traits or operating modes. Using these traits gives you satisfaction and a feeling of accomplishment. When you consider a particular job or career, ask yourself the following question: To what degree will it enable me to do what I am motivated to do?

To assist you in answering this question we have prepared the following lists indicating the built-in traits of persons with each motivational gift. Scan the items listed under your primary gift—and your secondary gift if it's a strong one—and check off all the things you would be able to do in a given job. If you check many items, you probably will be happy and successful in that work. If you check only a few, you are probably unsuited for it. Recognizing in advance whether or not you will enjoy a job could save you from untold frustration.

Statistics indicate two out of every three people are dissatisfied with their present jobs. How sad for so many people to spend their working years in employment that fails to utilize their motivational gifts and bring them joy.

God wills our occupational fulfillment. Adam may have been placed under the "curse" of work, but Jesus has set us free to *enjoy* it! Our motivational gifts should bless us and bless others.

MOTIVATIONAL GIFT OF PERCEPTION

admonish	defend	judge
advocate	discipline	negotiate
advise	dramatize	overcome
analyze	enforce	persevere
assess	evaluate	persuade
caution	evoke	preach
challenge	expose	prevail
change	forewarn	proclaim
combat	identify	reveal
convict	impact	solve
convince	inspire	strengthen
correct	intercede	urge
decide	moralize	warn

MOTIVATIONAL GIFT OF SERVING

assemble	fix	meet needs
assist	follow	minister
be useful	follow up	obey
carry through	fulfill expectations	operate
carry out plans	handle	perfect
build	help	persist
complete	host	produce
construct	implement	repair
detail	maintain	run effectively
develop	make	serve
do	make effective	tend
entertain guests	make work	wait on
finish	master	work for

MOTIVATIONAL GIFTS OF TEACHING

____analyze
____communicate
____comprehend
____discipline
____discover
____edit
____educate
____enlighten
____establish truth
____evaluate
____examine
____experiment
____expound

____figure out
____formulate
____improve
____inspire
____instruct
____interpret
____interview
____investigate
____learn
____lecture
____observe
____present truth
____publish

____recommend
____research
____search
____solve
____study
____systematize
____teach
____theorize
____train
____tutor
____use logic
____validate
____write

MOTIVATIONAL GIFT OF EXHORTATION

____achieve potential
____admonish
____advise
____advocate
____assure
____build up
____coach
____communicate
____convince
____counsel
____cultivate
____demonstrate
____develop

____direct
____edify
____endure
____encourage
____entreat
____exhort
____expound
____explain
____foster
____gain response
____give opinions
____guide
____improve

____influence
____inspire
____instruct
____modify
____motivate
____persuade
____prescribe
____relate
____stimulate
____strengthen
____talk
____teach (practical)
____urge

MOTIVATIONAL GIFT OF GIVING

____accommodate
____acquire
____advocate
____aid
____assist
____back up
____bargain
____benefit
____bless
____bolster
____budget
____contribute
____corroborate
____develop
____donate
____encourage

____endow
____entertain
____espouse
____evangelize
____expedite
____furnish
____gain
____give
____grant
____host
____help
____improve
____invent
____invest
____improvise
____make better

____modify
____multiply assets
____patronize
____perform
____proclaim
____procure
____prompt
____rescue
____share
____shore up
____succeed
____supply
____support
____sustain
____testify
____witness

MOTIVATIONAL GIFT OF ADMINISTRATION

_____achieve
_____accomplish
_____administrate
_____attain
_____authorize
_____be challenged
_____be in charge
_____be responsible
_____build
_____command
_____communicate
_____conduct
_____control
_____coordinate
_____create
_____delegate

_____develop
_____design
_____envision
_____establish
_____excel
_____explore
_____facilitate
_____govern
_____guide
_____handle projects
_____influence
_____initiate
_____instigate
_____lead
_____operate
_____organize

_____oversee
_____motivate
_____pioneer
_____plan
_____preside
_____proceduralize
_____promote
_____put together
_____rule
_____schedule
_____set goals
_____shape
_____shoulder
_____strategize
_____supervise
_____visualize

MOTIVATIONAL GIFT OF COMPASSION

_____accept
_____accommodate
_____affirm
_____assist
_____assure
_____avoid hurting
_____be gentle
_____be thoughtful
_____befriend
_____bring together
_____build relationships
_____build up
_____care for
_____cheer up
_____cherish
_____condole

_____comfort
_____compassionate
_____console
_____crusade
_____defer to
_____empathize
_____feel
_____forgive
_____give preference
_____heal
_____harmonize
_____help
_____intercede
_____look after
_____love
_____nurse

_____nurture
_____promote unity
_____relieve distress
_____relieve hurts
_____renew
_____repair hearts
_____rescue
_____respond
_____restore
_____serve
_____show kindness
_____show mercy
_____support
_____sustain
_____sympathize
_____trust

Apply these criteria when you are asked to help with a project, program, or task in your church, as well as in the selection of an appropriate ministry or volunteer work.

Now let's look at specific jobs and careers.

YOUR OCCUPATIONAL PROBABILITIES

The following charts list 180 career and job possibilities, indicating to what degree we feel each motivational gift would cause a person fulfillment and success in these fields. We hope these *opinions*, based on fifteen years of research and working with people in the area of the motivational gifts, will help you as you seek God's will for your life's work.

Remember, many other factors besides giftedness contribute to a person's success in any field: talents, special abilities, training, education, background, emotional stability, dependability, commitment, and adaptability. A person with little gifting in an area may succeed because of his eagerness to learn and apply himself. A person with considerable gifting in the same area may fail because of poor attitude, laziness, indifference, or unwillingness to make a nine-to-five commitment.

Some fields are so broad anyone can utilize his motivational gifts effectively. A look at writing careers demonstrates this point.

When I taught at a Billy Graham Writers' Conference my goal was not only to help writers discover their motivational gifts but to identify the various kinds of writing in which they might succeed.

Writers who are *perceivers* excel in high-pressure jobs such as news reporting and editing. They make good drama critics, probing interviewers, and challenging editorialists. Strictly interested in nonfiction, their writing is persuasive, highly opinionated, and often blunt. Their articles and books deal with good and evil, spiritual principles, politics, prophecy, prayer, character development, and spiritual growth.

Servers are unhappy in high-stress jobs or in leadership positions, but do well as editorial assistants, copy editors, or rewriters. They are supportive staff persons and are good at proofreading and detailed writing. Servers like to write fiction, poetry, and children's literature. They author excellent articles and short books dealing with the practical application of Christian principles, how-to subjects, and self-help ideas.

Teachers excel in almost every area of writing and make the finest editors and nonfiction book authors. They work well under stress and within schedules. Top-notch curriculum and Bible study writers, they do well on any biblical subject, loving research and often including generous amounts of information. They are good at writing about education, religion, science, medicine, history, and law. They write probing editorials, excellent descriptive pieces, textbooks, or research books. They are top-notch investigative reporters, and may also make good playwrights and superb poets.

Exhorters excel in writing anything with a self-help or how-to approach. Their writing is practical, encouraging, and often drawn from their own experience, focusing on people, not facts, places, or things. Among the most prolific and exceptionally readable of writers, they craft true-life stories, inspirational pieces, how-to articles and books, testimonies, advice columns, biographies, humor, poetry, and articles on counseling, psychology, ministry, interpersonal relationships—anything life-related.

246

Givers are so well-rounded they are able to write on a wide range of subjects and handle a variety of jobs. They make especially good editors or publishers and don't mind ghostwriting. They write both fiction and nonfiction, focusing on business, success, evangelism, and missionary endeavors.

Administrators also make excellent editors or publishers, and succeed in other management positions. Bored with copy editing or routine writing assignments, they'd rather pioneer. Their area is nonfiction, covering broad subjects comprehensively. Their material is well-organized and very readable. Freelancers will find disciplining themselves to "office hours" at the typewriter (or computer) a challenge because of their desire to interact with people. Routine writing tasks will be delegated to others, if possible.

Compassion people are the most creative of writers, focusing on fiction, from true confessions to science fantasies. Their children's stories, devotionals, and poetry are exceptionally well-done, as are their articles and books dealing with feelings, human interest episodes, interpersonal relationships, animals, inspiration, and overcoming handicaps. Not fond of research or heavy nonfiction, they are not suited to newspaper or magazine jobs unless these involve strictly human interest writing.

So, persons with each gift can find niches in the field of writing, and this applies to many other careers as well!

We have placed a plus sign (+) immediately following each of these something-for-everyone occupations in our list.

HOW TO SCORE

Here's how we've coded the 180 occupations.

If success in a job is *highly unlikely* for a person with a particular motivational gift (because it would not use his natural motivations, or because the demands of the job exceed his gift's capabilities), we gave the job a *minus sign* (−) in the column under the gift.

If success is *not likely*, but other factors (like a strong secondary gift) could enable him to enjoy this kind of work, we coded the job by leaving the *space blank*.

If success is *possible*, especially with other positive factors entering in, we coded it with an *asterisk* (*).

If success is *very possible*—if the person's motivational gift would be an asset in the job—we coded it with *two asterisks* (**).

If success is *highly probable*—if the person's motivational gift is especially suited to the job, and he would excel and be fulfilled—we coded it with *three asterisks* (***).

To score your probability for success circle all the three-star (***) and two-star (**) codes under your primary motivational gift. If you have a strong secondary gift, do the same in its column. Then place a check mark in front of all the occupations thus identified. Look to see which jobs have the highest number of stars. Write those occupations (except for ones you already know do not interest you) in the spaces provided at the end of the chapter. You can choose a career confidently from among these options knowing you are well-gifted for top performance in any of them.

If you've circled three-star codes on occupations beneath both your primary and secondary gifts, those careers would be among the best you could follow. Three-star and two-star codes lining up the same way also indicate probable success in a career.

Here's the scoring at a glance:

—	highly unlikely
(blank)	not likely
*	possible
**	very possible
***	highly probable

Now, record the occupations in which you have the highest number of stars. Remember, these "success probabilities" are just guidelines and suggestions. Take into consideration factors such as training, influences, circumstances, opportunities, anointing, interest, and talent; these would affect your success in any occupation. Talk with your parents, your school counselor, and persons in your prospective fields about your motivational gifts as they relate to career choice.

Most importantly seek the Lord's guidance, committing the choice (or change) of your vocation to Him. He created and gifted you, and He can reveal His specific plan for your life.

MY LIST OF OCCUPATIONAL POSSIBILITIES

1. _____
2. _____
3. _____
4. _____
5. _____
6. _____
7. _____
8. _____
9. _____
10. _____

	Perceiver	*Server*	*Teacher*	*Exhorter*	*Giver*	*Administrator*	*Compassion person*
accountant	**	***	*		***	—	
actor	***	*	—	*	***		*
advertising executive	*	—	**	***	**	***	—
agricultural worker	*	***			**	—	*
air traffic controller	***	**	**	*	*	***	—
airplane pilot	***	*	**	**	*	***	
ambassador	***	*	**	***	*	***	*
anthropologist	*	*	***	**	*	**	**
archaeologist	*	*	***	*	*	**	**
architect	**	***	**	*	*	**	
artist +	*	**	*	*	*	*	***
assembly line worker		***	—		**	—	*
astronomer	**	*	***	*	*	**	*
auctioneer	*	*		***	**	*	—
auditor	**	***	**	*	***	*	
automobile dealer		*		**	**	**	
bank teller	*	***	*	*	***	*	*
banker	**	*	*	*	***	**	
barber/beautician		***		*	**		***
biologist	*	*	***	*	*	**	*
bookkeeper	*	***	*		***		
botanist	*	**	***	*	**	*	**
builder	*	***	*	*	**	**	*
bus driver		***		*	**		*
business consultant	**	*	*	*	***	**	—
business owner +	**	*	**	**	***	***	
buyer	**	*	**	*	***	**	
cashier/checker		***		*	**		**

	Perceiver	Server	Teacher	Exhorter	Giver	Administrator	Compassion person
carpenter	*	***		*	***		*
chemist	**	*	***	*	*	**	
childcare provider	*	***		**	**		***
chiropractor	**	*	***	**	*	**	*
city planner	**	—	**	**	*	***	—
civil servant +	*	***	*	**	**	*	**
clerk	*	***	—	*	***	—	**
college professor	**		***	**	*	***	
conductor (music)	*		**	*		***	**
composer +	*	*	***	**	*	**	***
commercial artist	*	**	*	*	*	**	***
computer operator		***	*	*	***		**
computer programmer	*	***	***	*	***	**	
cook	*	***		*	**	*	**
conservationist	**	**	**	**	*	**	***
contractor	**	*	*	**	***	***	
criminologist	***	*	**	**	*	**	—
curator	*	*	***		*	**	
dental hygienist		***		*	**		*
dentist	**	*	**	**	*	*	
department store manager	**		**	**	**	***	
dietitian	**	**	*	**	*	*	**
dock worker		***	—	*	**	—	
doctor +	**	*	***	**	**	**	**
economist	*	*	**	*	***	**	
electrician	*	***		*	***	—	*
engineer	**	*	***	**	*	**	
evangelist	**	*		**	***	*	*
farmer	*	***			***	*	**

	Perceiver	Server	Teacher	Exhorter	Giver	Administrator	Compassion person
fashion designer		**		*	**	*	***
firefighter	*	***		*	**		*
fisherman		***	—	*	**	—	*
flight attendant	*	***		*	**	*	**
florist		**		*	**		***
forest ranger	*	***		*	**		**
funeral director	*	**		*	**		*
geographer	*	***	**	*	*	*	*
geologist	**	**	***		**	*	
guidance counselor	***	*	**	***	*	***	**
heavy equipment operator		***		*	**		
home economist	*	**	*	**	**	*	***
hospital administrator	**		**	**	*	***	
hotel manager	**		**	**	*	***	
industrial designer	*	***	**	*	**	*	
inspector	***	*	**	*	*	**	
interior decorator	*	***	*	*	**	*	***
investment fund manager	**		**	**	***	**	
janitor		***	—	*	**	—	**
journalist +	**	*	***	**	*	***	*
judge	***		**	*	*	***	—
landscaper		***		**	***		*
lawyer	***		**	*	*	***	—
librarian	*	***	***	*	**		**
licensed practical nurse	*	***		**	**		***
life insurance agent	***	*	*	**	***	**	*
manufacturer	**	*	*	*	***	**	
market researcher/analyst	***	*	***	**	*	***	*
marketing executive	**		*	**	**	***	

	Perceiver	Server	Teacher	Exhorter	Giver	Administrator	Compassion person
mason		***		*	***		*
mathematician	**	***	***	*	**	**	*
mechanic	*	***		*	***		*
mechanical drawing	*	***	*	*	**		**
medical technologist	**	**	***	**	**	*	*
metalworker		***		*	***		*
meteorologist	*	**	***	*	**	**	*
military officer	***		**	**	*	***	
miner	*	***			***		*
minister +	***	**	***	***	**	***	**
missionary +	***	**	**	**	***	**	***
model		**		**	*		***
musician +	*	**	**	*	**	*	***
nurse (RN) +	*	**	*	*	**	*	***
nutritionist	**	**	***	*	**	*	***
occupational therapist	*	**	*	***	**	*	***
oceanographer	*	**	***	*	**	*	*
office worker	*	***		*	***		***
optometrist	**	*	***	**	*	**	*
paramedic	***	**	**	**	***	*	*
personnel manager	*		*	***		***	*
pet groomer		***		*	**		***
performing artist +	**	*	*	**	**	*	***
pharmacist	*	**	***	*	**	*	**
philosopher	***		***	*	*	**	***
photographer	*	**	*	*	**	*	***
physical therapist	*	**	*	*	**		***
physician +	**	*	***	**	**	***	**
physicist	**		***	*		**	

Off to College, or Where?

	Perceiver	Server	Teacher	Exhorter	Giver	Administrator	Compassion person
plumber		***		*	**		*
politician	**	*	*	**	*	***	
postman		***		**	**		*
printer	*	**	*	*	**	**	*
professional housecleaner		***		*	**		**
proofreader	*	*	***	*	*	**	*
psychiatrist	**	*	***	***	*	**	*
psychologist	**		***	***		**	*
public administrator	**		**	**	*	***	
public relations director	*		*	***	*	***	*
purchasing agent	*	**	*	*	**	**	
radio/TV announcer	*		*	***	*	**	
radio/TV producer	**		**	**	*	***	
railroad engineer	*	**		*	**		
realtor	*	*	*	***	***	**	*
receptionist		***		***	**		**
recreation director	*	*		***	**	***	*
religious education director	**		**	***	*	***	*
reporter	***	*	***	**	*	***	*
research scientist	**	*	***		*	**	
researcher	**	*	***		*	**	
restaurant manager	**	*	*	**	**	***	
retailer +	**	*	*	**	***	**	
salesman	**	*	*	**	***	***	
school administrator	**		***	**	*	***	
scientist +	***	*	***	*	*	**	*
seamstress/tailor	*	***			**		**
secretary	*	***		*	***		**
shipbuilder	*	***		*	**		*

	Perceiver	Server	Teacher	Exhorter	Giver	Administrator	Compassion person
social worker	*	*		***	**	*	***
sociologist +	**	*	**	***	**	**	**
speech therapist		**	**	***	*	*	***
statistician	*	***	**	*	**	*	*
surgeon	*	***	***	*	*	**	
surveyor	*	***		*	**	*	*
systems analyst	***	**	**	*	**	**	
taxidermist		***			*		*
teacher (art)	*	**	**	*	*	*	***
teacher (business ed.)	*	***	*	**	***	*	**
teacher (drama)	***		**	**	*	*	***
teacher (elementary) +	*	*	*	**	**	*	***
teacher (English)	*	*	***	*	*	*	**
teacher (foreign language)	*	*	***	*	**	*	*
teacher (home economics)	*	**	*	**	*	*	***
teacher (history)	**	*	***	**	*	**	*
teacher (mathematics)	*	**	***	*	**	*	*
teacher (music) +	*	*	**	*	*	*	***
teacher (physical ed.)	*	*		***	**	***	
teacher (science)	***	*	***	*	**	**	*
teacher (social studies)	**	*	**	***	**	**	***
teacher (special ed.)	*	*	***	***	**	**	***
technician	*	***	**	*	***	*	*
telephone operator		***		*	**	*	***
theologian	***		***	*	*	***	
toolmaker		***			***		*
travel agent	*	*	*	***	***	***	*
truck driver	*	***		*	***		**
waiter/waitress		***		**	***		***

Off to College, or Where?

	Perceiver	Server	Teacher	Exhorter	Giver	Administrator	Compassion person
welder	*	***			***		**
wholesaler	*			*	***	***	
writer +	**	*	***	***	*	***	**
veterinarian		**			**	*	***
zookeeper		***			**		***
zoologist	*	***	**	*	**	**	***
X-ray technician	*	***		*	**		**

MARRIAGE: DO OPPOSITE GIFTS ATTRACT?

23

If your children are old enough to marry, or approaching that stage, you may wonder what impact the motivational gifts have on dating and marriage. Do opposite gifts attract? What if two persons with the same gift marry? What problems would crop up in either case? Concerned parents will consider these questions and discuss them with their children.

OPPOSITE GIFTS ATTRACT

Yes, opposite gifts usually attract in marriage. One spouse frequently has a speaking-type gift and the other has a serving-type gift. Or, a perceiver is attracted to a compassion person, a teacher to an exhorter, a server to an administrator—in all cases, seemingly opposite gifts.

Yes, these mates' opposite characteristics can pose significant challenges. But they may also complement one another nicely, with the advantages outweighing the disadvantages. Their levels of maturity and godliness will determine the outcome.

About 95 percent of the time people choose mates with motivational gifts different from their own. About five percent marry someone with the same gift. If the latter are mature for their ages, their similarities can be an asset; if they are immature, their problem areas will be amplified.

KNOW YOUR MATE'S MOTIVATIONAL GIFTS

We plan to write a whole book on this subject but let us emphasize one point: Many marriage conflicts and stresses will fade away when mates know and accept each other's motivational gifts.

Take Tim and Darlene. Tim, a boat builder by trade, is quiet, easily moved to tears, and easily swayed in the stands he takes. He likes to work with his hands. Darlene is outgoing, highly opinionated, unmovable in her standards, and drawn to a ministry of prayer.

At first they clashed often. Darlene got upset at Tim's apparent wishy-washiness and changeability. He disliked her dogmatic, unbending ways and was easily hurt by her outspokenness.

Then the motivational gift test revealed Darlene was a perceiver and Tim was a compassion person. Almost immediately their relationship improved. Darlene realized she needed to pray more and comment less. She began to appreciate her husband's sensitivity and gentleness as beautiful gifts from the Lord, and understood Tim could hear from God, too.

Tim realized Darlene's giftedness was from the Lord and learned to value, rather than be threatened by, her strong standards and ideas. He saw it was acceptable for her to be the more verbal of the two.

In encouraging each other's gifts instead of resisting them, Darlene and Tim began to see differences as assets. They have become one of the most loving and spiritually mature couples we know. "I realized if both of us were alike," Darlene said, "one of us wouldn't be needed."

Marriage partners, engaged persons, and young people who are dating seriously should consider each other's motivational gifts! If your child fits one of these situations, give him this book and have him analyze his giftedness and his spouse's, fiancee's or "steady's" giftedness as provided in the following chart. If possible they should work on it together, supporting each other as they seek changes in their own lives and in their relationship. Their broadened understandings of each other and consequent acceptance of each other's gifts will bring about new unity in their relationship, or, in premarital situations, could lead them to reconsider the wisdom of their choices.

IMPROVE YOUR RELATIONSHIPS

Use the following chart to help you gain insight into your mate's or potential mate's personality. If you have not already done so, be sure to take the youth or adult motivational gifts test. Refer to chapter 6 to help pinpoint your problem areas from the five problem characteristics of both your primary and secondary gifts. We've also listed some typical problem areas of each gift below:

Perceivers are often: strong-willed, judgmental, blunt, opinionated, intolerant, too idealistic, critical, prideful, domineering, controlling, pushy, unforgiving, loners, and plagued with poor self-images.

GIFTEDNESS IN MARRIAGE
POTENTIAL PROBLEMS AND POTENTIAL SOLUTIONS

HIS GIFTS:_____

          (primary gift)   (secondary gift)

HER GIFTS:_____

          (primary gift)   (secondary gift)

HIS POTENTIAL PROBLEMS:	POSSIBLE SOLUTIONS:

HER POTENTIAL PROBLEMS:	POSSIBLE SOLUTIONS:

OUR POTENTIAL PROBLEMS:	POSSIBLE SOLUTIONS:

OUR POTENTIAL ADVANTAGES:

Servers are often: easily embarrassed, overly shy, perfectionists, critical, interfering, and overdependent on appreciation.

Teachers are often: prideful, intolerant, legalistic, dogmatic, opinionated, unfriendly, aloof, prone to emit know-it-all attitudes.

Exhorters are often: opinionated, interruptive, compromising, overtalkative, pushy, found stretching the truth, and prone to give unsolicited advice.

Givers are often: stingy, too focused on money, tempted to steal, too frugal, manipulative, overworkers, and too generous.

Administrators are often: bossy, domineering, insensitive, callous, procrastinating, forgetful, messy, overzealous, overextended, and neglectful of routine work.

Compassion persons are: easily wounded, overemotional, compromising, indecisive, undependable, late, unrealistic, illogical, and overly empathetic.

Next we offer examples of gift-related potential problems and advantages sometimes found in marriage relationships. In each case the man's gift is listed first and the woman's second, except with identical gifts, in which case the positions are interchangeable. Take special note of examples fitting your marital gift combinations for other hints of possible conflict.

1. PERCEIVER (husband and wife)
   a) Potential problem: Conflicts over who's "right."
   b) Potential advantage: Both have strict standards.
2. PERCEIVER (husband)—SERVER (wife)
   a) Potential problem: Bossy, treats her like a servant.
   b) Potential advantage: Honest and loyal to her.
3. PERCEIVER (husband)—TEACHER (wife)
   a) Potential problem: Threatened by her opinions.
   b) Potential advantage: Both love to study the Word.
4. PERCEIVER (husband)—EXHORTER (wife)
   a) Potential problem: Irritation over her talkativeness.
   b) Potential advantage: Her gregariousness modifies his reclusiveness.
5. PERCEIVER (husband)—GIVER (wife)
   a) Potential problem: Controls her ability to give.
   b) Potential advantage: Joint intercessory prayer power.
6. PERCEIVER (husband)—ADMINISTRATOR (wife)
   a) Potential problem: Intimidates and squelches her leadership potential.
   b) Potential advantage: Her practical and organized approach balances his idealism.
7. PERCEIVER (husband)— COMPASSION (wife)
   a) Potential problem: Tendency to hurt her feelings.
   b) Potential advantage: Both sensitive to needs of others.
8. SERVER (husband)—PERCEIVER (wife)
   a) Potential problem: Tendency to feel overwhelmed by her strong personality.
   b) Potential advantage: Both are perfectionists in their own way.

9. SERVER (husband and wife)
   a) Potential problem: Try to outdo each other at serving, becoming competitive.
   b) Potential advantage: Work exceptionally well together as a team.
10. SERVER (husband)—TEACHER (wife)
   a) Potential problem: He resents her lack of practical helpfulness.
   b) Potential advantage: Opposite traits of doing (husband), and thinking (wife), balance each other.
11. SERVER (husband)—EXHORTER (wife)
   a) Potential problem: His interest in things conflicts with her interest in people.
   b) Potential advantage: She helps to draw him into social activities he'd otherwise miss.
12. SERVER (husband)—GIVER (wife)
   a) Potential problem: Need to do and to feel appreciated makes both partners insecure.
   b) Potential advantage: Helpful to each other and to everyone around them.
13. SERVER (husband)—ADMINISTRATOR (wife)
   a) Potential problem: He feels threatened by her leadership ability.
   b) Potential advantage: He's able to carry out effectively projects she initiates.
14. SERVER (husband)—COMPASSION (wife)
   a) Potential problem: His high energy level conflicts with her slowness and tardiness.
   b) Potential advantage: Both are gentle in spirit.
15. TEACHER (husband)—PERCEIVER (wife)
   a) Potential problem: Frustration over her emotional mood swings.
   b) Potential advantage: Both are highly analytical.
16. TEACHER (husband)—SERVER (wife)
   a) Potential problem: His intellectual emphasis makes her feel inferior.
   b) Potential advantage: She's glad to care for routine responsibilities while he reads or studies.
17. TEACHER (husband and wife)
   a) Potential problem: Differences in opinions easily become arguments.
   b) Potential advantage: Both love to read books.
18. TEACHER (husband)—EXHORTER (wife)
   a) Potential problem: Disagreements over how truth is arrived at cause friction.
   b) Potential advantage: Both love to talk.
19. TEACHER (husband)—GIVER (wife)
   a) Potential problem: He's threatened by her better business ability.
   b) Potential advantage: Both enjoy reading.
20. TEACHER (husband)—ADMINISTRATOR (wife)
   a) Potential problem: He gets upset with her procrastination and clutter.
   b) Potential advantage: Both enjoy learning.
21. TEACHER (husband)—COMPASSION (wife)
   a) Potential problem: His frustration with her illogical, irrational behavior.

b) Potential advantage: She compensates for his shyness in social situations.

22. EXHORTER (husband)—PERCEIVER (wife)
    a) Potential problem: He feels her perceptions are personal criticisms of him.
    b) Potential advantage: He encourages her in having broader social relationships.

23. EXHORTER (husband)—SERVER (wife)
    a) Potential problem: His talkativeness overwhelms her, causing further reserve.
    b) Potential advantage: She enjoys hostessing his many friends.

24. EXHORTER (husband)—TEACHER (wife)
    a) Potential problem: His frustration over her disinterest in social relationships.
    b) Potential advantage: He helps her to be more life-related and people-related.

25. EXHORTER (husband and wife)
    a) Potential problem: Competitiveness in talking.
    b) Potential advantage: Encouraging each other constantly.

26. EXHORTER (husband)—GIVER (wife)
    a) Potential problem: He resents her overemphasis on money.
    b) Potential advantage: Both enjoy many friends.

27. EXHORTER (husband)—ADMINISTRATOR (wife)
    a) Potential problem: He gets upset with her procrastination.
    b) Potential advantage: Both love being around lots of people.

28. EXHORTER (husband)—COMPASSION (wife)
    a) Potential problem: His frustration over her indecisiveness.
    b) Potential advantage: Both are great counselors.

29. GIVER (husband)—PERCEIVER (wife)
    a) Potential problem: He resents her telling him whom not to trust in business relationships.
    b) Potential advantage: Both are very honest.

30. GIVER (husband)—SERVER (wife)
    a) Potential problem: She's upset when he gives away things without consulting her.
    b) Potential advantage: Both are easygoing.

31. GIVER (husband)—TEACHER (wife)
    a) Potential problem: His focus on business conflicts with her interest in education.
    b) Potential advantage: Both operate diligently.

32. GIVER (husband)—EXHORTER (wife)
    a) Potential problem: He feels she wastes too much time on the phone and socializing.
    b) Potential advantage: He's a good provider, freeing her to help others with their problems.

33. GIVER (husband and wife)
    a) Potential problem: Their frugality can turn into stinginess.
    b) Potential advantage: Both enjoy offering help as well as gifts to others.

34. GIVER (husband)—ADMINISTRATOR (wife)
    a) Potential problem: He resents her telling him what to do, especially regarding business matters.
    b) Potential advantage: They can work together in business, but only if she submits to his authority.
35. GIVER (husband)—COMPASSION (wife)
    a) Potential problem: His frustration over her lack of industriousness and punctuality.
    b) Potential advantage: Both enjoy building interpersonal relationships.
36. ADMINISTRATOR (husband)—PERCEIVER (wife)
    a) Potential problem: He's upset when she judges his actions or decisions.
    b) Potential advantage: Both enjoy competition.
37. ADMINISTRATOR (husband)—SERVER (wife)
    a) Potential problem: He takes her for granted, forgetting to express appreciation.
    b) Potential advantage: She's glad to carry out his directions.
38. ADMINISTRATOR (husband)—TEACHER (wife)
    a) Potential problem: He resents her focus on reading and learning instead of on him.
    b) Potential advantage: Both are achievers.
39. ADMINISTRATOR (husband)—EXHORTER (wife)
    a) Potential problem: He saves everything; she throws away items with no more practical use.
    b) Potential advantage: They make a great team, working together with complementary characteristics.
40. ADMINISTRATOR (husband)—GIVER (wife)
    a) Potential problem: His bossiness offends her.
    b) Potential advantage: She's supportive of his projects.
41. ADMINISTRATOR (husband and wife)
    a) Potential problem: Organizational ideas conflict.
    b) Potential advantage: Harmonious relationship if individual areas of authority are clearly defined.
42. ADMINISTRATOR (husband)—COMPASSION (wife)
    a) Potential problem: He's perplexed by her emotional reactions.
    b) Potential advantage: He helps to keep her relatively organized and on schedule.
43. COMPASSION (husband)—PERCEIVER (wife)
    a) Potential problem: He often feels she dominates him.
    b) Potential advantage: He can soften her personality.
44. COMPASSION (husband)—SERVER (wife)
    a) Potential problem: They let others take advantage of them too often.
    b) Potential advantage: They do not criticize each other.
45. COMPASSION (husband)—TEACHER (wife)
    a) Potential problem: Difficult communication based on feeling/thinking differences.
    b) Potential advantage: Both enjoy the arts.

46. COMPASSION (husband)—EXHORTER (wife)
   a) Potential problem: He feels threatened by her decision-making abilities.
   b) Potential advantage: Very loving to each other.
47. COMPASSION (husband)—GIVER (wife)
   a) Potential problem: He resents her superior ability to handle finances.
   b) Potential advantage: They are very helpful to each other.
48. COMPASSION (husband)—ADMINISTRATOR (wife)
   a) Potential problem: He feels pressured by her organizational abilities.
   b) Potential advantage: He helps her focus more on personal relationships, instead of too much on achievements.
49. COMPASSION (husband and wife)
   a) Potential problem: Indecisiveness and lack of motivation.
   b) Potential advantage: Tremendous capacity to show love to one another.

Now list your actual or potential problems on the chart. Then list your spouse's. List conflicts you presently experience and ones that could logically develop between the two of you. Finally, jot down possible solutions. Consider how the understanding of your respective gifts can overcome problems and conflicts. Discuss needed changes in attitudes or actions. If the problems are deeper than you can handle, seek sound advice from your parents, your pastor, or a counselor.

Ask the Lord to guide you as you seek solutions. Remember, *you cannot change anyone else*, but *you can change yourself, your viewpoints, your attitudes, and actions*.

Next, look again at the list of combinations appearing earlier in this chapter and see what potential advantages your partnership might yield. Add others you already recognize. Appreciate and cultivate the dynamic possibilities of your gifts in your relationship.

HOW TO LEAD YOUR LOVED ONE TO THE LORD

Many young people fall in love and think they will lead an unsaved spouse to the Lord *after* the wedding. It's possible, but the statistics are against it. Your spouse will be ten times *less* likely to make a commitment to Christ after marriage.

Don't be unequally yoked. Lead your loved one to the Lord *before* you marry. With today's pressures and compromised values, a strong Christian foundation is essential for a good marriage.

Most classes and seminars on witnessing assume a basic formula that "works" for everyone. We have found this is not necessarily so. The effectiveness of witnessing approaches varies with each of the seven motivational gifts. We see great value in knowing something about a person's giftedness before sharing our faith, especially with someone we love dearly.

The following observations on witnessing within the framework of a person's gift should enable you to communicate the Gospel so as to gain your loved one's response.

1. A *perceiver* responds best to questions about right or wrong, good versus evil, God's justice, or other ultimate life concepts. Ask: "Why do you think there is so much evil in the world?" or, "How can God be both loving and just?" or, "Do

you know what happens to people when they die?" Depending on the answers you can lead into a discussion of your beliefs.

2. A *server* responds to a practical Gospel. Questions like, "What do you think is man's greatest need?" or, "Do you think 'good works' will help a person to get into heaven?" or, "Have you ever considered how much Jesus focused on the importance of having a servant's heart?" will arouse interest and response.

3. A *teacher* wants facts and reliable proof for what you share. Ask, "Why do you think God sent Jesus to live on this earth?" or, "Look at this verse. Isn't it compelling proof Jesus really was the Son of God?" or, "Have you ever considered the claims of Christ? Do you think they are valid?"

4. An *exhorter* is concerned about helping people with their problems. Questions like, "What do you consider the best way to help people overcome problems?" or, "What brings true fulfillment in life?" or, "Would you like to hear how I dealt with the same problem you are facing now?" will bring response.

5. A *giver* has an inborn, eager responsiveness to the Gospel. Your approach can be more direct: "Do you know what it means to be born again?" or, "What do you think the word *salvation* means in the Bible?" or, "What is the greatest gift you can give to God?"

6. An *administrator* is interested in an overall view of life, the universe—just about everything. Catch his attention with, "Why do you think God created people?" or, "What is the most important message the Bible teaches?" or, "What do you think will happen to the human race? "

7. A *compassion person* relates best on a feeling level; logic leaves him cold. Try, "How do you feel God wants people to treat each other?" or, "If Jesus were here today, what do you feel He'd spend His time doing?" or, "Do you feel hope for suffering people in the world?"

You'll develop your own questions also. Just remember: Each gift offers a different focus. After you've gained your loved one's interest, even *the way* he or she comes to Jesus will be influenced by the gifts.

1. The *perceiver* will probably feel the need to repent and make salvation a deliberate choice of the will.

2. The *server* will be attracted by Jesus' good works and receive Him because he longs to do good works, too.

3. The *teacher* may read through the New Testament, gaining the needed facts to make an intellectual decision.

4. The *exhorter* will respond eagerly to Jesus' methods of helping people, and want to join Him.

5. The *giver's* excitement when the Gospel suddenly makes sense will prompt him to witness to others right away.

6. The *administrator* will examine the whole story, from creation to the Millennium, before deciding Jesus is the Son of God.

7. The *compassion person* will shed joyful tears over God's great, personal love for him.

How to Restore Relationships with Grown Children

24

Because they have not understood the motivational gifts, many parents have allowed differences between themselves and their children to grow through the teenage and young adult years. Strains and conflicts have resulted in scars, wedges, even estrangements.

Perhaps you've noticed an aloofness in your grown son or daughter. Perhaps some hidden antagonism, never confronted and defused, maintains an invisible barrier between you. Open resentment may fester, occasionally erupting into verbal conflict. Or maybe your adult child is alienated, totally refusing contact with his family.

Now that you understand the differences in the motivational gifts you can begin to build better relationships with your grown children. Something innate in every person desires a good parent-child relationship. If adult children fail to honor their fathers and mothers their lives will be adversely affected. The apostle Paul pointed this out to the Ephesian Christians as the fifth of the Ten Commandments (Deuteronomy 5:16 and Exodus 20:12).

> "Honor your father and mother"—which is the first commandment with a promise—"that it may go well with you and that you may enjoy long life on the earth."
>
> Ephesians 6:2–3, NIV

Whether breaches are the result of real or felt hurts is irrelevant, and so is placing blame. The restoration of relationships is what matters. Each of us must do our part to bring healing if we want to draw closer to God and lead long, blessed lives. The next few pages detail important steps we can take in the restoration process.

CHOOSE TO HUMBLE YOURSELF

The person who has the light (understanding) should take the first step: humbling himself and assuming partial, perhaps even full, blame.

> Be completely humble and gentle; be patient,
> bearing with one another in love. Make every
> effort to keep the unity of the Spirit through the
> bond of peace.
> Ephesians 4:2–3, NIV

Even if your child was rebellious, contributed greatly to the conflict, or was totally wrong in attitudes or actions, rebuilding the relationship is your goal. Don't try to defend your "rightness"; it pales in importance compared to the loving unity the Lord wants your family to enjoy.

First, identify what has led to the relationship's problems. We've designed a simple chart to help clarify the situation. If possible, you and your spouse should work on it together. If he/she is unwilling (or no longer with you), do it yourself.

The chart includes a place for your gifts, and your spouse's. It also has a place to indicate what your child did wrong, but it is not your responsibility to make him own up to it. The only person you can deal with and change is *you*. By taking the humble position and saying you're sorry for what you have done (or not done), you release your grown child to say "I'm sorry," too. But if you hold on to your "right" to be right, you block the power of God's love to heal the relationship.

By now you should be able to identify your grown child's giftedness. List it, as well. From chapter 16, "Help! My Gift Conflicts with My Child's Gift," you should be able to spot circumstances in which your differences or similarities in gifting may have produced conflict. You cannot change how you handled those situations, but you can change the *feelings* you and your child have about the past and about each other.

Record on the chart past conflicts or problems causing the present less-than-perfect relationship between you and your child. Indicate your respective actions in each situation, as well as how your respective gifts may have contributed—knowingly or unknowingly—to the predicament.

REPENT

Here's where humility goes into action. In prayer, wholeheartedly repent of hurtful comments, neglected promises, lacks of love or patience, mistakes or misjudgments, lack of trust, ignorance resulting in poor decisions, un-Christlike actions, pre-Christian attitudes and actions, or out-and-out sin. Cover everything—great and small, important or seemingly insignificant—that worsened the parent-child relationship.

FORGIVE YOUR ADULT CHILD

Choose to forgive your grown child for whatever he has done to hurt you. Forgiveness is not a feeling; God's Word says it's a choice to follow His will.

> Be kind and compassionate to one another, forgiving each other, just as in Christ God forgave you.
>
> Ephesians 4:32, NIV

> "And when you stand praying, if you hold anything against anyone, forgive him, so that your Father in heaven may forgive you your sins. But if you do not forgive, neither will your Father who is in heaven forgive your sins."
>
> Mark 11:25, 26, NIV

When we hold anything against anyone we hamper answers to our own prayers and forgiveness of our own sins. God offers forgiveness to us so we can learn to forgive. In the parable of the unmerciful servant (Matthew 18:21–35) Jesus says our unwillingness to forgive a fellow human being will endanger our spiritual health and well-being. No one has sinned against us as we have sinned against a holy and just God; it's like comparing a debt of five dollars to a debt of several million.

God will not ask you to do something of which you are not capable. You can forgive—totally.

Write on the chart exactly what you need to forgive your grown child for. Then make a decision to forgive, and declare it—out loud. You and your spouse may want to do this together. No one else needs to hear you at this point, but God will hear, and delight in your obedience to Him.

MAKE IT RIGHT WITH THE LORD

Next, repent, asking the Lord to forgive your unforgiveness. He can and will—immediately!

MAKE IT RIGHT WITH YOUR GROWN CHILD

Now it's time to write in the space provided your plan of action for building a better relationship with your adult child.

Here are some ideas. Communicate with him as soon as possible. If he lives nearby, go to see him. If not, call or write. Initiate the forgiveness process, telling him you're sorry for what you've done, or left undone, in the past. Affirm your unconditional love and your desire for a good relationship. Don't sound too "spiritual," especially if he has not yet come to know Jesus Christ. Treat him as an adult, a peer; don't talk down to him. Keep an open, humble attitude, and demand nothing.

If your child questions your motives, explain how discovering your gifts has given you new insights concerning past conflicts. If possible, lend or give him a copy of this book or *Discover Your God-Given Gifts.* Or simply explain the concepts in your own way. Tell him you *think* you now know what his gifts are but suggest he take the test for himself. He will probably be curious: Most people are.

Ordinarily a grown child will delight in improving his relationship with his parents, but if yours is not willing, you have done your part. Continue to pray for him, and to reach out in any way the Lord leads you. The restoration is God's will, and He will work with you to accomplish it.

Once the restoration process has begun, extend your love, attention, and encouragement. Remember to make room for your grown child's motivational gifts.

RESTORING RIGHT RELATIONSHIPS

My motivational gifts: _____

My (husband's) (wife's) gifts: _____

My grown child's name: _____

My grown child's gifts: _____

The conflicts or problems: _____

_____

_____

_____

_____

My child's part in them:	My (our) part in them:
_____	_____
_____	_____
_____	_____
_____	_____
_____	_____
_____	_____
_____	_____
The way his/her gifts may have contributed to them:	The way my (our) gifts may have contributed to them.
_____	_____
_____	_____
_____	_____
_____	_____
_____	_____
_____	_____

In what areas do I (we) need to repent?: _____

_____

_____

What do I (we) need to forgive?: _____

_____

_____

What steps can I (we) take to restore our relationship?: _____

_____

_____

_____

Praise report: _____

_____

_____

DISCOVER YOUR GRANDCHILDREN'S GIFTS

25

If you've entered grandparenthood, you already know some of its privileges, including enjoying your grandchildren and sending them home to their parents for routine care! In this chapter we offer suggestions to help you relate more personally to each grandchild.

If you're a parent, share this book, or at least this chapter, with grandmas and grandpas. And be sure to see A SUGGESTION FOR PARENTS at the end of this chapter.

HOW TO DISCOVER YOUR GRANDCHILDREN'S GIFTS

The easiest way to discover your grandchildren's gifts is to test them. Give or loan a copy of this book to their parents, saying you are interested in knowing about your grandchildren's gifts. Or, purchase individual tests for each child, available as follows:

Youth Scoring Sheets Set—For teenagers, ages 13 to 19, grades 7 through 12.

Junior Children's Scoring Sheets Set—For ages 9 to 12, grades 4 through 6.

Primary Children's Scoring Sheets Set—For ages 6 to 8, grades 1 through 3.

Children's Survey Testing Sheets—For preschoolers, ages 2 to 5. (This can also cover a wider range of ages, though less precisely.)

Ministry Discovery Set—Designed to help teenagers and adults find opportunities for ministry based on their motivational gifts.

Occupational Success Test Set—Designed to help older teenagers and adults determine the jobs and careers in which they'd be successful, based on their motivational gifts.

Check "Additional Material Available" at the back of the book for ordering information.

Juniors and youth can test themselves, although juniors may need parental assistance to understand some concepts. Or you may prefer to give the tests directly to your junior and adolescent grandchildren. They will enjoy the challenge and want to share the results with you.

Parents complete the Primary and Children's Survey (preschool) tests. The preschool set contains tests for three children; all the rest are designed for one child.

If your children and/or grandchildren are not open to taking the tests, we suggest you fill out the relevant questionnaires. This may not be as accurate as their own self-testing, but you will discover a great deal about each grandchild as you complete a test with him in mind.

MAKE A PLAN

Fill out the quick reference chart in this chapter, listing each grandchild, his general sports interests (if any), and interest in pets. Be sure to read the chapters in Part II relating to his primary, and possibly his secondary, gifts, especially sections 15 through 20 in each chapter. You'll gain a handy, useful overview of your grandchildren.

Now map out some plans utilizing your new-found knowledge. Consider spending a day with one grandchild, doing things of special interest to him. If your granddaughter is a compassion child with a special interest in art, plan a trip to the local art museum, or try painting together with watercolors.

A second plan: Buy a good book for your grandchild, either for a special occasion or "just because." If you take him along to help pick it out, you'll know by your chart what sections to look in. If it's to be a surprise, he'll be sure to like it.

Plan three: Keep available in your home a box or basket of toys and games based on your grandchild's preferences. We filled a square plastic laundry basket with toys our grandson Jon enjoyed. He knew where it was kept and that he automatically had permission to get it out.

Information about your grandchild's favorite toys and games should help you pinpoint suitable Christmas and birthday presents quite easily. The more grandchildren you have the more difficult it is to remember who likes what; the chart will remind you.

Plan four: Use the information on your chart to tailor conversations and letters to your grandchild's interests. If your teacher grandson likes dinosaurs, clip out newspaper or magazine articles to send to him. Alert him to relevant museum exhibits or films and offer to take him. Check out a dinosaur film or video from the library and invite him over to see it. He will be delighted you've taken an interest.

Enjoy your grandchildren. They are a special blessing from the Lord!

A SUGGESTION FOR PARENTS

If it's impractical or impossible to share this book with your parents and/or in-laws, fill in the Quick Reference Chart on page 273 and give them a copy. (Be sure to include both sides of the family.) This will provide helpful information about each child and spark ideas for appropriate gifts. My mother-in-law always asked us what the children might like for Christmas or birthdays, and we never had to visit a returns department.

You can update the chart occasionally as each child grows and develops more precise interests.

QUICK REFERENCE CHART
MY GRANDCHILDREN'S MOTIVATIONAL GIFTS

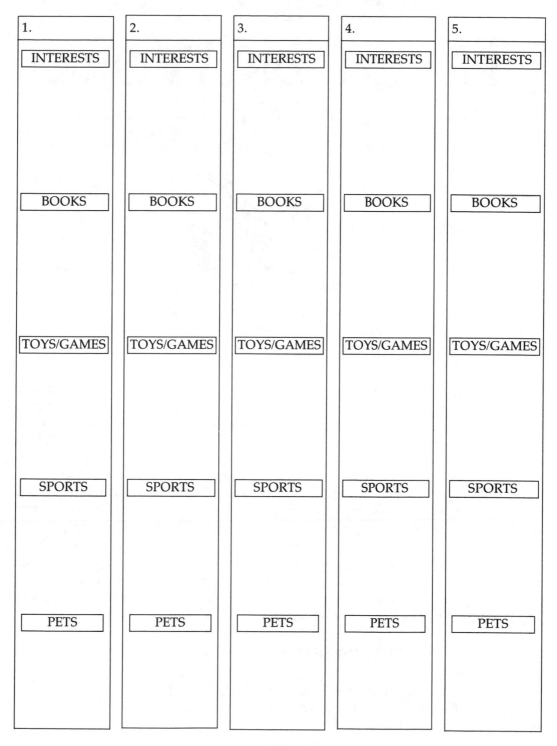

INSIGHTS FOR THOSE WHO TEACH OR WORK WITH CHILDREN

26

Are you a Sunday school teacher, a church youth or children's group leader, or a professional teacher in a public or private Christian school? Perhaps you're a scout leader, a Bible club teacher, an athletic coach, a children's counselor, a preschool teacher or daycare worker, or a regular babysitter. Maybe you're home schooling your own children. Whatever you do with children or young people you will do even better if you know and understand their motivational gifts.

We've been in many of the above roles ourselves, and have taught and worked with people who fill them. We've been invited into Christian schools to teach the teachers about motivational gifts, and to teach specific classes or age groups. We've spoken at youth retreats where participants have been excited about knowing their gifts. After teaching Sunday school classes and youth groups about the gifts we've been flooded with requests from parents, who wanted to know their own gifts, too. Some of the insights we've gained over the past fifteen years might help you as you minister to children.

YOUR GIFTS AFFECT YOUR TEACHING OR LEADING STYLE

Persons with every type of gift can teach. Persons with every type of gift can lead, to some extent. But the *way* you teach or lead is determined, for the most part, by your motivational gifts.

Perceivers usually spend much time in prayerful preparation for teaching or leading, and use the Bible as their basic text. They stress rules and standards, and expect everyone to fall into line. Disciplining comes easily to them, and they seldom make exceptions. They challenge students or followers to choose God's will in all things, and teach about or lead young people into prayer as often as possible.

Servers prefer to use already prepared materials when teaching, or when leading a group, and do detailed preparation. They usually prefer working with younger children. Their "hands-on" style leads them to utilize craft-type projects, and to allow for creativity and use of visual aids wherever possible. They are not strong leaders, but are practical, and assist young people to learn or to do.

Teachers enjoy researching and preparing their own teaching or program materials. Precise, systematic, and easy to follow, they offer clear, pointed directions, and their students find notetaking easy. Teachers often approach subject matter thematically, sometimes with a series in mind. They delight in teaching or sharing from the Bible and encourage Bible verse memorization.

Exhorters are the most interesting teachers or leaders because of their life-related approach. Their focus will always be on helping people—of any age—to grow and develop to their full potential. Exhorters relate easily to any age group, more as coaches than as instructors. They are glad to use prepared materials but pepper them with spontaneous illustrations drawn from their own lives or the lives of others.

Givers, like servers, are not strong leaders or teachers, but can perform well with careful planning, using prepared materials and their own ideas. They work hard at whatever they do, encouraging their charges to do likewise. Givers challenge students or followers to witness to their friends about Jesus Christ, motivating them to get results. They emphasize missions and initiate practical projects to get money and people on the field.

Administrators love teaching and thrive on leadership, quickly and thoroughly putting together their own materials (often eclectic), to benefit and motivate those they teach or lead. They advocate thinking big, planning ahead, and developing one's full potential. Their capabilities are extensive, their zeal is contagious, and they will try just about anything once, encouraging broad perspectives and various approaches. Administrators bring in resource people to enrich curriculum and programming. Children follow their leadership enthusiastically, though administrators prefer older followers.

Compassion people prefer prepared materials but always look for ways to make them more interesting or creative. Though they prepare well, their teaching or leading sometimes takes a spontaneous course, occasionally winding up far from their original goals and purposes. No matter! As long as everyone enjoys the sessions and gets to know others better, compassion people are satisfied. Whatever they prepare to teach or share, they end up focusing on love and/or right relationships. Children they work with feel loved, needed, and wanted, but compassion people are not good disciplinarians and therefore do better with younger children.

All of these approaches to teaching and leading are valid. Each child benefits from exposure to the different gifts, but produces and performs best under those whose gifting is the same as their own. An identification, almost a bonding, often develops with such a teacher or leader.

Be yourself. Abide as much by the rules, curriculum, or requirements as necessary, but utilize your God-given gifts in working with children and young people. A word of caution: Any group of children will represent several or all of the seven gifts. Don't expect every child to love or respond eagerly to your teaching style all the time.

Talk about "learning styles" has reverberated in educational circles during recent years. Researchers use several approaches to define them, but the consensus remains: Children learn in a variety of different ways. We agree.

The longest-established approach, the Myers-Briggs Type Indicator, plots four pairs of approaches to life: extroversion/introversion, sensing/intuition, thinking/feeling, and judging/perceptive.

Another approach, detailed by Rita and Kenneth Dunn, focuses on the channels of perceptivity, namely: visual (seeing), auditory (hearing), and kinesthetic (doing). The Dunns believe children learn best through one or a combination of the three channels.

Anthony Gregorc developed still another approach, identifying four basic ways children perceive reality: abstract random, concrete random, abstract sequential, and concrete sequential.

While all of these are useful, especially under the direction of someone trained to test and interpret, the layman may have difficulty understanding or utilizing them outside an academic setting. In contrast we have found the motivational gifts easy for any parent, teacher, or leader to understand and apply to everyday life.

TEACH THEM TO APPRECIATE THE DIFFERENT GIFTS

Teach the children you work with about the motivational gifts. Help them learn to appreciate the differences, and to accept others with gifts differing from their own.

Draw from the material in this book, adapting it to the age level with which you are working. Junior and senior high students could participate in the research and sharing, also studying some of the biblical characters. Juniors respond well to the subject and enjoy role-playing or participating in dramatizations. An introductory overview unit plus one unit for each gift can be presented in eight consecutive sessions or on eight consecutive days.

We have used role-playing and various dramatics to present important concepts about the motivational gifts. In one school teachers prepared their fifth and sixth grade students with a bird's-eye view of the seven gifts. A delightful poem by John Godfrey Sax served to help them see the danger in thinking everyone else should think and act like them. Students volunteered to portray six blind men from India who went to see an elephant. The day of the presentation two students—bent over, seat to seat—pretended to be the elephant, with swinging trunk and tail. Another student narrated as the blind men acted out their parts, wearing blindfolds for effect, and quoting their lines on cue.

It was six men of Indostan,
  To learning much inclined,
Who went to see the Elephant
  (though all of them were blind)
That each by observation
  Might satisfy his mind.

The First approached the Elephant
  And, happening to fall
Against his broad and sturdy side,
  At once began to bawl:
"God bless me! But the Elephant
  Is very like a wall!"

The Second, feeling of the tusk,
  Cried: "Ho! what have we here
So very round and smooth and sharp?
  To me 'tis mighty clear
This wonder of an Elephant
  Is very like a spear!"

The Third approached the animal,
  And, happening to take
The squirming trunk within his hands,
  Thus boldly up and spake:
"I see," quote he, "the Elephant
  Is very like a snake!"

The Fourth reached out his eager hand
  And felt about the knee:
"What most this wondrous beast is like
  Is mighty plain," quoth he;
" 'Tis clear enough the Elephant
  Is very like a tree!"

The Fifth, who chanced to touch the ear,
  Said: "E'en the blindest man
Can tell what this resembles most;
  Deny the fact who can,
This marvel of an Elephant
  Is very like a fan!"

The Sixth no sooner had begun
  About the beast to grope,
Than, seizing on the swinging tail
  That fell within his scope,
"I see," quoth he, "the Elephant
  Is very like a rope!"

And so these men of Indostan
 Disputed loud and long,
Each in his own opinion
 Exceeding stiff and strong,
Though each was partly in the right
 And all were in the wrong![1]

The children got the point: Each of us is somewhat *blind* to the perspectives of those with the other six motivational gifts. We are each *partly right*. We need each other's perspectives in order to see the *whole* picture of life.

We used another tool with the same class at the end of the study, a dramatization with the following introduction:

"The scene is a birthday party to which seven children have been invited. Each one has a different motivational gift. The young host brings three plates of ice cream and cake to the dining area, and as he tries to put one on the table it slips off, crashes to the floor, and scatters plate, ice cream, and cake in one big mess. How does each person react to the situation?"[2]

One student played the host, and seven students acted as the seven guests with signs hung around their necks to indicate their seven distinct motivational gifts. Students set up a round table with seven chairs, and prepared three paper plates with cotton balls shaped like scoops of ice cream and chocolate brown paper folded to look like slices of cake. The narrator read the paragraph above and the group went into action.

PERCEIVER: "That's what happens when you try to carry too many plates!"

SERVER: "I'll clean it up!"

TEACHER: "The reason you dropped that plate is that it was not balanced properly."

EXHORTER: "Next time, let someone help you carry the plates!"

GIVER: "I'll be happy to help you make another dessert."

COMPASSION: "Don't feel bad, it could have happened to anyone!"

ADMINISTRATOR: "John, get the broom and dust pan; Sally, get the mop; Marie, help me fix another plate!"

Applied to any crisis situation, this type of role-playing demonstrates the unique reactions of each motivational gift. Let your students come up with their own ideas.

GIVE THEM THE TEST

If possible, test the children or young people you work with after you've given some introductory material.

Each student should have individual test materials suited to his age category. These are listed below, and are available as indicated on the "Additional Materials Available" pages at the end of the book. Please do not photocopy.

---

[1] Quoted in *Sounds of a Young Hunter* by Bill Martin, Jr. (Holt, Rinehart & Winston, Inc., 1967).
[2] Our thanks to Bill Gothard for this idea.

Youth Scoring Sheets Set—For teenagers, ages 13 to 19.

Junior Scoring Sheets Set—For ages 9 to 12.

Primary Scoring Sheets Set—For ages 6 to 8.

Children's Survey Testing Sheets—For preschoolers, 2 to 5.

Ministry Discovery Set—For teenagers and adults.

Occupational Success Test Set—For older teenagers.

The Primary and Children's Survey (preschool) tests should be sent home for parents to complete. (The preschool test is suitable for testing three children; all the rest are designed for one child.) Have the parents return the test for you to evaluate and record. Discussing the completed motivational gifts test results during individual parent-teacher conferences may be helpful.

We suggest you photocopy the *completed* profile sheet for each primary child, and the Scoring Records Chart (page 26) and three pages of *circled* characteristics for the preschool child. This will provide a much larger perspective on the child, enabling you to work more effectively with him in the future.

Juniors and youth can complete their own tests although juniors may need assistance from the teacher or leader in understanding some concepts. Administer the tests to the whole group, reading the characteristics one at a time, giving additional explanations or illustrations, and having the students score themselves. Allow for questions.

Junior and senior high students can also take the Ministry Discovery Test and/or the Occupational Success Test (either in class or youth group, or at home) after they have completed the Youth Test. The tests will interest them, and may produce good small or large group follow-up discussions. One youth leader divided his group into seven sections, one for each of the motivational gifts. An informed adult discussion leader asked probing questions and led a lively discussion in each group. The young people were so interested they didn't want to go home when meeting time was over, so they continued the discussion groups the following week.

Another group found it helpful to focus on ministry, and how individual members could use their gifts effectively to serve others. Within two weeks of the testing and discussion almost everyone in the youth group found a place of ministry within their local church.

Secondary schools offer other tests to help students discover how their interests and abilities fit them for various jobs or occupations, but the Occupational Success Test seems more personal once the student knows his motivational gifts. The section on built-in traits may also aid them in finding satisfying part-time work or summer jobs.

GROUP THE GIFTS FOR SPECIAL PROJECTS AND LEARNING OPPORTUNITIES

The two broad categories of gifts defined in 1 Peter 4:11, as indicated below, are very useful in grouping children for special events, projects, and learning opportunities.

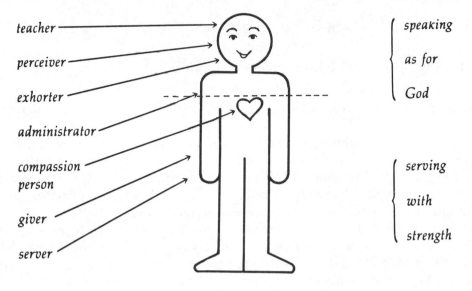

The teacher, the mind of the body, must speak in order to teach. The perceiver, the eye of the body, must speak in order to proclaim what is right or wrong. The exhorter, the mouth of the body, has a fluid speaking-gift. And the administrator, the shoulders of the body, has facility of speech in order to lead.

These children ordinarily thrive in educational systems and cultures where facility of speech and competitiveness are rewarded.

Children with serving gifts, however, often fare poorly, overwhelmed by the competitiveness and talkativeness of their speaking-gift peers. Feeling it useless to compete, they may settle for less than they should.

The compassion child, the heart of the body, prefers working behind the scenes to speaking publicly, delighting to serve others through the abundance of love God has given him. The giver, the arms of the body, also shuns the limelight to give preference and support to others. And the server, the hands of the body, excels in dexterity and focuses on helping others.

These children focus more on cooperation than competition, and are excellent team members. Their joy comes in helping or serving others, not outshining them.

Most children with serving gifts who do C work academically are putting out just as much effort as are children with speaking gifts who achieve As and Bs.

In one Christian school we taught the teachers, and then their fifth and sixth graders, about the motivational gifts. Later the teachers separated the children with serving gifts from the children with speaking gifts during special learning times. The serving children handled a project in geography superbly when they were not being dominated by children with more extroverted gifts. They were more willing to practice speeches out loud when surrounded by their helpful server counterparts. And the children with speaking gifts polished their speeches even more, thriving on the critical evaluations of their counterparts.

This sort of separation for some projects and play groups encourages the less expressive children in youth and children's groups as well as in preschools. The constant presence of dominating children will only force shy children further into their shells. Give them opportunities for time segments with similar children.

FIND WAYS TO ENCOURAGE EACH CHILD

As teachers or leaders, do what you can to encourage each child or young person to use his gifts properly and to develop his full potential. Be aware of each child's gifts as they relate to group interaction and individual growth:

Encourage the perceiver to be less critical of others and to pray more for his peers.

Give the server extra handwork and show appreciation for his help.

Allow the teacher to dig out interesting facts to share with the class or group.

Help the exhorter to channel his talkativeness into productive outlets like speeches, reports, and leadership.

Let the giver use his industriousness in projects and in helping others to accomplish tasks.

Release the administrator to lead and organize his peers.

Permit the compassion child to use his creativity to bless other group members.

ASSIGN RESPONSIBILITIES TO FIT GIFTEDNESS

If your class or group is planning a special event or project, assign responsibilities to those whose giftedness will handle them well. Children with assignments will benefit, but so will the group or class as a whole.

Let's suppose your group or class has decided to sponsor a "Fun Night"—with various booths, food, and entertainments—to raise money for a missionary project. How can you best assign responsibilities to fit students' giftedness?

Give administrators overall organizational responsibilities, but place *one* administrator in charge. (Others can head up subcommittees.)

Have givers plan and organize the entertainment project, and even produce a dramatization themselves. They'd also handle finances efficiently.

Servers could construct and man the booths, make posters, and bake cookies and cakes.

Perceivers' persuasiveness will enhance the publicity campaign.

Assign teachers to tell about the event at church or in the school assembly. They'll also be glad to research, through the library or other people, good ideas for booths.

Place at least one exhorter on each committee. Their enthusiasm will be contagious and they'll come up with lots of good ideas.

Compassion children will help anywhere and will work especially well in the booths, ensuring fun for everyone.

What else are you planning? A missions project? A retreat? A fundraiser? A national observance week? A contest? A play? Use your children's or young people's gifts to full advantage, thereby blessing everyone and enhancing the event's prospects for success.

STUDY THE BIBLICAL CHARACTERS

Studying biblical characters in light of their motivational gifts can be lots of fun, and incorporates easily into a series on the seven types of gifts. Make a game out of it. Challenge students to see how many characteristics they can find about one biblical character. (This works well as an individual home project or in small search and find groups.)

If you are studying the gift of perception, for instance, give students fifteen minutes to look up references to John the Baptist (Matthew 21:32, Luke 3:2–20, and 7:18–29). Instruct them to write down all the perceiver characteristics they identify, both specific and implied, using the Youth Test from chapter 6 or the Junior Test from chapter 5 for reference. Here's an example using the Youth Test characteristics:

> So he said to the crowds that came out to be baptized by him, You offspring of vipers! Who secretly warned you to flee from the coming wrath?
>
> Luke 3:7, TAB

Obvious characteristics
   #1. He identified evil.
   #3. He sized up the group's character.
   #9. He was frank and outspoken.

Implied characteristics:
   #4. He wanted to encourage repentance.
   #12. He saw their blind spots.
   #18. He expressed a strong opinion.

Here's an example using the Junior Test characteristics:

Obvious characteristics:
   #18. He identified evil.
   #19. He sized up the group's character.
   #21. He was frank and outspoken.

Implied characteristics:

#2. He wanted them to do right.

#23. He expressed a strong opinion.

#24. He was upset over their sins.

For a thorough look at biblical characters and their characteristics, see the seven chapters on biblical examples of motivational gifts in Part II (chapters 9, 12, 15, 18, 21, 24, and 27) of our first book, *Discover Your God-Given Gifts*.

Other ways to arrange a study of biblical characters include:

1. Assigning teams from your class or group to examine and report about biblical characters representative of each motivational gift.

2. Dividing students into seven groups, according to their motivational gifts, and assigning them biblical characters matching their giftedness.

Biblical characters will come alive as children study about them as real people with real motivational gifts.

You will discover additional innovative ways to use the motivational gift materials with your students or young people. We trust knowing about these wonderful, God-given gifts will continue to bless you all!

CLOSING THOUGHTS

27

The day I was finishing the last chapter of this book eight inches of new-fallen snow covered the Seattle area, an unusual occurrence for this part of the country on March 1. But it helped to keep me in the house, persistently pounding out manuscript pages on the computer, and wondering how we should end the book.

That afternoon Don tromped through the snow to our roadside mailbox and returned with a package from our son Dave and his wife, Scotti. We knew it was Don's birthday present—Dave had called several nights before to say the present was on its way.

I looked over Don's shoulder as he opened the card, first. It was lovingly handmade by Scotti, a new tradition since she became part of our family two years ago, and contained a handwritten note from Dave expressing his love and appreciation for his father. A tribute to Don's investment in parenting, it was a gift far more precious than anything money could buy. Overwhelmed, Don could hardly read through his tears.

Later I asked Dave if we could use his note to end our book. We offer it here—in closing.

Closing Thoughts

Happy Birthday Dad!

I wish I could be with you to celebrate this grand day. But as it is, I am far away.

A few weeks ago, Scotti and I were at a concert and Chet Atkins ("Nashville's finest") sang a song about his relationship with his father. I cried. I kept thinking about all of the time we have spent together over these 24 years. I can remember a lot of special times.

I can remember throwing a football with you, shooting baskets with you, "helping" you on the roof of our house, being spanked by you (I am grateful now), and talking to you about the many "problems" I have had over the years.

I can remember praying with you, having family devotions with you, having "family time" with you, listening to you tell stories, laughing at your jokes and puns, camping with you, fishing with you, hiking with you, and walking on the beach with you.

I can remember cutting down Christmas trees in the backyard, weeding at the cabin, and being hugged and kissed by you before I went to sleep when I was a child.

I already have a lifetime of special memories with you that will always be with me while we are apart. I appreciate and cherish these memories, and I covet our relationship to come. I marvel at how wonderful a father you have been to me, and when I am a father, I hope I can be a lot like you!

I love you, Dad.

Dave

13-WEEK
STUDY GUIDE

28

This study plan is designed to help you teach the material in this book. Organized as a 13-week study, it may be lengthened or shortened to fit any time frame. Assign the chapters and questions in advance of the discussion time.

FIRST WEEK: READ CHAPTERS 1–6.

Chapter 1: "Every Child is Gifted by God"

   a) When does a child receive his motivational gifts? What is the evidence?
   b) How does a motivational gift affect a child's viewpoint and personality?
   c) Are all seven motivational gifts of equal value? Why do you think so?
   d) In what ways are different basic needs met by the seven motivational gifts?

Chapter 2: "Motivational Gifts: A Portrait"

   e) How does a child's gift influence the way a parent trains and disciplines him?
   f) How can understanding the speaking gifts and the serving gifts help children?

Chapters 3–5: "Testing Materials"

g) What insights did you gain about preschoolers? Primaries?
h) How can juniors benefit from knowing their motivational gifts?

Chapter 6: "Discover Your Teenager's Gifts"

i) What important decisions can be affected when a teenager knows his gifts?

SECOND WEEK: READ CHAPTERS 7–8

Chapter 7: "Every Child Has a Gift"

Chapter 8: "Train Up Your Perceiver"

a) Why is the perceiver the most challenging child to raise?
b) Why does the perceiver experience such extremes in his emotions?
c) Why shouldn't he speak openly and bluntly if his expressions are based on truth?
d) Why does the perceiver often have self-image problems?
e) What are the perceiver's blind spots and how can you help him to eliminate them?
f) Discuss the pros and cons of disciplining the perceiver with a rod.
g) How could you modify his tattletale tendency?
h) How would you cope with his argumentativeness?
j) How could you assist him in becoming a better leader?
k) Discuss the perceiver's four major traits.
l) Why are family activities so vital to every child?

THIRD WEEK: READ CHAPTER 9

Chapter 9: "Train Up Your Server"

a) Why is the server one of the easiest of children to raise?
b) Discuss some possible solutions to problems caused by the server's shyness.
c) How does a server communicate, besides verbally?
d) How can you help your server develop a better self-image?
e) Discuss some ways to enhance a server's creativity.
f) How should you deal with a server's academic performance?
g) What areas of achievement can you encourage in your server?
h) How can you gracefully tell a server you don't want his help with something?
i) Why shouldn't you push a server into leadership positions?

j) Discuss the server's four major traits.

k) How can you help a server feel more loved and appreciated?

FOURTH WEEK: READ CHAPTER 10

Chapter 10: "Train Up Your Teacher"

a) How can you help your teacher to become more demonstrative?

b) How can you cope with his persistent questioning?

c) Why is pride a potential problem for a teacher?

d) Is it possible to change a teacher's opinions? How?

e) Should you insist a teacher be imaginative? Why?

f) How can you effectively cope with a legalistic or dogmatic teacher?

g) What should you do when your teacher starts rationalizing instead of obeying?

h) How can you help him to develop friendships?

i) What should you do when your teacher wants to study too much?

j) How can you help him become an achiever in areas other than academics?

k) What resources would be helpful to have at home for the teacher?

l) Discuss the teacher's four major traits.

FIFTH WEEK: READ CHAPTER 11

Chapter 11: "Train Up Your Exhorter"

a) How can you cope with the exhorter's overtalkativeness?

b) How can the exhorter learn to accept others without compromising?

c) What other "mouth" problems does the exhorter have? How can you help him?

d) What problems develop if he joins too many groups?

e) What should you do if your exhorter keeps giving unsolicited advice?

f) What achievements should you expect from an exhorter?

g) Why do you think exhorters should be involved in sports?

h) Discuss the exhorter's four major traits.

i) What jobs and careers should an exhorter consider? What are the criteria?

SIXTH WEEK: READ CHAPTER 12

Chapter 12: "Train Up Your Giver"

a) Why is it sometimes difficult to identify a giver?

b) How can you deal with the giver's shyness?

c) Why should you encourage a good prayer life in your giver?
d) What two habits stand out uniquely in the giver?
e) In what problems can the giver's generosity involve him?
f) Why should he be confident if he pursues a career in business?
g) What special achievements should you expect from the giver?
h) Discuss the giver's four major traits.
i) Describe the ways in which givers excel in handling money.
j) Why are givers good witnesses and capable of becoming evangelists?

SEVENTH WEEK: READ CHAPTER 13

Chapter 13: "Train Up Your Administrator"

a) In what ways does the administrator have good communication skills?
b) Why should you teach him to have a humble and grateful heart?
c) In what way is he a visionary?
d) How can the administrator's organizational ability become irritating to his family?
e) What are some of the administrator's good and bad habits?
f) Why does the administrator continually need to keep lists of things to do?
g) Why does the administrator relate well to almost everyone?
h) In what areas would you expect him to achieve?
i) What leadership qualities do administrators usually have?
j) Discuss the administrator's traits.
k) Why does your administrator have wide areas of interest?

EIGHTH WEEK: READ CHAPTER 14

Chapter 14: "Train Up Your Compassion Child"

a) Why is the compassion child the most easily damaged?
b) What keeps him from being confident in communication?
c) How could you help a compassion child overcome his serious self-image problems?
d) In what ways can his idealism get him into trouble?
e) How does the compassion child's creativity help him to excel in certain areas?
f) In what ways can he be both a blessing and a problem?
g) How can you help him deal with procrastination and tardiness?
h) Why is the compassion child drawn to those who are hurting or in distress?
i) What would help him to better his academic achievements?
j) Why is it essential for a compassion child to have a pet?
k) Discuss the compassion child's four major traits.

NINTH WEEK: READ CHAPTERS 15–16

Chapter 15: "How to Cope with Combination Gifts"

a) Describe the differences between a classical gift and a combination gift.

b) Why does the Lord give some children more than one strong motivational gift?

c) How can you cope with children who have seemingly opposite gifts?

d) Circle the combination scales for your children and share one with the class.

Chapter 16: "Help! My Gift Conflicts with My Child's Gift!"

e) Name some challenges of parenting a child whose gift conflicts with your own.

f) Fill out the chart on page 183 and share how you are solving these conflicts.

g) From the list of gift combinations beginning on page 182 select three and give suggestions to help.

TENTH WEEK: READ CHAPTERS 17–18

Chapter 17: "How to Enhance Your Parenting Style"

a) Why is it important for a husband and wife to agree on their parenting style?

b) Have each class member share thoughts about one or two of the "ABC's of Christian Parenting."

c) Select several Scripture verses to share on Christian parenting.

Chapter 18: "How to Bring Healing to Wounded Children"

d) Explain why compassion children are more easily wounded than are persons with other gifts.

e) How does a child react to overt rejection? To covert rejection?

f) Share an example of negative treatment and how help was provided.

g) Describe five steps to bring healing to a wounded child.

ELEVENTH WEEK: READ CHAPTERS 19–20

Chapter 19: "How to Change a Negative Home Atmosphere"

a) What constitutes a negative home atmosphere?

b) How do our actions impact the home atmosphere?

c) Why do words have such strong effects on family members?

d) What role does forgiveness play in creating a positive home atmosphere?

Chapter 20: "How to Eliminate Negative Generational Influences"

e) Why do the influences of one generation impact future ones?

f) How can negative generational influences already in motion be stopped?

g) Complete the chart on page 222 and share insights about one item with the class.

TWELFTH WEEK: READ CHAPTERS 21–22

Chapter 21: "How to Minister to Your Child"

a) How can knowing your child's motivational gifts help you to minister to him?

b) Report some fresh insight you've received on ministering to one of the seven gifts.

c) Complete the chart on page 237 and share the steps you are taking to help one child.

Chapter 22: "Off to College, or Where?"

d) Look into what's available in your area for one of the eight items on page 238.

e) Why is it important for your child to use his built-in traits in a job or career?

f) If you have a teenager, have him score himself on the Occupational Success Test.

THIRTEENTH WEEK: READ CHAPTERS 23–27

Chapter 23: "Marriage: Do Opposite Gifts Attract?"

a) Why do opposite gifts usually attract?

b) If you have a married or engaged child, have him do the chart on page 258.

c) Share some of the problems and solutions you've found in dealing with conflicting spousal gifts.

d) Select one gift and share how you could witness effectively to a person who has it.

Chapter 24: "How to Restore Relationships with Grown Children"

e) Why must you be first to humble yourself in order to restore a relationship?

f) Complete the chart on page 269 and share with the class some insights you've gained.

Chapter 25: "Discover Your Grandchildren's Gifts"

g) Fill out the sheet on page 273 and give it to your children's grand-parents.

h) If you're a grandparent, have your grandchildren (or their parents) fill out page 273.

i) Why would knowing your grandchildren's gifts help you?

Chapter 26: "Insights for Those Who Teach or Work With Children"

j) How do the motivational gifts affect teaching and leading styles?

k) Why would knowing the gifts of the children you work with help you to function better?

l) How can serving and speaking children benefit from separate grouping?

m) How can a leader's knowing children's gifts help them develop to their full potential?

Chapter 27: Closing Thoughts

n) What insights have you gained from this study of children's motivational gifts?

o) What has been most helpful in enhancing your parenting style?

p) How have your children benefited from what you have learned?

ADDITIONAL MATERIAL AVAILABLE
29

To assist you in testing yourself, your children or others, or in presenting the material in this or other books by Don and Katie Fortune in a teaching or sharing situation, the authors make the following items available:

1. *Adult Questionnaire Scoring Set* (16 pp.). This includes the seven adult testing sheets from *Discover Your God-Given Gifts*, along with a profile sheet for final scoring. Tie-breakers (enabling a person to determine which gift is stronger when scores are close or the same) are also included.

2. *Youth Questionnaire Scoring Set* (16 pp.). Designed for teenagers (grades 7–12) and college-age young adults, this set is based on the material in chapter 6 of *Discover Your Children's Gifts*. It includes the seven scoring sheets for teens, a profile sheet and tie-breakers.

3. *Junior Children's Questionnaire Scoring Set* (16 pp.). Designed for grade-schoolers (grades 4–6), this test should be adminis-

tered by a parent, teacher or other adult. It is based on the material in chapter 5 of *Discover Your Children's Gifts*. Tie-breakers included.

4. *Primary Children's Questionnaire Scoring Set* (16 pp.). Designed to be completed by parents of primaries (grades 1–3), this testing set is based on material in chapter 4 of *Discover Your Children's Gifts*. Tie-breakers included.

5. *Children's Survey Testing Sheets: Preschool* (16 pp.). This packet includes three sets of scoring sheets from the material in chapter 3 of *Discover Your Children's Gifts*. Use these to help determine the gifts of children from toddler through kindergarten age. The tests can also help determine the gifts of older children and help adults clarify their own scores by comparing the survey characteristics with those from their own childhood.

6. *Objective Questionnaire Testing Set* (16 pp.). Designed to be used for objective (not

teaching) testing situations. The adult questionnaire is arranged randomly so a person taking the test cannot tell how the gifts relate to each characteristic. Tie-breakers, scoring key and decoder sheet included.

7. *Ministry Discovery Set* (16 pp.). This set contains expanded material from chapter 31 of *Discover Your God-Given Gifts* and a listing of ministries most fulfilling for persons with each gift. Selected material from chapter 30, "Living Your Gift," helps the user put gifts into practical action.

8. *Occupational Success Testing Set* (16 pp.). This set contains information from chapter 32, "Careers and Jobs," of *Discover Your God-Given Gifts*, along with a detailed analysis of the 180 most common careers and jobs, showing the degree to which each gift is likely to be successful. Also included is an evaluation of built-in traits that bring joy and satisfaction to persons with each gift.

9. *Secular Objective Questionnaire Testing Set* (16 pp.). This test is arranged randomly and designed to be used in situations where secular adult objective testing is desired. Christian terms and interests have been replaced by generic ones. Tie-breakers, scoring key and decoder sheet included.

10. *Children's Gifts Teaching Tape Set* (6 cassettes). Nine hours of seminar teaching on the book *Discover Your Children's Gifts*, recorded on six 90-minute cassette tapes and packaged in an attractive case. By following the teaching outline in the back of the book, the tapes can be used for teaching others. The following syllabus is recommended for use with the tapes.

11. *Children's Gifts Seminar Syllabus* (48 pp.). This workbook is designed for use in seminars or with the seminar teaching tapes, and covers the subjects discussed in *Discover Your Children's Gifts*. Many charts and practical application ideas included.

12. *Forms & Charts Packet* (32 pp.). This includes enough forms and charts from Part III, "Practical Insights," in *Discover Your Children's Gifts* to keep records for a family of four or five children. In 8 1/2" x 11" size it constitutes a permanent family record, but individual forms or charts can be removed. (It does *not* contain the motivational gifts testing sets.)

13. *The ABCs of Christian Parenting* (parchment). This inspirational reminder, taken from *Discover Your Children's Gifts*, makes a thoughtful gift for new parents or anyone with children. It is available on 9" x 12" parchment-type paper suitable for framing.

14. *Variety Packet, Children* (13 items). This packet contains one each of the above items: all testing and discovery sets, syllabus, tapes, a parchment and the Forms & Charts Packet—everything needed to teach the material from *Discover Your Children's Gifts*.

15. *Discover Your God-Given Gifts* (book, 276 pp.). Here is how to discover the gifts God has built into every person according to Romans 12:6–8. This book, a comprehensive study complete with study guide, is fun as well as revealing. A continuing bestseller, it is used by pastors and educators to help people understand the motivating forces of their lives and get involved in vital ministry.

16. *Motivational Gifts Seminar Tape Set* (6 tapes). This set includes nine hours of seminar teaching on motivational gifts based on the book *Discover Your God-Given Gifts*, recorded on six 90-minute cassette tapes and packaged in an attractive case. The following syllabus is recommended for use with the tapes.

17. *Motivational Gifts Seminar Syllabus* (48 pp.). This attractive workbook is designed for use in motivational gifts seminars or with the seminar teaching tapes above, and

covers the material and subjects in *Discover Your God-Given Gifts*. Testing sheets and tie-breakers for adults included, as well as biblical examples and practical application material.

18. *Video Teaching Tape Sets* (two tapes per set). Each of these two sets contains material from the nationally broadcast Canadian TV program *It's a New Day*, featuring Don and Katie Fortune. Each of the segments, in an interview format, is about 45 minutes long but can be shown in shorter units. Each is informal and lively, including introductory and life-related material, and can be used in teaching a smaller group.

The first set contains five segments on the motivational gifts, covering the adult testing material for all seven gifts from *Discover Your God-Given Gifts*. The second set contains four segments on the book *Discover Your Children's Gifts*, covering the characteristics for all seven types of gifted children. To order specify *Adult Gifts* or *Children's Gifts* teaching videos.

19. *Foreign Language Adult Questionnaire Scoring Sets* (8 pp. each). The adult testing sets have been translated so far into Danish, Finnish, French, German, Indonesian, Japanese, Korean, Polish, Portuguese, Norwegian, Russian, Spanish and Swedish. More translations are in process. Inquire about special permissions for missionaries and those teaching in foreign countries. To order specify the language needed.

20. *Free Information Packet #1*. Information about the procedure for having the authors present a motivational gifts seminar (or other subject) for a group, church, retreat or conference.

21. *Free Information Packet #2*. Information about the authors' books, tapes and materials on various subjects.

22. *Variety Packet, Adult* (11 items). This packet contains one each of the above items 1–9 and 16–17: testing material, syllabus, tapes and everything needed to teach the material from the book *Discover Your God-Given Gifts*.

23. *Discover Your Spouse's Gifts* (book, 352 pp.). Here is how the discovery of the motivational gifts of Romans 12:6–8 can enhance a marriage relationship. Based on an extensive marital survey conducted by the Fortunes, the book gives valuable information on how the gifts affect marriage, how to identify problems that stem from not knowing about the motivational gifts and how to overcome those problems and release a couple into the freedom and joy of a God-given, God-gifted marriage.

24. *Survey Your Marriage* (16 pp.). Based on an extensive marriage survey conducted by the Fortunes, this personal copy of the survey will enable you and your spouse to pinpoint the differences you have and the problem areas in your marriage. It will give you insight and understanding that will greatly enhance your marital relationship. It is also an excellent tool for couples' groups or classes and in premarital or marital counseling. The survey is based on the twenty most common categories of problems in marriage.

25. *Marriage Seminar Tape Set* (6 tapes). Nine hours of seminar teaching on the book *Discover Your Spouse's Gifts*, recorded on six 90-minute cassette tapes and packaged in an attractive case. By following the teaching outline in the back of the book, the tapes can be used for teaching others. The following syllabus is recommended for use with the tapes.

26. *Marriage Seminar Syllabus* (48 pp.). This attractive workbook is designed for use in marriage seminars or with the sem-

inar teaching tapes above, and covers the material and subjects of the book *Discover Your Spouse's Gifts*. Dual motivational gift testing sheets for couples are included, as well as a personal copy of the marriage survey and practical application material. Ideal for teaching couples who want to make their marriages better.

27. *The ABCs of Christian Marriage* (parchment). This inspirational reminder, taken from *Discover Your Spouse's Gifts*, makes a thoughtful gift for engaged couples, newlyweds or any Christian couple. It is available on 9" x 12" parchment-type paper suitable for framing.

28. *Dealing with Anger* (tape and book). Katie Fortune shares a life-changing teaching based on Matthew 5:21–26 on how to get free from the negative effects of anger in the heart. Couples and individuals will discover the scriptural key to dealing with anger. Christian counselors will have a tool for helping people with the number-one problem: buried anger.

For orders or a free price list write:

The Foundation of Faith, Family and Friends
1532 U.S. 41 By-pass, Suite 265
Venice, FL 34293
toll free: 1-866-395-2291
web site: thefoundationonline.com
email: info@thefoundationonline.com

authors:
Don and Katie Fortune
Heart to Heart International Ministries
P.O. Box 101
Kingston, WA 98346
(360) 297-8878
web site: heart2heart.org
e-mail: fortune@heart2heart.org